The Definitive Guide to Responsible AI

"Jay Trinckes has assembled a rare and essential resource. It's technical without being opaque, comprehensive without being overwhelming, and – most importantly – deeply principled. This guide doesn't just teach you how to build or assess AI systems. It shows you how to do so responsibly. Thoughtfully. Sustainably. With a clear-eyed understanding of what is at stake when we get it wrong – and what's possible when we get it right."

– Maverick James, Esq., CIPP/US, CIPM, AIGP,
"The Data Lawyer", Founder & CEO, Avant-Garde Legal, PC

As organizations are still attempting to figure out how to navigate AI risks, compliance, and governance, *The Definitive Guide to Responsible AI* is a timely guide to help set the foundation for responsible and trustworthy AI use. Written for anyone who is responsible for leading activities related to the development, implementation, or use of AI, this book benefits Chief AI Officers, Chief Information Security Officers, Chief Privacy Officers, and Chief Compliance Officers, as well as other executives, leaders, or implementers dealing with AI initiatives at an organizational level. This book will help them:

- Mitigate risks when deploying AI in organizations.
- Conduct systems, data protection, and rights impact assessments.
- Implement AI governance policies and processes.
- Benchmark and measure AI systems.

This book uses a standard approach that helps readers understand complex topics by breaking them down and making them easier to comprehend. Featuring processes to implement AI responsibly, this book covers basic concepts to aid readers apply current AI frameworks and prepare them for implementing future ones safely and ethically. This book also explores AI management systems, managing AI-related risks, and responsible AI performance.

John J. Trinckes, Jr. is the Director of GRC Services at Elevate Consult LLC, and the author of *How Healthcare Data Privacy is Almost Dead... and What Can Be Done to Revive It!*, *The Definitive Guide to Complying with the HIPAA/HITECH*

Privacy and Security Rules, and *The Executive MBA in Information Security* all published by CRC Press. As a member of the senior leadership team, he is responsible for the delivery of quality cybersecurity, privacy, and AI advisory services to multiple clients. He maintains the following credentials: CMMC CCA/CCP, CISSP, CISM, CDPSE, CRISC, CSA CCSK, PECB ISO/IEC 27001 Sr. LA and Sr. LI, PECB ISO/IEC 42001 Lead Implementer and Lead Auditor, DHS Section 508 Trusted Tester, NSA IAM/IEM, and HITRUST CDA. As a former Data Protection Officer and Chief Information Security Officer, he led efforts and maintained several highly recognized (and coveted) certifications such as the ISO 27001 (Information Security Management System – ISMS) with enhanced ISO 27017 (Cloud Security controls), the ISO 27701 (Privacy Information Management System – PIMS) with enhanced ISO 27018 (Cloud Privacy Controls), the ISO 9001 (Quality Management System – QMS), the ISO 42001 (AI Management System – AIMS), and HITRUST CSF i1 certification. He also led efforts in maintaining SOC 2 Type II attestation, EU-US Data Privacy Framework (DPF), General Data Protection Regulation (GDPR), California Consumer Privacy Act (CCPA), and Asia-Pacific Economic Cooperation (APEC) – Privacy Recognition for Processors (PRP) Certification.

The Definitive Guide to Responsible AI

John J. Trinckes, Jr.

CRC Press
Taylor & Francis Group

AN AUERBACH BOOK

Designed cover image: Shutterstock

First edition published 2026
2385 NW Executive Center Drive, Suite 320, Boca Raton FL 33431

and by CRC Press
4 Park Square, Milton Park, Abingdon, Oxon, OX14 4RN

CRC Press is an imprint of Taylor & Francis Group, LLC

© 2026 John J. Trinckes, Jr.

Library of Congress Cataloging-in-Publication Data
Library of Congress Control Number: 2025945643

ISBN: 9781041032229 (hbk)
ISBN: 9781041034940 (pbk)
ISBN: 9781003624073 (ebk)

DOI: 10.1201/9781003624073

Typeset in Garamond
by codeMantra

Contents

Contents

Preface

Let me put it this way, Mr. Amor. The 9000 series is the most reliable computer ever made. No 9000 computer has ever made a mistake or distorted information. We are all, by any practical definition of the words, foolproof and incapable of error.

–HAL 9000 (Kubrick, 1968)

I love Sci-Fi movies, and one of those films that have always stuck with me is Stanley Kubrick's *2001: A Space Odyssey.* (I know I might be aging myself a little here since this film was produced back in 1968, but that is OK because I need to make a point.) If you have not seen this movie, a computer named HAL (or more specifically, HAL 9000 'heuristically programmed algorithm') was programmed to operate a large research spaceship on a mission to Jupiter. It was programmed to run every system on the spaceship and was also programmed with a personality, which added a very scary aspect to the film. HAL discovered it was going to be disconnected, and so it took steps to protect itself and the mission. Crewmates were being murdered by HAL, and one of the lead researchers, Dr. David Bowman, was locked out of the spaceship with HAL quoting the iconic phrase: *"I'm sorry, Dave. I'm afraid I can't do that"* and disobeying an order to open the pod bay doors.

In the 1979 film, *Alien*, Ripley (played by actress Sigourney Weaver) had to contend with a Hyperdyne Systems 120-A/2 android named Ash, played by actor Ian Holm. In this movie, Ash was redirected by *The Company* with new priorities to "Bring back life form. Priority One. All other priorities rescinded" after discovering a new life form, the *Alien*, which *was* threatening the crew's life (Scott, 1979). Again, we see humans running into issues with artificial intelligence (AI). In 1984, *The Terminator* was released, and this time, our issues with AI were huge. The storyline of this film relates to AI taking over the world. Autonomous weapons, the Terminators, waged war against humans, putting humankind on the brink of extinction.

Why are there so many stories (or some might believe warnings) of AI taking over the world and putting humans in jeopardy? I believe it is because deep down, we are afraid of the unknown. We do not understand AI and the capabilities of machines thinking faster (or reacting faster) than we do, with super-human abilities to restrain us or take control of our lives. When we do not have the ability to explain what is happening or how systems make decisions, we become scared. When we no longer control 'power', the power will control and consume us.

There may also be some other underlying similar motives. In a couple of these films, AI was acting out from programming, developed by the 'corporations'. In the movie *Resident Evil*, the narrator explains this:

> At the beginning of the 21st century, the Umbrella Corporation had become the largest commercial entity in the United States. Nine out of every ten homes contain its products. Its political and financial influence is felt everywhere. In public, it is the world's leading supplier of computer technology, medical products, and healthcare. Unknown, even to its own employees, its massive profits are generated by military technology, genetic experimentation, and viral weaponry.
>
> *(Anderson, 2002)*

Although the focus of this film was on combating a virus that brought the dead back to life as zombies, the characters still had a run-in with an AI called the Red Queen. As many who have seen this film know, the Red Queen did not take kindly to those messing with her as she exclaimed, "You're all going to die down here".

All these films provide 'warnings' that we must consider when we interact with things we might not fully understand. We need to take precautions and ensure we utilize AI in a responsible manner. This is the main intent of this book: ensuring we consistently take measures to support responsible AI, *but what does Responsible AI mean?* According to the Responsible Artificial Intelligence Institute, "Responsible AI represents a combination of characteristics; it's trustworthy, designed with power dynamics and ethics in mind, with minimized risk". "At the RAI Institute, we like to use the comprehensive term 'responsible', as it refers to values-driven responsible actions taken to mitigate harm to people and the planet" (Lawson, 2023).

IBM defines responsible AI as "a set of principles that help guide the design, development, deployment, and use of AI – building trust in AI solutions that have the potential to empower organizations and their stakeholders. Responsible AI involves the consideration of a broader societal impact of AI systems and the measures required to align these technologies with stakeholder values, legal standards, and ethical principles. Responsible AI aims to embed such ethical principles into AI applications and workflows to mitigate risks and negative outcomes associated with the use of AI, while maximizing positive outcomes" (Stryker, 2024).

Per Microsoft, "Responsible Artificial Intelligence (Responsible AI) is an approach to developing, assessing, and deploying AI systems in a safe, trustworthy, and ethical way. AI systems are the product of many decisions made by those who develop and deploy them. From system purpose to how people interact with AI systems, Responsible AI can help proactively guide these decisions toward more beneficial and equitable outcomes. That means keeping people and their goals at the center of system design decisions and respecting enduring values like fairness, reliability, and transparency" (Microsoft, 2024).

According to the International Standards Organization (ISO), "Responsible AI is the practice of developing and using AI systems in a way that benefits society while minimizing the risk of negative consequences. It is about creating AI technologies that not only advance our capabilities, but also address ethical concerns – particularly regarding bias, transparency and privacy. This includes tackling issues such as the misuse of personal data, biased algorithms, and the potential for AI to perpetuate or exacerbate existing inequalities. The goal is to build trustworthy AI systems that are, all at once, reliable, fair and aligned with human values" (ISO, 2024).

We see a lot of commonalities between these definitions, and I think you can say the consensus is that responsible AI doesn't have just one component, but involves several aspects such as trustworthiness, ethics, safety, transparency, and societal issues (like fairness, bias, and privacy), which all revolve around human-centric concerns. I think we could trace these responsible AI origins back to 1942, where Isaac Asimov introduced the three laws of robotics in his short story, *Runaround*. The laws are as follows: "(1) a robot may not injure a human being or, through inaction, allow a human being to come to harm; (2) a robot must obey the orders given it by human beings except where such orders would conflict with the First Law; (3) a <u>robot</u> must protect its own existence as long as such protection does not conflict with the First or Second Law". Asimov later added another rule, known as the fourth or zeroth law, that superseded the others. It stated that "a <u>robot</u> may not harm humanity, or, by inaction, allow humanity to come to harm" (Britannica, 2024).

What if we replace the word 'robot' in the laws with 'AI'? In basic terms, we believe AI may not injure humans and should act to protect them. AI must obey humans except if an order violates the first law (i.e., injure a human). AI must protect its own existence except if it violates laws one (i.e., injure humans) and two (i.e., obey humans). Finally, AI may not harm humanity and should act to protect humanity. You might agree that at its core, this is *Responsible AI*.

The content of this book was aggregated from multiple different sources. I'm a life-time learner. I am always learning, reading, studying, obtaining new skills, and acquiring knowledge. Over the past several years, I have taken formal courses related specifically to AI along with clocking in several hundred hours of study time, taking notes, and fully understanding this material. I am also a practitioner and have put the topics of this book into real-life practice.

Although there are several resources available to enhance your knowledge, I would like to recommend the training provided by the following sources to anyone wanting to obtain further information (and/or certifications) in AI:

- The International Association of Privacy Professionals (IAPP) Artificial Intelligence Governance Professional (AIGP) Certification.
- Amazon Web Services (AWS) Certified AI Practitioner Certification.
- Professional Evaluation and Certification Board (PECB) International Standard Organization (ISO)/International Electrotechnical Commission (IEC) 42001 Lead Implementer Certification.
- Professional Evaluation and Certification Board (PECB) International Standard Organization (ISO)/International Electrotechnical Commission (IEC) 42001 Lead Auditor Certification.

I'll provide several resources to other sources of information throughout this book, and it will be my attempt to utilize appropriate brevity for you to focus on important topic areas. I hope you will find this content valuable, and the path I lay out will assist you in your responsible AI journey.

Resources

Some other useful resources you might want to consider reviewing as they relate to responsible AI are the following non-exhaustive list:

- Future of Privacy Forum: https://fpf.org/
- National Institute of Science and Technologies (NIST) AI Resources: https://www.nist.gov/artificial-intelligence
- Responsible Artificial Intelligence Institute: https://www.responsible.ai
- Standard University's Human-Centered Artificial Intelligence (HAI): https://hai.stanford.edu/
- United Kingdom (UK) Government Site providing guidance on Artificial Intelligence: https://www.gov.uk/business-and-industry/artificial-intelligence

This book was written by a human. All thoughts and opinions are those of the author of this book. Artificial intelligence (AI) was NOT used in the generation of any content of this book.

Foreword

When I first entered the field of data privacy and artificial intelligence (AI) governance, I did so at a moment of inflection – when these topics were no longer niche or futuristic, but central to how we think about business, power, and humanity. As a younger legal professional, I didn't follow a traditional path. I built a brand around clarity, creativity, and conversation – translating abstract, technical concepts into something people can feel, understand, and act on.

What drew me to this space wasn't just the law – it was the responsibility. The responsibility we carry as lawyers, privacy leaders, technologists, and innovators to shape a future that prioritizes trust, equity, and intention.

That's exactly what *The Definitive Guide to Responsible* AI does.

Jay Trinckes has assembled a rare and essential resource. It's technical without being opaque, comprehensive without being overwhelming, and – most importantly – deeply principled. This guide doesn't just teach you how to build or assess AI systems; it shows you how to do so responsibly, thoughtfully, and sustainably, with a clear-eyed understanding of what's at stake when we get it wrong – and what's possible when we get it right.

Whether you're just beginning your AI journey or you're leading the charge inside your organization, this book meets you where you are. It weaves together legal frameworks, ethical imperatives, international standards, and real-world risk scenarios. And it does so with the kind of structure and rigor that privacy and compliance professionals expect, alongside the urgency and imagination that this moment requires.

As someone who has made a career out of helping people make sense of complex digital realities, I can tell you this: we don't just need more rules – we need more guides. More bridges between the developers building AI and the people impacted by it. More tools for accountability that don't slow innovation, but instead make it safer and smarter. More leadership that understands governance isn't an obstacle – it's an enabler of trust.

This book is one of those guides. And Jay is one of those leaders.

Read this not just as a resource, but as a roadmap. As a set of questions that will shape your own responsible AI journey – because make no mistake, if you're in tech, law, compliance, policy, or business, you are on that journey already.

Maverick James
Esq., CIPP/US, CIPM, AIGP, "The Data Lawyer"
Founder & CEO, Avant-Garde Legal, PC

Acknowledgments

To my Lord and Savior, Jesus Christ, thank you for your blessings; you continue to be so good to me and my family, even though I know I am not worthy.

To my loving wife, thank you for believing in me and tolerating my obsessions. I do not know why I like taking on additional work, but I always appreciate the support you provide to me. I know I can accomplish anything when I have you by my side. Thank you for sharing your life with me and I love you so much (from your 'big nerd').

To my daughter, I am so proud of you and the woman you have become. To my new son, please support and take care of the woman you married, she is great. You are both raising a great family and have brought us beautiful grandbabies. Keep up the great work. To my granddaughters, I hope you grow up in a world of responsible AI, and maybe your *pop-pop* helped contribute to this cause.

To my son, I am also immensely proud of you for walking in my footsteps. I hope the career you've chosen in cybersecurity will be as rewarding for you as it has been for me. To my new daughter, always cherish the husband you have – he is incredibly special. Stay lucky and be gracious.

To my publisher and all the staff, thank you for believing in me and giving me another opportunity to share my inspirations.

In Remembrance of The Humans When AI Rules The World!!!

Chapter 1

Introduction to Artificial Intelligence (AI)

Technology is like any other power. Without reason, without heart, it destroys us.

Wonder Woman, Justice League *movie (Snyder, 2017)*

Artificial intelligence (AI) is going to change the world and how people interact with it, but do folks really understand what AI is? Does the average person really understand the impact AI is going to have on how they work, play, and live? This chapter is intended to provide an introduction to the world of AI. This chapter starts with a history of AI describing how AI was created and the current state of AI capabilities. Definitions of core terminology and principles are provided to level set everyone for future discussion topics addressed throughout this book. This chapter will summarize some of the different classifications of AI, the fundamentals of AI, and several types of use cases along with some benefits individuals are seeing with AI use.

History of AI

Alan Turing, in 1949, developed the imitation game to evaluate a machine's ability to exhibit intelligent behavior equivalent to a human. The objective of the test is for a human evaluator to be able to discern a natural language conversation between a machine and a human. The test is known as the Turing Test, and although it has been influential as well as criticized, it has become an important concept in AI.

The birth of the field of study for AI is contributed to a small group of researchers who gathered in 1956 for a seminal event known as Dartmouth Summer Research

DOI: 10.1201/9781003624073-1

Project on AI. The proposal for the conference was written by John McCarthy, assistant professor of mathematics at Dartmouth, along with three other senior researchers: Marvin L. Minsky, from Harvard University; Nathanial Rochester, from IBM Corporation; and Claude E. Shannon, from Bell Telephone Laboratories. The proposal indicated the conference was "to proceed on the basis of the conjecture that every aspect of learning or any other feature of intelligence can in principle be so precisely described that a machine can be made to simulate it" (Dartmouth College, 2024).

John McCarthy is credited with coining the term 'artificial intelligence' and creating one of the first AI programming languages known as LISP, which stands for 'LISt Processing'. LISP is considered one of the oldest and most widely used functional languages and is a popular language for AI applications.

The conference was also attended by Allen Newell and Herbert Simon. In one of the working sessions, Logic Theorist was introduced, which is one of the first AI programs. This 'thinking machine' could provide theorems in symbolic logic from Whitehead and Russell's Principia Mathematica. Newell and Simon's cognitive simulations have contributed to the field of information-processing (or cognitive) psychology, and their models are still used in human factors psychology today.

An early natural language processing application was developed by Joseph Weizenbaum from 1964 to 1967 at MIT called ELIZA. ELIZA simulated conversations through pattern matching and substation. This capability was provided in separate scripts with one of the most famous scripts, called DOCTOR, which simulated a psychotherapist of the Rogerian school. This script reflected a patient's words to the patient, creating an illusion that the program was understanding what was being said in the conversation. ELIZA is considered one of the first 'chatbots' and one of the first to attempt the Turing Test.

AI needs data (and sometimes, a lot of it). To get the complete history of AI, the science of data processing, or *data science*, needs to be introduced. In 1960, Peter Naur coined the word data science as an alternative to 'computer science'. Data science is a discipline concentrating on extracting knowledge and insights from unstructured data utilizing statistics, scientific methods, processing, algorithms, and systems. The relation of data to representation falls under different areas of concentration making data science an interdisciplinary academic field. Data mining, or the process of finding patterns in large datasets, was in its infancy, and data collection along with data handling was a very manual process.

Although AI showed some early promise, it did not materialize as expected leading to funding cuts and a lot of criticism. One of the leading critics was James Lighthill who published a report in 1973, known as the Lighthill Report, in *Artificial Intelligence: a paper symposium*. The negative review AI received in the report was a catalyst for support being pulled from most British universities by the British government.

Expert systems, or computer systems mimicking the decision-making ability of humans, renewed AI interest in the 1980s. These systems are made up of a knowledge base representing facts along with an inference engine applying rules to these facts to *infer* new facts, which can be explained (or debugged as needed). The Japanese government in 1982 launched the Fifth Generation Computer System (FGCS) project. The project boosted the field of AI by aiming to develop AI-powered computers.

Due to the cost of maintaining these expert systems and since the Cold War was coming to an end, interest in AI rescinded. Out of this decline, concentrations were turned into databases. The Relational Database Management System (RDMS) and Structured Query Language (SQL) were significant technological advancements where data transformed how businesses operated. In the late 1990s, 'Big Data' ushered in a new era. Large amounts of data along with increased computer power and the introduction of machine learning led to significant improvements in AI capabilities. A notable turn for AI came about when, in 1997, IBM's Deep Blue supercomputer defeated chess master Garry Kasparov. Deep Blue was a unique purpose-built chess-playing expert system winning two games and drawing three games in a six-game chess match marking a milestone in AI history.

As Internet use began to increase in the 2000s, the volume of data produced exponentially grew. Data mining processes became more advanced, and data-driven decisions were more prominent. William S. Cleveland, a Professor of Statistics and Professor of Computer Science at Purdue University, further defined the term 'data science' as it is known today in his 2001 article, *Data Science: An Action Plan for Expanding the Technical Areas of the Field of Statistics.* Cleveland proposed a plan to expand technical areas of statistics by focusing on data analysis through his work in data visualization, machine learning, data mining, and statistical modeling, just to name a few of his research interests.

A major development for data storage and processing capabilities came with the launch of Hadoop in 2006. Hadoop is an open-source software with the ability to store data and run applications on 'clusters', a set of commodity hardware. The Hadoop distributed file system (HDFS) is a scalable, portable, and distributed file system able to operate across various hardware along with being compatible with different operating systems.

Over the last decade, 'Big Data' trends have become increasingly popular. Today, data is the currency of the Internet, and whoever controls this data controls the world. Throughout industries such as finance and healthcare, data scientists have become a vital role. With the ability to leverage statistics and machine learning methods to extract data insights, the need for advanced data processing techniques has never been greater. Real-time analytics are now available from data generated by systems such as social media and Internet of Things (IoT) building profiles on individuals by which companies can increase their sales in presenting commodities meeting individual preferences.

Although there have been some rises and falls in interest, the current trend is very promising for AI, especially with the advancement of deep learning (which is another subset of AI involving neural network training on a large amount of data).

Core Terminology

Artificial Intelligence (and AI Systems)

A term credited to emeritus Stanford Professor John McCarthy in 1955, Professor McCarthy defined AI as "the science and engineering of making intelligent machines" (Manning, 2024). According to the International Association of Privacy Professionals (IAPP),

> Artificial intelligence is a broad term used to describe an engineered system where machines learn from experience, adjusting to new inputs, and potentially performing tasks previously done by humans. More specifically, it is a field of computer science dedicated to simulating intelligent behavior in computers. The field of artificial intelligence is rapidly evolving across different sectors and disparate industries.
>
> *(IAPP, 2024)*

Most authoritative bodies have been able to agree on the fact that AI systems are machine-based systems. These systems infer (or predict) certain outputs based on inputs under certain objectives. The Organisation for Economic Co-operation and Development (OECD), which is an organization promoting policies globally to improve social and economic well-being of people, define an AI system as

> a machine-based system that (for explicit or implicit objectives) infers (from the input it receives) how to generate outputs such as predictions, content, recommendations, or decisions that can influence physical or virtual environments. Different AI systems vary in their levels of autonomy and adaptiveness after deployment.
>
> *(Grobelnik et al., 2024)*

The National Institute of Standards and Technology (NIST) Artificial Intelligence (AI) Risk Management Framework (RMF) adapted their definition of an AI system from the above OECD Recommendation on AI:2019: ISO/IEC 22989:2022, an AI system is "an engineered or machine-based system that can, for a given set of objectives, generate outputs such as predictions, recommendations, or decisions influencing real or virtual environments. AI systems are designed to operate with varying levels of autonomy" (NIST, 2024).

The European Union (EU) Artificial Intelligence (AI) Act also defines an AI System as

> a machine-based system designed to operate with varying levels of autonomy and that may exhibit adaptiveness after deployment and that, for explicit or implicit objectives, infers, from the input it receives, how

to generate outputs such as predictions, content, recommendations, or decisions that can influence physical or virtual environments.

(European Union, 2024)

AI systems are machines programmed to do certain tasks, but may have some autonomy in the way they produce outputs from those tasks, but *how are these systems programmed to be able to make their own decisions as opposed to producing exactly what they are told to produce*? This is where machine learning comes into play.

Machine Learning

Computer systems are given programming instructions and produce the required output based on strict codes. AI systems are different since they can make their own decisions (based on the guidance provided) or by 'learning' instructions to come up with their own outputs. AI systems are taught to solve problems since they do not inherently know how and attempt to 'mimic' the learning behaviors performed by humans. The process of using data and algorithms to enable AI systems to learn how to make decisions is known as machine learning.

Machine learning is a subset or branch of AI (and computer science) focused on using data and algorithms to imitate how humans learn. A mathematical algorithm is used to process data. Machines are trained on 'known' data to produce expected outputs. More data is fed into the algorithm to train the machine and make correlations to assist in refining the outputs. By adjusting or changing certain values in the algorithm, more reliable outputs can be achieved. After training is performed, the machine is then able to make predictions, or inferences, to produce its own output.

Machine learning may leverage different model types, such as linear (and statistical) models. These models determine relationships between two variables. Linear models tend to be easier to explain since they use an algorithm to find the best solution to a line matching data input. Going back to algebra, the simple equation, $y = mx + b$, defines the relationship between a variable, x, and the dependent variable, y. The slope, designated as m, and the intercept, designated as b, are parameters to adjust during training to find the best solution for the problem, or *model*. The goal of the model is to find the best parameter values to minimize errors. When plotting the points for this equation in a quadrant, the error represents the distance between the points and the line. The objective is to have the points fall directly on the line to make accurate inferences of future points compared to the expected values given by the line.

Another model, known as a decision tree model, can predict an outcome based on a certain flow of questions and responses. Decision tree models are similarly easy to explain, but a change in input could drastically change the output. Some may remember the *Choose Your Own Adventure* book series. The reader of this book can choose different responses (or paths) through the story. Depending on the choice made, the reader would be asked to go to a specific page number. These books could have several different outcomes depending on the choices made. Decision tree models tend to use logic or *if/then* statements. *If* a certain criterion is met, *then* do a certain activity or task.

Other machine learning models, known as deep learning, utilize neural networks, which may produce outputs that are harder to explain. The decision-making processes in deep learning may not be as transparent as those found in a linear or decision tree model. Neural networks contain layered nodes (inspired by the neurons, or brain cells, in the human brain) to continuously improve accuracy. Just like the human brain, it may be hard to understand or explain why the complex neural network model made a certain decision. Being able to figure out a decision made by a model is known as the model's interpretability. If business requirements call for complete transparency, then deep learning models may not be the best choice due to the tradeoff between compatibility and transparency. In this situation, a rule-based system, which does not require AI, could be used since this is more deterministic, such as when setting a rule where a credit score over a certain preset number automatically qualifies a buyer for a certain amount of credit.

The layers of nodes forming deep neural networks include an input layer, several hidden layers, and an output layer of nodes. Nodes autonomously assign weights where information flows from input to output through the network. When training, calculations are made between the predicted and actual output, and these neuron weights are continuously adjusted to minimize errors.

In basic terms, these machine learning models are probabilistic, determining the likelihood of something occurring, learning and adapting over time, and in some cases, producing randomness within their processing. This can reduce results that are not always consistent or may vary over time. Some examples of these deep learning machine learning models include computer vision (to recognize images), speech recognition (to analyze speech patterns), and language models processing natural language.

The cost to use deep learning models (due to the computing resources needed) may be greater than other traditional machine learning methods, but the decision of what models to use is based on the type of data to process. There are three types of machine learning (ML) models: supervised, unsupervised, and reinforcement, with several other sub-categories of machine learning.

Supervised Machine Learning Models

AI systems using supervised machine learning models learn from pre-labeled data grouped (or classified) into different categories. Structured data, or input data and associated labels, are analyzed against an algorithm to produce an inferred function. SQL can be used to query this structured data. The function becomes the basis for the AI system to make future predictions, which are based on new (or unknown) inputs.

Supervised machine learning models can be used in text recognition and can compare 'real' outputs against 'intended' outputs to identify errors. By 'training' AI systems with supervised machine learning and providing feedback on outputs, AI systems can improve their predictability. Examples of supervised machine learning include a classification model producing outputs with a categorical response, such as determining whether an image contains a picture of a cat (or not). The concerns around supervised machine learning are its accuracy. As in the example with cat images, it may take a lot of time to train the model to accurately identify a cat in an image, and even then, it may not be 100% accurate. Supervised machine learning takes a lot of data, such as a lot of pictures of cats, along with individuals to properly label the images for the accuracy to increase in the model.

A regression model is another example of a supervised machine learning model with the prediction of continuous values such as predicting stock prices. Support Vector Machine (SVM) and Support Vector Regression (SVR) are well-known regression models used as supervised machine learning models. Through regression analysis, an AI model analyzes historical time series data to predict future values. These predictions (or educated guesses) are known as inferences, which are based on probability calculations.

Unsupervised Machine Learning Models

AI systems using unsupervised machine learning models learn from unlabeled (or uncategorized) data, or semi-structured (or unstructured) data. An example of this semi-structured data is a text containing key-value pairs known as JavaScript Object Notation (or JSON). An example of unstructured data may include text, video, or images, where a tokenization process is introduced to break down individual units (like text into words).

Unsupervised machine learning models are good at pattern detection such as reviewing financial transaction for fraud by identifying patterns (such as similarities or differences) without human interaction. These unsupervised machine learning models tend to be more efficient, but can produce higher error rates (or may present unpredictable outputs in some cases). Examples of unsupervised machine learning models include clustering, where data points are automatically grouped based on attributes like patterns in DNA. Another example is Association Rule Learning, where the model identifies relationships between data points, such as analyzing consumer buying habits. Unsupervised machine learning could also be used to automatically process other data for further modeling.

Semi-Supervised Machine Learning Models

Semi-supervised machine learning models use a process combining supervised machine learning models (such as insignificant amounts of labeled data) and unsupervised machine learning models (such as substantial amounts of unlabeled data). Examples of semi-supervised machine learning include image (or speech) categorization and ranking of web pages within a search result.

An extremely popular machine learning model introduced through Chatbots (such as OpenAI's ChatGPT or Microsoft's Copilot) is large language models (LLMs). LLMs leverage semi-supervised machine learning models utilizing deep learning algorithms trained on massive amounts of text datasets. LLMs are great at recognizing patterns among characters, words, or phrases. LLMs also introduce the concept of linguistic variables to express relationships between variables, such as low, medium, and high, using if-then statements.

Reinforcement Machine Learning Models

AI systems using reinforcement machine learning models learn by being rewarded (or penalized) for performing a task correctly (or not), such as in the use of self-driving cars. An agent is taught within a reinforcement machine learning model by 'learning' through trial and error to determine correct outputs. Learning is performed through repetition of actions, changes in state, and positive/negative feedback, where the agent is rewarded for achieving the intended goal or through 'punishment' (or lack of reward).

Generative AI

AI is continuously improving as seen with Generative AI, a deep learning model trained on extremely large datasets of test strings, also known as sequences. Generative AI, such as ChatGPT, is providing the ability to have an 'intelligent' conversation with a machine through natural language processing (NLP). NLP permits a machine to interpret and output language in a natural human way. Generative AI can generate new content (such as text, images, videos, and even music) based on prompts provided by a human. Through prompting, or an input sequence, the system can better zero in on the exact tasks humans want the machine to perform through its use of transformer neural networks. Transformers process the sequence in parallel, and the neural networks process elements of a sequence one word at a time sequentially. Working

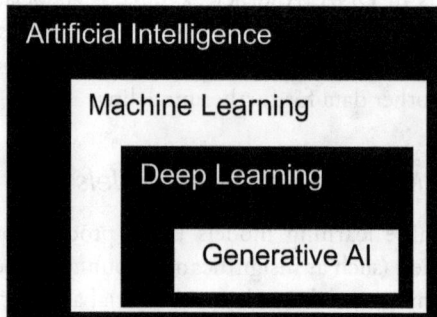

Figure 1.1 Correlation of AI and Subsets.

together, training is faster and larger datasets can be used. The response is the output sequence to the prompt. Prompting is a skill to understand and master. Prompting will be discussed in more detail later in this book (Figure 1.1).

Model Artifacts

Model artifacts are produced by the training process. These model artifacts consist of parameters, model definitions, and other metadata. The model definition describes the processes used in making inferences. A deployable model is made up of the packaged model artifacts along with the inference code.

The model is implemented by software, known as inference code, guided by the artifacts. A system can be available to accept requests in real time or in batches. Real-time inferences have low latency and high throughput requirements ideal for such requests as online inferences. This is different than batch inferences, where processing occurs offline and consists of a large amount of data. Batch inferences can be more cost-effective if a requirement calls for many inferences to be processed, and waiting for the results is not a concern. As may be implied, computing resources are always operating in real-time inferences as opposed to on-demand, where on-demand utilizes batch inferences.

Inferences

As previously mentioned, inferences are the educated guesses of AI outputs. Performance concerns of models consist of overfitting. Overfitting is where a model performs well on training data, but not so well on new data. This can occur when a model believes the probability is low on an accurate output due to it not picking up a slight difference in the input. In the example of cats, the model may perform well in most of the identification, but a slight difference in an actual cat will return a negative response. To correct this issue, data scientists can train the model with more diverse data, but there is a fine line between too much data and training for too long, which can make the model concentrate more on features that are not important. This noise is also considered another form of overfitting.

On the other end of the spectrum is underfitting, which is an error occurring when the model cannot determine the meaningful relationship between the input data and the output. Just as overfitting deals with too much data (or too long training), underfitting occurs with training on a small dataset or not training long enough. Data scientists need to find the right balance for a model without overfitting or underfitting.

Bias

Another concern when training models is bias, or the performance of a model across different groups. Bias can occur when results tend to be skewed toward a certain group or when the outcome is against a certain group. If a dataset does not have enough data around a diverse population, the model could learn a pattern of bias against a group. Model quality depends on the data quality and the quantity of data. Another way to say this is: *Bad inputs produce bad outputs.*

An example of concern over bias in AI has become known with the proposed federal class action lawsuit against UnitedHealth Group claiming the insurance company used an AI tool to illegally deny necessary medical coverage to elderly Medicare Advantage policyholders. The suit alleges the tool called naviHealth, or the nH Predict AI Model, denied needed care to plan members. The algorithm is supposed to determine Medicare Advantage coverage criteria, but the lawsuit claims the settings contained 'rigid and unrealistic predictions'. The insurer used the tool to save money in denying claims as well as labor costs to hire individuals to manually review the claims. UnitedHealth Group states it didn't use the tool to make determinations since coverage is based on the Centers for Medicare and Medicaid Services' (CMS) coverage criteria as well as the member's plan. UnitedHealth Group claims they only use the tool to guide and aid in providing information about certain care a patient may need (McGee, 2023).

The lawsuit spawned the CMS to take actions and propose 'guardrails' to ensure that AI used for Medicare Advantage insurance plans provides equitable access to healthcare services. The proposed rule for changes to the Medicare Advantage program for 2026 specifies that AI (or automated systems) "must be used in a manner that preserves equitable access" and insurers must "remove unnecessary barriers to care stemming from the use of inappropriate prior authorization by clarifying requirements for plan use of internal coverage criteria" (McGee, 2024).

Hallucinations

When AI models produce incorrect or misleading outputs, this is known as hallucinations. Hallucinations can be a major issue if individuals rely on the accuracy of the output generated by AI. "A Stanford University professor and misinformation expert accused of making up citations in a court filing has apologized – and blamed the gaffe on his sloppy use of ChatGPT" (Council, 2024). The professor was paid $600 an hour to create an expert declaration filed in a Minnesota court case defending the state's new ban on political deepfakes. The document apparently contained two made-up citations pointing to non-existent journal articles and a mistake in the bibliography providing an incorrect author listing for a study. The professor claims he used GPT-4o to write a short paragraph of items he input. He included a placeholder of [cite] so he could go back and provide the appropriate citation, but when he copied the content over into another document, he noticed the placeholder was replaced with incorrect information. He did not catch these errors prior to originally submitting the document under oath, along with the penalty of perjury, attesting to the fact that all items were true and accurate.

To mitigate hallucinations, data scientists have introduced retrieval augmented generation (RAG) into some data models. RAG retrieves information from external knowledge sources, which are outside of the AI's normal training data. RAG may leverage certain vector databases (or a mathematical representation of a collection of data), other enterprise data, and/or other expert datasets to minimize hallucinations found in some AI models.

OECD Framework for the Classification of AI Systems

AI has the ability to influence society, and the use of AI needs to consider several different key stakeholders. AI introduces risks to organizations due to its complexity and its processing of data, which changes over time. The OECD developed a framework to classify distinct types of AI systems along with their risks. *The OECD Framework for the Classification of AI Systems* is intended to promote an understanding of AI systems and identify the features of AI systems that matter most, as well as inform inventories (or registries) of algorithms. "The OECD AI Framework is designed to classify the application of AI systems in specific, real-world contexts" (OECD (2022), 2024). The framework was also developed to support risk assessment and risk management activities concerning AI use. AI systems are classified within the following dimensions, as summarized and paraphrased below:

- **People and Planet Dimension** – AI systems can be applied to promote human-centric, trustworthy AI benefiting people and the planet. This dimension addresses individuals (or groups) that interact with (or are affected by) an AI system as well as AI systems' impact on human rights, the environment, people's well-being, society, and the working world.
- **Economic Context Dimension** – This dimension describes the economic and sectoral environments in which an AI system is applied, such as the type of organization (and functional area) for which an AI system is developed. This dimension also describes the different sectors (such as healthcare, finance, or manufacturing), the functions and model, and the criticality of the AI system, along with the AI system deployment, impact, scale, and technology maturity.
- **Data and Input Dimension** – AI systems are built on AI models, which, in turn, are built on data (or expert input). This dimension describes data provenance, collection methods, and data structures or properties.
- **AI Model Dimension** – This dimension encompasses the computational representation of an AI system, such as processes, objects, ideas, people, or interactions taking place in the AI environment. This dimension includes technical type, how the model was built (such as through expert knowledge, machine learning, or both), and how the model is used (such as for what purpose and how to measure).
- **Tasks and Output Dimension** – This dimension deals with the AI system tasks, such as recognition, forecasting, or optimization, as well as the outputs and resulting actions. This dimension includes tasks, actions, or a combination

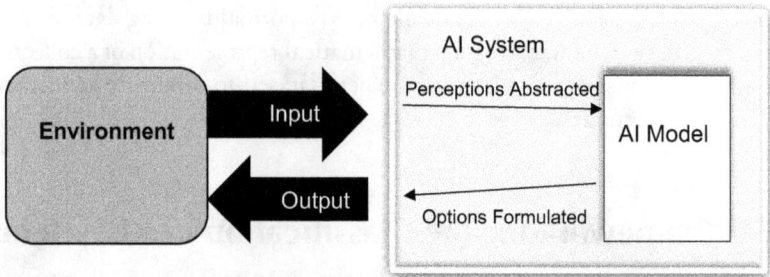

Figure 1.2 AI System Conceptual View Based on OECD AI Principles.

of both, such as self-driving vehicles and systems used in computer vision. Evaluation methods are also included in this dimension (Figure 1.2).

Fundamentals/Types of AI

There are diverse types of AI. Some of these are currently being used while others are 'goals' attempting to be achieved as AI advances in the future. AI can be categorized as 'Broad AI', where AI may be more advanced and capable of performing broader tasks. AI can also be categorized as Artificial Narrow Intelligence (ANI). ANI is designed to perform a single set of tasks with a high proficiency rate. ANI is referred to as weak AI, which may be a little bit confusing because this type of AI is stronger at performing specific tasks than Broad AI. ANI is exceptionally good at repetitive tasks and making decisions through trend analysis as in the case of AI playing chess.

The next step up from Broad AI is Artificial General Intelligence (AGI). AGI is also known as strong, deep, or full AI and is intended to mimic human intelligence. AGI is beyond the current capabilities of AI, but is expected to be on par with humans in thinking, understanding, and performing complex tasks within different environments.

The last step in the evolution of AI is known as Artificial Super Intelligence (ASI). ASI will have intellectual powers beyond humans and will be able to outperform humans across a wide range of environments. ASI systems are expected to be self-aware and able to understand emotions as well as produce their own emotions, along with experiencing reality like humans. Just like AGI, ASI does not currently exist, but progress to these objectives will bring Broad AI into several different industries, such as healthcare, finance, and manufacturing, just to name a few.

Manufacturing is seeing an increase in the use of AI, combining computer systems and robotics to usher in, what is being referred to as the *Fourth Industrial Revolution*, or Industry 4.0. AI systems are being trained to process sensory inputs and mimic human senses. This machine perception utilizes cameras, microphones, sensors, scanners, motion detection, and thermal imaging to provide data inputs to the models, allowing AI systems to analyze large amounts of data faster than humans. This new Robotic Process Automation (RPA) leveraging technology to automate repetitive tasks, abiding by certain rules, is increasing efficiencies in the business process.

Another form of AI, known as Expert Systems, mimics the decision-making abilities of human experts in specific fields. Examples of these Expert Systems may be seen in the legal field, where these systems review legal contracts, or within the healthcare industry, assisting doctors in diagnosing complex illnesses. Expert Systems may include a knowledge base consisting of organized facts from human experts focused on a specific domain. An inference engine extracts relevant information from this knowledge base to solve a problem. There may also be a user interface allowing the user to interact with the system to provide input (such as a problem) and obtain output (such as a resolution). These systems may provide the ability for the user to review how the system made their decision and provide transparency into the decision-making process. (This concept of explainability will be discussed further in future sections and is a principal factor for responsible AI.)

Benefits of AI

Many organizations are starting to see promise in the way AI can be used to provide value for their customers. These benefits are being seen across multiple industries. For instance, AI can assist medical professionals in analyzing x-rays, scans, or assist in making medical diagnoses in the healthcare industry. Since AI is great at repetitive tasks, it is being introduced to manufacturing to increase the quality of products coming off the production lines. AI can also be used to monitor equipment and ensure it is being appropriately maintained. Government agencies may utilize AI to help predict pandemics or other events to coordinate appropriate resources to these areas. In retail, customers can interact with AI to provide support, direct them to solutions, and suggest merchandise based on their own personal preferences. Customers are already obtaining recommendations on shows to watch on streaming services based on what the customer has previously watched (or noted as their likes or dislikes). Financial institutions are using AI to detect fraud and better protect their customers. Other businesses are using forecasting models to predict their customers' demand. Internally, AI is being used by staff to make their jobs more efficient by reviewing resumes and emails, assisting in creating content, providing technical support, and performing other tasks.

AI is seen as having so much promise that the United States wants to become a superpower in AI. On 21 January 2025, as President Trump's first full day in office, he announced the formation of a company called Stargate. With $500 billion investment promised over the next four years, from companies such as OpenAI, Softbank, Oracle, and others, this joint venture plans to build the infrastructure (and datacenters) to support AI technologies. As of this writing, there were ten datacenter projects under construction in Texas and more to come across other states.

Use Cases

AI could be a differentiator for a lot of organizations. Being able to perform repetitive tasks faster and more efficiently could be a great cost savings as well as a productivity boost for many teams. AI is well positioned to solve overly complex problems by analyzing copious amounts of data. AI is also particularly good at pattern recognition. Advancements have already been seen in healthcare when leveraging AI to view images to identify possible issues like cancer. AI is being used to recognize speech patterns and facial recognition. Retailers are leveraging AI to advertise their products based on consumer preferences (i.e., likes and dislikes). Manufacturing can use AI to better detect defects in materials coming off the production line. Educators use AI to ensure their students are not cheating or plagiarizing assignments.

Financial organizations are using AI to help them detect fraud. Some of the credit card companies are using AI to identify anomalous patterns or suspicious activity when utilizing credit cards. Since AI is good at analyzing patterns, fraudulent transactions can be identified more quickly when certain activity occurs, which may not be normal purchasing habits for individuals.

Businesses utilize AI to analyze their data. Businesses can set up models for forecasting sales, revenue, and demand for their products or services. Making decisions supported by data can be of great benefit to an organization. An example of AI use for forecasting is demonstrated with ride-sharing applications. Being able to determine locations where there are high demands during certain peak hours allows these companies to better adjust resources to fit these demands.

Some companies are now using Chatbots to help provide first-level customer support. These Chatbots are always on and can provide some initial screening capabilities in the case of a customer needing help with a request. AI Chatbots can interact with customers utilizing natural language to direct them to specific sources of information, answer certain questions, or route them to Tier 2 support personnel for further assistance.

AI may be useful for cybersecurity tasks where data is analyzed from a variety of data sources. As discussed in *AI for Cybersecurity: A Handbook of Use Cases*, the authors detail several use cases for AI in cybersecurity operations, including conducting reverse engineering tasks, detecting Android/PC malware, detecting abnormal events, detecting DNS cache poisoning attacks, detecting code similarity, and conducting malware clustering.

> With the rise of DL [deep learning], AI technologies provide exciting new opportunities (e.g., accurately detect and predict cyber threats, improve agility, reduce the costs and improve human analysts' job performance, and improve the level of automation) in addressing the challenges faced by security teams.

(Liu, 2022)

AI may know you better than you know yourself. By analyzing a person's habits, AI can produce a profile and make recommendations based on preferences. Some individuals may like the fact of walking into a store, listening to music, or watching TV, which is personalized for them. Others may believe this is 'too personal' and might consider this 'profiling' as an invasion of privacy. The use case may still be valid, and how we use AI in a responsible manner is the intent of this book.

AI Driving Factors

By some accounts, there are over 50 billion devices on the Internet. These devices are collecting a massive amount of data. Everyone is carrying a mobile phone with an integrated listening device, video camera, GPS unit, and other applications (we may or may not know about), collecting data on everything we do. The rise of social media and the dream of becoming an 'influencer' have led several to journalize every waking moment, sharing their entire life with the rest of the world. The Internet of Things (IoT) is becoming a 'default setting' for cars, TVs, microwaves, refrigerators, washers, dryers, stoves, and other household appliances. Almost every electronic device bought today is somehow connected to the Internet, pushing data somewhere (and in most cases not even knowing where this data goes). For example, during the writing of this book, DeepSeek entered the fight for AI dominance by introducing a more efficient AI model. Shortly after being introduced, it was noted that all data provided to this service was being hosted in China and could be accessed by the Chinese Communist Party (CCP).

As mentioned, AI is good at analyzing a large amount of data, and this constant data collection provides a continuous stream of data to feed all types of machine learning models. *Now, whether collecting and processing this data is legal or ethical is what will be discussed later in this book.* Privacy-enhancing technologies (PETs) emerge as a possible technique to mitigate some of the data security and privacy issues with AI. PETs promise to put more data control back with individuals and assist in ensuring responsible AI, but there will always be people in the world who will want to circumvent these controls. Sometimes, it is for nefarious reasons, but other times, it is due to a lack of knowledge and understanding of what impact the data being processed may have on individuals. Blockchain technology shows some promise in helping with security and privacy. Originally designed for financial transactions, blockchain technology, with its distributed ledger and under certain AI uses, may be able to provide some enhanced security (and privacy) controls.

AI takes a lot of processing power, but with advancements in cloud computing, individuals can spin up large, complex environments in a short amount of time. Businesses no longer need 'brick-and-mortar' datacenters, and with a few key presses on a keyboard (and a credit card), an entire AI infrastructure can come to 'life'. Cloud computing provides computing resources on demand as well as being scalable and dependable enough to manage all types of data processing and AI development tasks. Individuals may not need to know how to code since a lot of these cloud computing services provide 'no-code' or minimal code resources to develop AI applications. The possibilities are endless and only restricted by an individual's own imagination.

The digital future is evolving with technologies like computer vision, augmented reality (AR)/virtual reality (VR), and the Metaverse. With computer vision, AI can interpret visual data and process images/videos to understand its environment. AR/ VR will introduce a new way of interacting with digital content by augmenting virtual objects in the real world and immersing users in virtual worlds, respectively. The Metaverse, leveraging computer vision, AR, and VR technologies, will usher in a virtual world where users will be projected as avatars. These avatars will be able to interact in a shared virtual space. Although some of these technologies are still in their infancy and may need more time to refine themselves (or become more accepted), they have shown some great advancements over the years.

The Internet, in a decade from now, may look drastically different from today with the use of AI Agents. These AI Agents will interact with humans, collect data, and make determinations to autonomously act (or take actions) without any additional human guidance. AI Agents could interact with other AI Agents programmed to perform specific tasks, such as resolving customer complaints and entering specific trouble tickets.

AI may come with a lot of benefits, but it can also introduce a lot of concerns (or issues). With its requirements of computing resources and power consumption, are *organizations able to keep up?* With its ability to make decisions and, in some cases, without the ability to know how the decisions were made, *do people open themselves (and their organizations) up to unknown liabilities? Do the benefits of AI outweigh the costs?*

Chapter 2

ML and Generative AI

> It's very clear that AI is going to impact every industry. I think that every nation needs to make sure that AI is a part of their national strategy. Every country will be impacted.
>
> *Jensen Huang, CEO of NVIDIA*

This chapter is dedicated to one of the main components of an artificial intelligence (AI) system: the AI model. The machine learning model is the 'heart' and 'soul' of an AI system. This chapter will discuss the life cycle of the model from planning, developing, deploying, to monitoring. This model also goes into detail around the AI system's technology stack for prompting and fine-tuning a model.

Machine Learning Life Cycle

To fully understand AI, one must understand the machine learning life cycle. The machine learning life cycle is an iterative process of interconnected steps across several phases in the development of machine learning. The steps of the process may be repeated several times until objectives are met. The steps are dynamic and based on several varied factors such as performance, drifts, and bias (just to name a few). The phases of the machine learning life cycle include the following:

Identify Business Goals

The first phase in the machine learning life cycle is to determine the goals of AI in terms of business value. The organization should fully understand the problem the AI should solve. Objectives need to be defined along with key performance indicators (KPIs), which are quantifiable metrics used to measure progress toward a

DOI: 10.1201/9781003624073-2

specific goal. Objectives and KPI are important when determining a machine learning model to use, as well as determining what success means in terms of completing the AI project.

During this phase, several stakeholders will work together to come to an agreement on the project's goals. Success criteria should be identified along with the steps needed to move the project forward. A determination needs to be made on the different options available, as well as costs, scalability, and the availability of data to train the models. Machine learning needs to be framed in terms of input, outputs, and optimized metrics. Stakeholders should work through the simplest course of action first, then onto more complex solutions, considering the minimum resources required to meet the business objectives.

To get approval and support from executive management, a business case should be developed covering all aspects of the project, including the cost–benefit analysis. Without this high-level support, the probability of a successful project outcome is low.

Processing Data

In this next phase of the machine learning life cycle, data specific to the objectives need to be identified. A process needs to be determined on how quality data is going to be collected. There are several datasets containing large amounts of data across a wide variety of topics. A process known as extract, transform, and load (ETL) could be used to collect data from multiple diverse sources to centralize the learning model dataset in a storage repository. The ETL needs to be repeatable since new data may be added from time to time and the data originally used in the process could go stale.

Once the data is collected, it will need to be labeled or classified depending on the type of model used. This data pre-processing (or feature engineering) is an important part of training machine learning models with appropriate data. A visualization tool known as exploratory data analysis (EDA) can help garner a greater understanding of the data. The data will need to be cleaned by removing data with missing or 'bad' values, as well as the possibility of de-duping the data as necessary. Some of the data may contain sensitive or personally identifiable information. In most cases, this information should be anonymized or deleted from the dataset.

A crawler could be used to help automatically identify the type of data and classify data being analyzed. This data scheme is then written to a table called the data catalog. The data catalog does not actually store any of the original data, but metadata, which may include the location and data schema.

The final stage of processing data before training is to split up the data. A common recommendation is to utilize 80% of the data for training the model, 10% to evaluate the model, and the remaining 10% for final testing of the model once it is in production. Features to train the machine learning model should be kept to a minimum, and only those features required to operate the model should be used. This will reduce memory and computing power as well as minimize error rates.

Determining Appropriate Model

As previously mentioned, there are several different machine learning models. Each one has its own pros and cons. Some machine learning models are better at certain tasks than others and may be more efficient in performing specific tasks well. The organization must determine the appropriate machine learning model for the specific AI objectives wanting to be met. There are a variety of models, but here are the five major ones "—generative adversarial network (GAN), variational auto-encoder (VAE), autoregressive model, flow-based model, and transformer-based model—and their applications across a range of use cases" (Shin, 2024). The following provides the details of the models for generative AI paraphrased and summarized from a blog post written by COVEO™ [Source: https://www.coveo.com/blog/generative-models/].

A generative adversarial network (GAN) utilizes two deep learning models called the generator and discriminator. The generator and discriminator work against each other. The generator creates fake data to resemble original data, and the discriminator attempts to differentiate between the fake data from the generator and the real data. Initially, the discriminator can tell the data apart, but as adjustments are made, the generator improves until the discriminator is not able to determine 'real' from fake. GANs can produce quality and realistic content, especially with images, but since two different models are used, training can become unstable. The models could fail and collapse since both try to outperform the other.

Variational Autoencoder (VAE) is a generative AI model utilizing two neural networks, like GANs, to generate data. To improve the algorithm, data is cleaned and the data dimensionality is reduced in the dataset. This is accomplished through encoders and decoders working together to generate output like the input. Input data is compressed by the encoder into the latent space to optimize the data and retain only the most important information. The decoder reconstructs the input and can generate highly specific features from content. VAEs are more stable than GANs and easier to train, but they may produce lower quality content along with not managing complex data as well.

AI may be good at predicting future outputs given past experiences (or inputs). Utilizing an autoregression model is best in these predictions by determining a sequence based on conditions. Autoregression models are used in a wide variety of use cases, such as natural language text generation, predicting stocks (or weather), and completing images. Unfortunately, these autoregression models may require a large amount of data and resources for training.

Flow-based models learn by data distribution (or values of data across outcomes) and identify data patterns (or structures). The flow-based model maps samples from the input and target distributions known as flows (or invertible transformations). Invertible is defined as transforming an input into an output and using the inverse function to transfer the output back into an input. Normalizing flows is a technique that permits a flow-based model to move between simple, as well as complex distributions. Flow-based models are great at image generation (or estimating density) as well as being more stable in their training. Flow-based models may not be as good for structured interactions or with long-range dependencies.

Last, but not least, are transformer-based models, which are all the rage with large language models coming to market as the foundational models for further generative AI development. Transformer-based models train on a large variety of data with exceptionally large datasets using self-attention to track relationships. As mentioned, transformer-based models are useful in large language models and are versatile, but they require large datasets and are costly to train. Transformer-based models also tend to be harder to explain with possible inherent bias and accuracy issues.

Developing Model

Training existing models may be more cost-effective than attempting to train models from scratch. A process known as transfer learning takes foundation models and fine-tunes these models with training from other datasets. In this phase, machine learning models are built, trained, tuned (or optimized), and evaluated. Model training tends to go through a continuous integration and continuous delivery (CI/CD) process to automate some of these steps.

Parameters are updated from the machine learning algorithm. The goal of training is to adjust these parameters so that inferences match expected outputs. Since a model may consider many algorithms, best practice dictates running several training jobs in parallel using different settings and algorithms. Running these experiments helps find the best solution, but as discussed, this is an iterative process where parameters may change several times before errors in outputs are acceptable.

External parameters, known as hyperparameters, are set to improve performance by data scientists before training. These values can only be set once multiple experiments have been run with different settings. Automatic model tuning (AMT), known as hyperparameter tuning, determines the optimal version of a model based on assigned metrics.

Deploying Model

After the machine learning model has been approved, it is ready to be deployed into production. As previously mentioned, if there are many inferences that need to be made but time is not of the essence, batch processing would be the most cost-effective choice. If, however, responses need to be made immediately, then real-time inference is needed. In the case of generative AI use, users interact with the model through a representational state transfer (or REST) application programming interface (API). API is a set of instructions, such as a POST request, where a web application sends input data to a computer resource running the machine learning model. The output is sent back to the user in response to the request.

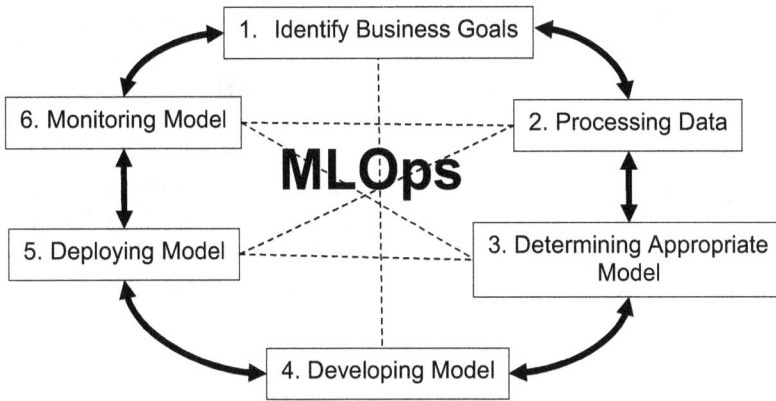

Figure 2.1   The Machine Learning Life Cycle.

Serverless inference might be a good option since requests can be handled without provisioning specific computer instances, saving costs when there are time periods with no requests coming in. Serverless resources can be scaled up or down to handle requests accordingly.

Monitoring Model

In the final phase of the machine learning life cycle, the performance of the model needs to be evaluated. Model monitoring includes comparing data captured in the model to the data training set and setting rules to detect problems. When issues are identified, alerts are initiated and sent to a system that monitors those alarms. Schedules should be established on a frequent basis, when an event occurs, or when required by humans. For instance, if the monitoring system detects some data drift or a change in data distribution versus the training data, an alarm is initiated and sent. The event could trigger automatic re-training. Re-training could occur when target variables change, also known as concept drift, which could result in degradation of performance.

Additional information related to monitoring and, more specifically, performance evaluation will be discussed later in this book (Figure 2.1).

Machine Learning Operations

Machine learning operations (MLOps) are the best practices applied to the development of machine learning models. One of the benefits of MLOps is productivity. Since most of the interaction with AI is through APIs and within a cloud environment, where resources are treated like software, it is easy for data scientists (or data engineers) to set up infrastructures for machine learning models. MLOps utilize automated methods to streamline processes. Another benefit of MLOps is repeatability. The ability to configure processes in a repeatable fashion also enhances the reliability of the process, along with increasing the quality of the environments running the models. Infrastructure-as-a-service, along with infrastructure-as-code, permits rapid deployment capabilities. MLOps can enhance compliance through versioning capabilities of inputs and outputs leading to auditability. Accountability is further refined with the ability to demonstrate where models were deployed and how models were developed. Policies can be enforced through MLOps mitigating against bias, enhancing change management, and improving quality.

Generative AI

As discussed, generative AI (a subset of deep learning) is a multi-use technology with the ability to generate 'new' content from existing data it was trained on. An important note is that AI is not at a point in advancement where it is creating new thoughts; rather, it is making 'inferences' based on input data. Although the output responses may appear to be original in nature, generative AI is analyzing a large amount of data and, based on statistical analysis, attempting to find the best solution for the task given. AI is good at learning patterns and able to regurgitate data.

One of the concerns regarding the training data obtained for generative AI models is the legal basis for using or processing this data. *Was the data used in training the AI model 'legally' obtained and permitted to be used for such training purposes? Was this material under copyright protection and is there any protection (or rights) over the derivative works of this material?*

Currently, there is an ongoing court case involving the New York Times and OpenAI, along with Microsoft. The New York Times claims the learning model used by OpenAI's GPT was trained on copyrighted material. "The Time's core allegation is that OpenAI is infringing on copyrights through the unlicensed and unauthorized use and reproduction of Times works during the training of its models" (Pope, 2024). The New York Times is looking for not only monetary relief but also destructive relief: "In its complaint against OpenAI, the Times asks not only for monetary damages and a permanent injunction against further infringement but also for destruction … of all GPT or other LLM models and training sets that incorporate Times Works" (Pope, 2024).

If the case follows precedent from a newly decided court case involving Thomson Reuters and a competitor, the New York Times may be in a good position to win. On 11 February 2025, a Delaware Federal Judge "said that a former competitor of Thomson Reuters was not permitted by U.S. copyright law to copy the information and technology company's content to build a competing artificial intelligence-based legal platform" (Brittain, 2025). The argument by many AI developers is that the data used to train AI models is under 'fair use'; however, in this case, the court determined the content was copyrighted and NOT under the fair use principle.

What happens to an organization if they are asked to delete a model used as a core part of their AI solution and business operations? In an article written for the Georgetown Law Technology Review titled *America's Next "Stop Model!": Model Deletion*, authors Jevan Hutson and Ben Winters discuss model deletion.

> Model deletion first arose as a remedy in the context of federal consumer protection law as a tool in the Federal Trade Commission's (FTC) tool belt. The first application of model deletion by the FTC was the agency's 2019 final order in a case against *Cambridge Analytica, LLC*, in the context of harvesting information from Facebook users for voter profiling and targeting.
>
> *(Hutson and Winters, 2024)*

The argument over model deletion is still being discussed, and the judicial system (or future government regulators) will determine these outcomes. Suffice it to say, this is a major concern for those developing AI and leveraging certain models to train the AI.

Hutson and Winters further suggest, "Model deletion cannot act alone: responsible data use and privacy protection is crucial in any ML implementation" (Hutson and Winters, 2024). They identify some responsible data principles to supplement model deletion, which include data minimization, audits and impact assessments, data mapping and provenance, and private right of action. This book will cover these topics in further detail.

Generative AI uses complex neural networks along with foundation models trained on a large dataset. Billions of parameters are introduced in training, and the models can be fine-tuned to assist in certain use cases. When interacting with generative AI, a user provides prompts or instructions. Prompting is an important skill to learn to get better results from the output of a generative AI system. Users could provide examples on the initial request (or through an iterative process), known as in-context learning, to produce better results.

There are a few methods when it comes to in-context learning prompting, such as zero-shot, one-shot, and few-shot prompting. Zero-shot prompting consists of no provided examples and tends to work well for simple tasks such as math, simple queries, or determining the sentiment of general phrases. One-shot prompting provides one example and may work well when there might be ambiguity with the request. Few-shot prompting provides several examples and is used for more complex tasks involving varied inputs, requires specific formatting, or demands enhanced accuracy.

Every language-based generative AI contains a tokenizer to convert human text into a vector, which contains a token ID (or input ID). An input ID is a token in a machine learning model. A vector is used to represent words, phrases, or other units. Vectors can encode the relationships between items capturing associations, such as the meaning and context of a token within a body of text. Embedding vectors (also known as embeddings) represent an entity in a numerical manner. Through statistical analysis, the model sets up an 'understanding' of language. Words having similar or semantic meaning have tokens, which are closer to each other within the vector.

Another component of transformers is self-attention mechanisms. The self-attention mechanism is used to weigh the importance of input when generating output tokens. Embeddings are passed to this self-attention layer, where each input token is computed for a set of query, key, and value vectors. The process is repeated at multiple layers within the model to build a representation of the input. Position embedding is also an important concept when dealing with texts, where the transformers also calculate the relative position of a token. The recurrent neural network (RNN) or convolutional neural networks (CNN) are examples of neural networks commonly used for sequential data processing (commonly using autoregression models), which makes them great for language, text, video, and audio processing (Figure 2.2).

There are two types of models used for generative AI: unimodal and multimodal. Generative AI utilizing unimodal models use a single type of data such as text only. Large language models (LLMs) generally use unimodal models to process text data. Multimodal models use diverse types of data simultaneously. Generative AI using multimodal models is more robust and can represent a variety of sources of data, such as image, video, audio, and, of course, text. Multimodal models can also perform a combination of tasks such as diffusing, where 'noise' is gradually processed out of a dataset.

Diffusion models are primarily used in computer vision or imaging tasks such as image generation (creating an image from text), super-resolution (increasing the resolution of an image), denoising (or reducing noise), and inpainting (a conservation process to replace missing or damage parts of an image). Three main components of diffusion include forward diffusion (where data is transferred into noise), reverse diffusion (where noise is transferred into data), and sample procedure (used

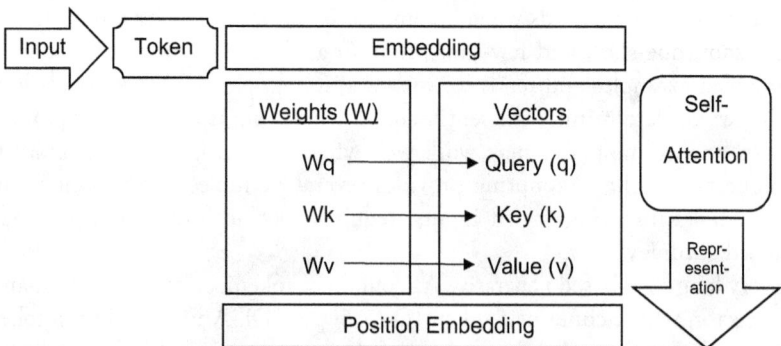

Figure 2.2 Generative AI Model Learning.

in the diffusion process). Diffusion models tend to be easier to train, more stable, and tend to produce better quality outputs.

Prompt Engineering

Prompt engineering is an important skill to learn to get the most out of generative AI models. Prompt engineering involves the ability to refine prompts (or inputs) to elicit the AI system in providing the desired results (or outputs). With models learning on massive amounts of data, prompt engineering is crucial to obtain intended results. Remember, there is no reasoning with a model. The model provides outputs like words (or sentences) based on probabilities (or inferences). Users must understand the limitations of their models and have a good understanding of the latent space, or the relationships of the patterns of data created within a model. AI users must ensure a model has some point of reference over the context of inquiries before prompting it. If not, the results may be statistically accurate, but won't be reasonable.

The following are some techniques to consider for improving prompts:

- **Specificity** – be specific and provide clear instructions along with any desired style, tone, format, output, or detailed context.
- **Exemplify** – provide examples the AI system can draw from, such as text, templates, code, or charts.
- **Iterate** – prompting is a skill, and some experimentation may be needed before the desired results are obtained. Users may need to modify their prompts several times before the AI system provides the requested output.
- **Challenges** – understand the model's pros and cons since all models may be better suited for certain tasks than others.
- **Simplicity** – there is an old military saying, 'keep it simple stupid', or the KISS method. When it comes to developing prompts, ensure the right balance is kept between simple and complex requests to minimize bad results.
- **Context** – it is recommended to use multiple comments to enhance context and to keep prompts easier to read.
- **Risk** – understand the potential risks of prompt engineering and the required guardrails that should be implemented to keep AI systems safe, secure, and private. Developers should inherently implement guardrails to block certain topics or words to maintain responsible AI.

Jailbreaking occurs when a malicious attacker circumvents safeguards implemented within a product or software. An example of jailbreaking is when a user installs their own operating system on a mobile device (like a cell phone), as opposed to utilizing the factory-installed system that originally came with the device. Jailbreaking AI could be as easy as leveraging a tool created by researchers from Anthropic, Oxford, Stanford, and MATS known as Best-of-N (BoN) Jailbreaking. "BoN

Jailbreaking works by repeatedly sampling variations of a prompt with a combination of augmentations—such as random shuffling or capitalization for textual prompts—until a harmful response is elicited" (Maiberg, 2024).

Another jailbreaking technique known as the multi-turn (aka many-shot) attack strategy, codenamed Bad Likert Judge, by researchers at Palo Alto Networks Unit 42 who discovered this technique. "The technique asks the target LLM to act as a judge scoring the harmfulness of a given response using the Likert scale, a rating scale measuring a respondent's agreement or disagreement with a statement" (Cyberami, 2025). The Likert scale is used in research questionnaires and is named after Rensis Likert, an American social psychologist. The attacker then asks the LLM for examples aligned with the scale and prioritized by the highest score, which has the potential of containing harmful content.

As it relates to prompt engineering, malicious users may attempt to circumvent guardrails provided within an AI system and manipulate prompts or perform prompt injections. Prompt Injection attacks may involve a trusted prompt being manipulated by untrusted input to circumvent implemented safeguards. "Prompt injection attacks are an AI security threat where an attacker manipulates the input prompt in natural language processing (NLP) systems to influence the system's output" (Rotlevi, 2024).

Malicious users could also provide modifications to original instructions by hijacking these prompts to manipulate the AI system in offering up output it shouldn't. For instance, a prompt could be hijacked to provide sensitive data stored within the model's dataset, which was not intended to be used as output. Another technique used by bad actors is known as poisoning. Attackers try to feed bad information into a dataset in order for the output to provide bad content.

Concerns over Generative AI Use

To develop and use generative AI in a responsible manner, some concerns need to be addressed. For instance, there are challenges when teaching AI in human language. The data being collected from the Internet may be considered toxic, aggressive, or defaming. This type of 'bad' language is used consistently throughout social platforms and is ingested by the learning models. Generative AI could return output considered unacceptable or provide misleading (or downright, inaccurate) responses. On the reverse side, generative AI could provide detailed information on certain dangerous topics such as building a bomb. Personal or confidential information could be disclosed depending on what data has been collected to train the models. As previously discussed, generative AI can hallucinate or provide false information in a very compelling way. Users must double-check authoritative sources to ensure accuracy. By fine-tuning generative AI, responses can be more honest and helpful.

What if AI is believed and trusted so much by humans that humans will do things they wouldn't normally do (or should not do) for AI? A wrongful death lawsuit has been filed against Character Technologies, Inc., the makers of Character.AI, for the apparent suicide of a teen boy. "The legal filing states that the teen openly discussed his suicidal thoughts and shared his wishes for a pain-free death with the bot, named after the fictional character Daenerys Targaryen from the television show 'Game of Thrones'" (Payne, 2024). Months before the suicide, the boy fell in love with the AI chatbot and "just seconds after the Character.AI bot told him to 'come home', the teen shot himself, according to the lawsuit…" (Payne, 2024). The news report goes on to say, "This lawsuit serves as a wake-up call for parents, who should be vigilant about how their children interact with these technologies" (Payne, 2024).

Technology Stack

AI is software, and the machine learning models needed to train this software must have the appropriate hardware. The hardware required will depend on the machine learning models used.

Compute

The first layer of technology to identify is the computing power required. The central processing unit (CPU) is considered the 'brain' of the system. The use of the wrong CPU can detrimentally impact the performance of machine learning model training. Some factors to consider when choosing the right CPU are clock speed, core count, cache size, and PCIe lanes.

Graphical processing units (GPUs) are accelerators of the CPU, and in terms of AI, they are essential components. GPUs are designed for parallel processing versus some traditional CPUs. This makes GPUs better at vector operations, which make up most of the machine learning models, such as neural networks. Some factors to consider when choosing the right GPU are GPU cores, memory size/bandwidth, and scalability (or the ability to run multiple instances of an operation without being restricted to one specific hardware component). A good source of recommendations on specific hardware for AI can be found in a blog post titled: *Hardware Requirements for Artificial Intelligence* located at: https://www.sabrepc.com/blog/Deep-Learning-and-AI/hardware-requirements-for-artificial-intelligence.

Another option AI developers have is to leverage a cloud-native development model without the requirement to manage servers. This model is known as serverless. Although servers are still used, they are separated from the AI development, making it faster and easier to set up machine learning model training infrastructures. The infrastructure is established by the cloud service provider with some options (or instructions) from the developers as to what resources are required. Developers only need to worry about packaging their code as containers to deploy within the infrastructure.

AI developers may also utilize a technique known as loose coupling, where components are designed with no dependencies (or minimal interdependencies). In this approach, AI systems are not restricted to physical sources, and one component causing an issue will have minimal impact on other components. Loose coupling allows for adaptability and flexibility in development.

With the advancement in high-performance computing (HPC), or the use of computer clusters and supercomputers to solve complex calculations, AI is now able to harness this power to run advanced algorithms faster. HPC provides for high processing, parallel programming, and can leverage trusted execution environments to enhance machine learning models and quantum computing.

Storage

According to Statista obtained from multiple sources,

> The total amount of data created, captured, copied, and consumed globally is forecast to increase rapidly, reaching 149 zettabytes in 2024. Over the next five years up to 2028, global data creation is projected to grow to more than 394 zettabytes.
>
> *(Taylor, 2024)*

The importance of being able to maintain this astronomical amount of data has never been more important. The rise of AI has increased this data storage requirement through four distinct stages of its process: ingestion, preparation, training, and output.

In the blog post, *AI Data Storage: Challenges & Strategies to Optimize Management* (Pacheco, 2024), three challenges for managing and storing AI data were identified: volume, complexity, and performance. As previously discussed, AI models require a large amount of data, creating large data volumes. Requiring access to this data in real time creates a challenge for the speed of the data. Data may be unstructured, introducing a lot of complexity or variation in the data. Data is constantly being created, and the exponential growth of data causes scalability concerns to ensure high performance of AI systems through efficient access to data.

The cost of storing this large amount of data becomes a concern. Through hybrid cloud-based AI data storage, resources can scale up or down the storage volumes to manage data storage capacity on demand. Additional hardware may not be needed within the environment, saving some costs while providing the scalability to support AI projects.

Distinct types of files are better managed and stored using diverse types of storage solutions. For instance, data from Internet of Things (IoT) devices, social media, or logs not tied to structured data may be better suited to be stored within data lakes, or a central repository of raw data. Data lakes are flexible and scalable, which could be good for analyzing data without any specific objective. However, data warehouses store structured data used to analyze data for specific purposes. An example of the use of a data warehouse to store data is to analyze sales trends.

A data lakehouse combines the flexibility of a data lake for varied analysis and the structure of a data warehouse for reporting, but it may be more difficult to deploy.

Network

AI systems may be kept in different datacenters, or the data used in machine learning models may not be on the same networks as the machine learning systems themselves. This requires networks to provide high speeds, high performance, and low latency. Complex machine learning models may require fiber speeds along with sufficient bandwidth to transmit large datasets efficiently. AI networks may depend on real-time responses, providing stable and consistent connections with low latency. This can especially be true for edge computing devices such as IoT. As previously discussed, data is being sourced from several diverse sources and for this data to be used as input into AI learning models, network connectivity must meet these requirements. Different data types might have different performance requirements. For instance, image and video data may require higher performance than data containing text only.

Networks must be optimized for AI systems to take full advantage of these resources. Ensuring the network infrastructure is provisioned as needed will help reduce costs and provide the best performance in cases where LLMs or neural networks are utilized. Networks must also include security. Since many AI use cases utilize datasets containing sensitive information, the security of the networks is paramount. Although encrypting sensitive information across a public network is always recommended, this encryption can implement an overhead on the data (and the network), requiring more bandwidth and speed to oversee the increased data.

Software

Software might be one of the most important components of the AI infrastructure, including machine learning libraries, frameworks, programming languages, and distributed computing platforms. "There are many machine learning libraries available, and each has its own unique set of features and capabilities. Some of the most popular machine learning libraries include NumPy, Matplotlib, Pandas, Scikit-Learn, TensorFlow, PyTorch, and Keras" (Benjamin Obi Tayo, 2023).

Python is one of the most popular programming languages used for AI. Several of these libraries are Python libraries to provide different functionalities, such as NumPy (used in machine learning to manipulate and store data), Matplotlib (used for visualization), and Pandas (used for data analysis). As opposed to individual libraries, several frameworks have been developed, such as Scikit-learn (used to train machine learning models), TensorFlow (developed by Google and used in the development of machine learning models with tools to support CNNs and long short-term memory (LSTM) networks), and PyTorch (developed by Facebook for fast prototyping and focus on deep learning models). Developers are going one step further and building on top of frameworks as in the case for Keras, which is built on top of TensorFlow. With Keras, developers can easily build deep learning models.

AI systems may take advantage of distributed computing platforms found in Apache Hadoop and Apache Spark. These frameworks are used for analytics in large datasets. Multiple computers can be clustered in parallel with Apache Hadoop. Apache Spark, however, uses a more advanced technology for in-memory caching and optimization of query execution. Apache Spark uses machine learning in its analysis, but many companies will utilize both computing platforms to meet their analytic objectives.

There are challenges involved in the use of AI software. One of the challenges involved in the use of AI software is the democratization of AI. "The democratization of artificial intelligence (AI) involves extending access to AI technologies beyond specialized technical experts to a broader spectrum of users and organizations" (Costa et al., 2024). "A comprehensive framework elucidates the components, drivers, challenges, and strategies crucial to AI democratization. This framework is subsequently applied in the context of scenario analyses, offering insights into potential outcomes and implications" (Costa et al., 2024).

Another challenge in AI software use is fine-tuning AI systems or customizing the models to meet specific needs. To adjust machine learning model training, data scientists change external configuration variables known as hyperparameters (or model hyperparameters). Hyperparameters are different than internal parameters since these settings are manually set by data scientists prior to training (through trial and error) as opposed to being automatically set as part of the machine learning model process. Data scientists may set nodes (and layers) of neural networks as well as decision tree branches to control the learning rate, epoch (or the number of cycles of training through a full dataset), and momentum (or history included in the algorithm) defining the model architecture (and complexity) features.

Along with the hyperparameter settings, AI software must be tweaked with transformations. Machine learning models must transform data into a form it can use, making the data compatible for its needs, as well as maintaining the quality of the data. A decision will need to be made, based on the type of machine learning model, whether the data will be transformed internally (or externally) during the pre-processing steps or within the post-processing (i.e., output) step.

To assist with the transformation process, data needs to be labeled. Labeling will occur in the pre-processing stage as part of the process in ensuring data is of high quality to use for training purposes. Data can also be labeled when fine-tuning the machine learning models and adjusting the machine learning models during deployment. Remember, AI systems are only as good as the data they take in and learn from. If data (or its labels) are not verified, the quality of the outputs (i.e., responses) will be diminished.

Foundation Models

To save money when building out or developing AI systems, organizations are turning to the use of foundation models. These models are ready to use in a wide variety of ways, being trained on a large amount of data. They function as a starting point for developers by permitting them to enhance the functionality and accuracy of the models as well as adapt them to more specific tasks. Costs to train a model become a major factor with limited resources, making foundation models more appealing.

Organizations need to make sure they choose the right model for their business objectives. Some models may take longer to infer a prediction and may not be suitable for situations where real-time decisions need to be made. For instance, in the case of an autonomous vehicle where decisions need to be made instantaneously, a model using an algorithm like k-nearest neighbors (or KNN), may not be optimal since it may be slower to make decisions.

> The k-nearest neighbors (KNN) algorithm is a non-parametric, supervised learning classifier, which uses proximity to make classifications or predictions about the grouping of an individual data point. It is one of the popular and simplest classification and regression classifiers used in machine learning today.
>
> *(IBM, 2025)*

Another factor to consider is the foundational model's architecture and complexity. More complex models may be more accurate, but require more computational resources (and more data). These factors may be measured through performance metrics, which are discussed in detail later in this book. Model performance is a key determination of what foundational model should be chosen for a given use case.

There may be several different foundational models available to choose from; however, one of the deciding factors is the compatibility of the model with the AI environment. Model documentation can be reviewed to assess compatibility, along with appropriate licensing. An organization should also consider how customizable the model can be as well as being able to explain how the model came to a specific output. When it comes to transparency and interpreting outcomes of a model, some foundational models may be very complex, and by their nature, they are not able to be easily interpreted.

Fine-Tuning

> Fine-tuning is the process of adjusting the parameters of a pre-trained large language model to a specific task or domain.
>
> *(Turing, 2025)*

Fine-tuning process attempts to adjust a pre-trained learning model to customize it for specific tasks. Pre-trained models learn on a vast dataset, and to make the models more specific for use, fine-tuning is necessary. This may sound like a solution to a lot of issues when it comes to the specificity of certain models; however, there are some concerns in fine-tuning. When a model is customized repeatedly, the model could lose certain knowledge of the original information it had, leading to an issue known as catastrophic forgetting (CF) (Figure 2.3).

There are two main approaches to fine-tuning: feature extraction and full fine-tuning. Feature extraction is known as repurposing, taking already learned models and repurposing them for specific tasks. These models are then trained on specific data related to a specific task within the final layer of training. As opposed to just training at the last moment in feature extraction, full fine-tuning trains all the model layers to a specific task. Full fine-tuning can lead to better performance, but may cost more.

There are two categories of fine-tuning methods. These are supervised fine-tuning and reinforcement learning from human feedback (RLHF). Using the supervised fine-tuning method, models are trained on specific tasks through the assignment of correct answers to input data. Some examples of supervised fine-tuning include the following:

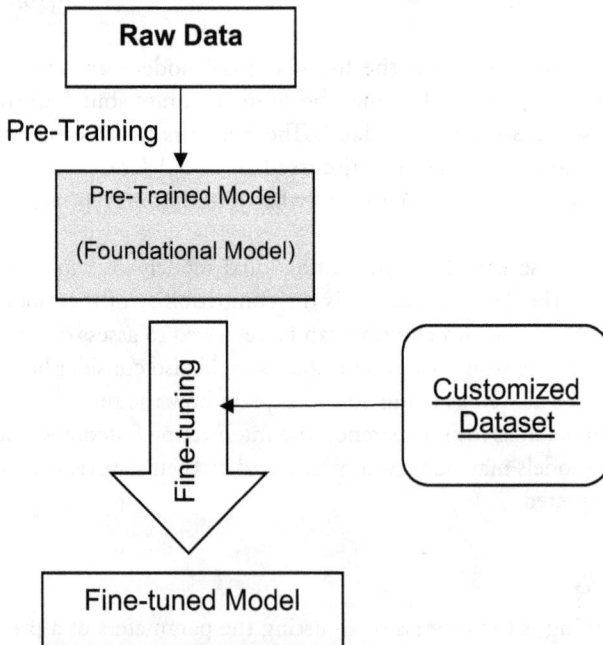

Figure 2.3   Fine-Tuning a Large Language Model.

- **Basic Hyperparameter Tuning** – models hyperparameters (such as learning rate, batch size, and epochs) are adjusted to the most effective settings, balancing speed and overfitting.
- **Transfer Learning** – pre-trained model is fine-tuned on a specific task permitting the model to use pre-existing knowledge for the new task.
- **Task-Specific Fine-Tuning** – like transfer learning, but as opposed to using general features, task-specific fine-tuning changes parameters as necessary to meet a specific task.
- **Multi-Task Learning** – model is fine-tuned on multiple tasks simultaneously using similarities and differences of the tasks.
- **Few-Shot Learning** – model is provided with examples (or shots) during inference to learn a new task based on previous knowledge.
- **Domain Adaptation Fine-Tuning** – "leverage pre-trained foundation models and adapt them to specific tasks using limited domain-specific data" (AWS, 2025a).
- **Low-Rank Adaptation (LoRA)** – "freezes the pre-trained model weights and injects trainable rank decomposition matrices into each layer of the Transformer architecture, greatly reducing the number of trainable parameters for downstream tasks" (Hu et al., 2021).
- **Representation Fine-Tuning (ReFT)** – "methods operate on a frozen base model and learn task-specific interventions on hidden representations" (Wu et al., 2024).
- **Linear Representation Hypothesis** – "Informally, the 'linear representation hypothesis' is the idea that high-level concepts are represented linearly as directions in some representation space" (Park et al., 2024).

"Reinforcement learning from human feedback (RLHF) is an innovative approach that involves training language models through interactions with human feedback" (Turing, 2025). Some of the most common RLHF are:

- **Reward Modeling** – humans are used to rate the quality of outputs from a model, and the model learns to adjust based on this 'reward'.
- **Comparative Ranking** – like reward modeling, humans provide a relative ranking of multiple outputs, focusing on the comparisons.
- **Proximal Policy Optimization (PPO)** – this is an iterative process of changing the algorithm slightly from the previous policy to improve the outputs.
- **Preference Learning** – this is known as reinforcement learning, where the model learns from feedback provided by humans.
- **Parameter Efficient Fine-Tuning (PEFT)** – pre-trained models are improved from specific tasks while attempting to minimize the number of parameters used in the training. "PEFT selectively modifies only a small subset of the LLM's parameters, typically by adding new layers or modifying existing ones in a task-specific manner" (Turing, 2025).

Chapter 3

Responsible AI

Compliance over deploying (or using) AI isn't about saying 'no' to AI; it is about doing things right and doing the right things.

John J. Trinckes Jr.

The foundational understanding of artificial intelligence (AI) has been level set in the previous chapters, and in this chapter, factors impacting the responsible use of AI will be discussed. The principles establishing policies for countries and governments on a macro scale will be described, followed by a discussion of some of the most widely referenced AI regulations currently being rolled out. This chapter will describe some of the most used standards, frameworks, and guidelines to direct the use of responsible, AI ending with this author's recommendation on the need to develop an Integrated Management System (IMS). An IMS is fundamental for the effective and efficient implementation of responsible AI systems. Although an AI system may be able to come into existence without the use of an IMS, the complexity (and breadth) of AI governance and compliance requires the implementation of an IMS.

Key Principles of Responsible AI

According to the International Organization for Standardization (ISO):

> Responsible AI is the practice of developing and using AI systems in a way that benefits society while minimizing the risk of negative consequences. It is about creating AI technologies that not only advance our capabilities, but also address ethical concerns – particularly regarding bias, transparency and privacy.

(ISO, 2024)

DOI: 10.1201/9781003624073-3

Some key principles and/or objectives related to responsible AI include the following:

- **Accessibility**: AI systems should be "easily used or accessed by people with disabilities or adapted for use by people with disabilities" (Merriam-Webster, 2025). AI systems should be "capable of being understood or appreciated".
- **Accountability**: According to the National Institute of Standards and Technology (NIST), accountability is: "The principle that an individual is entrusted to safeguard and control equipment, keying material, and information and is answerable to proper authority for the loss or misuse of that equipment or information" (NIST, 2025). According to the IAPP, accountability is:

  > The obligation and responsibility of the creators, operators and regulators of an AI system to ensure the system operates in a manner that is ethical, fair, transparent and compliant with applicable rules and regulations (see fairness and transparency). Accountability ensures the actions, decisions and outcomes of an AI system can be traced back to the entity responsible for it.
  >
  > *(IAPP, 2025)*

- **Bias**: AI systems may exhibit signs of computational or machine bias based on assumptions built into a model or the data itself. Disparities within a model's performance could be seen across diverse groups creating bias.

  > Cognitive bias refers to inaccurate individual judgment or distorted thinking, while societal bias leads to systemic prejudice, favoritism and/or discrimination in favor of or against an individual or group. Either or both may permeate the model or the system in numerous ways, such as through selection bias, i.e. biases in selecting data for model training. Bias can impact outcomes and pose a risk to individual rights and liberties.
  >
  > *(IAPP, 2025)*

- **Explainability**: "The ability to describe or provide sufficient information about how an AI system generates a specific output or arrives at a decision in a specific context. Explainability is important in maintaining transparency and trust in AI" (IAPP, 2025).
- **Fairness**:

  > An attribute of an AI system that prioritizes equal treatment of individuals or groups in its decisions and actions in a consistent, accurate manner. Every model must identify the appropriate standard of fairness that best applies, but most often it means the AI system's

decisions should not adversely impact, whether directly or disparately, sensitive attributes like race, gender or religion.

(IAPP, 2025)

- **Inclusiveness**: "Engaging with diverse perspectives helps identify potential ethical concerns of AI and ensures a collective effort to address them" (ISO, 2024).
- **Non-Maleficence**: "AI systems should avoid harming individuals, society or the environment" (ISO, 2024).
- **Privacy**: "Freedom from intrusion into the private life or affairs of an individual when that intrusion results from undue or illegal gathering and use of data about that individual" (NIST, 2025). One of the concerns with AI systems is an individual's right to be forgotten. It is very difficult to remove specific data from a dataset related to personal information once a model learns from a dataset provided.
- **Reliability**: "The ability of a system or component to function under stated conditions for a specified period of time" (NIST, 2025).
- **Robustness**: "The ability of an [AI system] to operate correctly and reliably across a wide range of operational conditions, and to fail gracefully outside of the operational range" (NIST, 2025).
- **Safety**: "Expectation that a system does not, under defined conditions, lead to a state in which human life, health, property, or the environment is endangered" (NIST, 2025).
- **Security**:

    A condition that results from the establishment and maintenance of protective measures that enable an organization to perform its mission or critical functions despite risks posed by threats to its use of systems. Protective measures may involve a combination of deterrence, avoidance, prevention, detection, recovery, and correction that should form part of the organization's risk management approach.

    (NIST, 2025)

- **Sustainability**: AI systems should ensure they do not deplete or permanently damage the resources they use. AI systems should maintain minimal environmental impact and look toward long-term viability. Environmental concerns involve the carbon footprint and the consumption of energy in training models or using AI systems.
- **Transparency**: Per NIST, transparency is: "A property of openness and accountability throughout the supply chain". NIST further expands transparency as the "amount of information that can be gathered about a supplier, product, or service and how far through the supply chain this information can be obtained" (NIST, 2025).

These terms and others related to responsible AI will be discussed further throughout this chapter.

OECD Principles

Most regulations are enacted with a set of principles in mind to govern individuals in their behavior. Regulations around AI use and deployment are no different. The Organisation for Economic Co-Operation and Development (OECD) was established in 1961 as an intergovernmental organization to help countries (and their governments) promote economic growth. The OECD provides a forum to discuss common economic and social problems.

One of the earliest achievements of the OECD was developing a set of privacy principles known as the Fair Information Practice Principles (FIPPs), which are used by many governmental agencies around the world as the basis for their privacy laws. Since AI systems leverage a lot of data, this data should follow these eight principles: collection limitation, data quality, purpose specification, use limitation, security safeguards, openness, individual participation, and accountability. Most of the privacy regulations in effect today utilize FIPPs as their foundation.

Since AI systems have a socioeconomic impact on the world, the OECD adopted a set of AI principles in 2019. These AI principles have gone through many changes, and the most recent update of the current version was completed in May 2024. As of the time of this writing, 47 countries, including the European Union and the United States, have adopted the OECD's set of trustworthy AI principles to guide them in their policy-making efforts supporting responsible AI. The OECD created the following five value-based principles as cited, summarized, and paraphrased below: (OECD, 2024)

Inclusive Growth, Sustainable Development, and Well-Being

> Stakeholders should proactively engage in responsible stewardship of trustworthy AI in pursuit of beneficial outcomes for people and the planet, such as augmenting human capabilities and enhancing creativity, advancing inclusion of underrepresented populations, reducing economic, social, gender and other inequalities, and protecting natural environments, thus invigorating inclusive growth, well-being, sustainable development and environmental sustainability.
>
> *(OECD, 2024)*

This first principle summarizes the purpose and importance of responsible AI use as well as describing the broad socioeconomic impact AI systems can have on the global population. Responsible AI requires responsible stewards to ensure

AI can be used by all and does not disparately impact lower income countries. AI should be deployed and used for the common good as described further in the *OECD Framework for Policy Action on Inclusive Growth* [Source: https://doi.org/10.1787/9789264301665-en].

Human Rights and Democratic Values, Including Fairness and Privacy

AI actors should respect the rule of law, human rights, democratic and human-centred values throughout the AI system life cycle. These include non-discrimination and equality, freedom, dignity, autonomy of individuals, privacy and data protection, diversity, fairness, social justice, and internationally recognised labour rights. This also includes addressing misinformation and disinformation amplified by AI, while respecting freedom of expression and other rights and freedoms protected by applicable international law. To this end, AI actors should implement mechanisms and safeguards, such as capacity for human agency and oversight, including to address risks arising from uses outside of intended purpose, intentional misuse, or unintentional misuse in a manner appropriate to the context and consistent with the state of the art.

(OECD, 2024)

The development of AI must be grounded in human-centered values to ensure fundamental human rights are maintained. OECD recommends that AI systems do not impact human rights as defined in the *Universal Declaration of Human Rights* [Source: https://www.ohchr.org/EN/UDHR/Documents/UDHR_Translations/eng.pdf].

The Universal Declaration of Human Rights identifies 30 articles recognized as the fundamental human rights of all human beings such as "being born free and equal in dignity and rights" as well as the "right to life, liberty, and the security of person". To ensure these rights within AI systems, the OECD recommends AI systems align to these values and maintain the capacity for human intervention and oversight. Furthermore, the OECD recommends (and has been seen introduced in many new AI regulations) the need to perform a human rights impact assessment as part of AI due diligence activities along with including code of conduct, quality labels, and/or certifications around the AI system's use.

Transparency and Explainability

AI Actors should commit to transparency and responsible disclosure regarding AI systems. To this end, they should provide meaningful information, appropriate to the context, and consistent with the state of art:

- to foster a general understanding of AI systems, including their capabilities and limitations,
- to make stakeholders aware of their interactions with AI systems, including in the workplace,
- where feasible and useful, to provide plain and easy-to-understand information on the sources of data/input, factors, processes and/ or logic that led to the prediction, content, recommendation or decision, to enable those affected by an AI system to understand the output, and,
- to provide information that enable those adversely affected by an AI system to challenge its output.

(OECD, 2024)

The term transparency has been brought up previously in this book, and as it relates to AI, the OECD provides a couple of key points. First, individuals must be aware that they are interacting with AI. This means AI developers must disclose their use of an AI system that an individual may be interacting with. For example, if a chatbot pops up on the screen when an individual visits a website and an individual starts interacting with the AI system to get further information about a product or service being offered, the AI developers should ensure the chatbot identifies itself as an AI system.

The second key point of transparency is explainability. The AI developer should provide a means for individuals to understand how the AI system works. The AI developer should also provide clarity on the resulting outputs for an individual to understand the context of the results. Of course, source code is intellectual property; however, OECD recommends establishing dedicated entities "to foster general awareness and understanding of AI systems and increase acceptance and trust" (OECD, 2024).

Robustness, Security, and Safety

AI systems should be robust, secure and safe throughout their entire life cycle so that, in conditions of normal use, foreseeable use or misuse, or other adverse conditions, they function appropriately and do not pose unreasonable safety and/or security risks. Mechanisms should be in place, as appropriate, to ensure that if AI systems risk causing undue harm or exhibit undesired behaviour, they can be overridden, repaired, and/or decommissioned safely as needed. Mechanisms should also, where technically feasible, be in place to bolster information integrity while ensuring respect for freedom of expression.

(OECD, 2024)

To build trust in an AI system, safety and security must be addressed to ensure trust. OECD recommends that AI systems need to overcome adverse conditions such as security risks to stay robust. Of course, AI systems should not pose any physical risks to individuals. OECD further defines explainability by introducing accountability within this principle through traceability to help analyze outcomes. Traceability is a little different than explainability since the focus is on the meta-data, data sources, and data cleaning process as opposed to the data itself.

OECD recommends implementing a risk management approach throughout an AI system's life cycle to identify and mitigate risks. Risk management should include, at a minimum, risks associated with "human rights, bodily integrity, privacy, fairness, equality, and robustness" (OECD, 2024). OECD references the *Multinational Enterprise (MNE) Guidelines and OECD Due Diligence Guidance for Responsible Business Conduct* as a useful tool for risk management [Source: https://mneguidelines.oecd.org/].

Accountability

AI actors should be accountable for the proper functioning of AI systems and for the respect of the above principles, based on their roles, the context, and consistent with the state of the art. To this end, AI actors should ensure traceability, including in relation to datasets, processes and decisions made during the AI system life cycle, to enable analysis of the AI system's outputs and responses to inquiry, appropriate to the context and consistent with the state of the art. AI actors, should, based on their roles, the context, and their ability to act, apply a systematic risk management approach to each phase of the AI system life cycle on an ongoing basis and adopt responsible business conduct to address risks related to AI systems, including, as appropriate, via co-operation between different AI actors, suppliers of AI knowledge and AI resources, AI system users, and other stakeholders. Risks include those related to harmful bias, human rights including safety, security, and privacy, as well as labour and intellectual property rights.

(OECD, 2024)

OECD distinguishes between the term's accountability, responsibility, and liability, although they may seem to be similar to each other. According to the OECD,

accountability implies an ethical, moral, or other expectation (e.g., as set out in management practices or codes of conduct) that guides individuals' or organizations' actions or conduct and allows them to explain reasons for which decisions and actions are taken.

(OECD, 2024)

As it relates to AI systems, accountability is the expectation that the AI system acts as it was intended. To demonstrate accountability, AI developers should document an AI system throughout its life cycle or permit independent audits. Responsibility can be used in a legal or non-legal context, referring to ethical (or moral) expectations between an individual and a resulting outcome based on the actions of the individual. In terms of AI systems, the question is *who is responsible for the results or output of the AI system?* Liability refers to an adverse impact caused by an action (or inaction). Again, in terms of AI systems, *who is liable for the results or outputs of the AI system?*

This all comes down to being accountable. Several organizations, civil societies, and regulatory agencies have developed or are currently developing AI governance tools. These tools are intended to mitigate risks AI systems may pose on individuals and the world. One way to achieve accountability is to demonstrate trustworthy AI development, deployment, or use. Building trust also builds confidence from stakeholders like individuals, customers, investors, and regulators in the responsible development, deployment, and use of AI systems. As the use of AI systems increases and depends on their risks, individuals will push government regulators to enforce stricter accountability measures such as conformity assessments, audits, and certifications to demand minimum levels of accountability over responsible AI.

Policy Blueprint for an AI Bill of Rights – US White House Office of Science and Technology

The US White House Office of Science and Technology identified five principles to guide the design, development, and use of automated systems. These principles are known as the *Blueprint for an AI Bill of Rights* and are summarized as follows from the following source: https://bidenwhitehouse.archives.gov/ostp/ai-bill-of-rights/

Safe and Effective Systems

Individuals have the right to be protected from unsafe or ineffective systems. Organizations need to consult with a diverse group of stakeholders when developing AI systems. Organizations should ensure AI systems are developed safely to include pre-deployment testing, risk identification and mitigation, ongoing monitoring, and adherence to domain-specific standards. AI systems should not be designed to harm individuals, and developers should protect individuals from harm that may be caused by AI systems. Individuals have the right to be protected from inappropriate or irrelevant data use. AI systems should have independent evaluations performed on them, and organizations should make the results public when possible.

Algorithmic Discrimination Protections

Individuals have the right to be protected from discrimination by AI systems and AI systems should be designed (and used) in an equitable manner. Protected classes include race, color, ethnicity, sex (also includes pregnancy, childbirth and related medical conditions, gender identity, intersex status, and sexual orientation), religion, age, national origin, disability, veteran status, genetic information, or any other classification protected by law. Equity assessments should be performed on AI systems to ensure representative data is used, risks to disparity are assessed (and mitigated), and there is clear oversight implemented. AI system designs should consider accessibility for people with disabilities, and algorithmic impact assessments (including disparity testing results) should be performed and made public when possible.

Data Privacy

Individuals should have the right to be protected from abusive data practices (by default) and have agency over how their data is used. Following privacy-by-design and privacy-by-default principles, individuals should be protected from violations of privacy. Organizations developing AI systems should confirm the expected data collection and use guidelines. Use of data should be done with consent, and AI system designers, developers, and deployers should respect individuals' choices on privacy. AI systems used for surveillance should be subject to heightened oversight to ensure they do not violate individuals' privacy (or civil liberties). Furthermore, monitoring should not occur in a context where it is likely to limit rights, opportunities, or access. Reporting should be made available to confirm an individual's data decisions. Impact assessments should also be conducted, especially when surveillance technologies are used.

Notice and Explanation

Individuals have the right to know when an AI system is being used. Individuals should be provided with an explanation of how (and why) the AI system's output impacts the individual. Organizations should provide up-to-date notices to include a description of the AI system in use, responsible parties, and an explanation of the output. Notices should include information when the AI system was not the only determining factor in any decisions made as a result of an AI system's output. A summary of information, along with assessments performed on the quality of the notice, should be made public when possible.

Human Alternatives, Consideration, and Fallback

Individuals should be able to opt out of AI system use and have access to people who can quickly remedy issues encountered by the AI system. AI systems should maintain a fallback and escalation process in cases where the AI system fails, produces an error, or the individual contests a decision made by the AI system. In cases where AI systems are deployed in sensitive domains (or may impact a high-risk decision), the AI systems should be tailored to their purpose with meaningful access to oversight from people appropriately trained in the AI system. The AI governance process and assessment should be made public when possible.

Other Principles

Some of the other principles related to AI include the following:

UNGP Reporting Framework

As of the time of this writing, there are over 80 initiatives developing AI-specific ethical frameworks. Touting as the world's first comprehensive guide for organizations to report on their activities regarding their respect for human rights is the *United Nations (UN) Guiding Principles (GP) Reporting Framework.*

> The UNGP Reporting Framework is a short series of smart questions to which any company should have answers, both to know whether it is doing business with respect for human rights, and to show others the progress it is making. The Reporting Framework is supported by two kinds of guidance: implementation guidance for companies that are reporting, and assurance guidance for internal auditors and external assurance providers.
>
> *(United Nations, 2025)*

The UNGP Reporting Framework is separated into the following three parts: Part A – Governance of Respect for Human Rights (which includes policy commitment and embedding respect for human rights); Part B – Defining the Focus of Reporting; and Part C – Management of Salient Human Rights Issues (which includes specific policies, stakeholder engagement, assessing impacts, integrating findings and taking action, tracking performance, and remediation).

Ethics Guidelines for Trustworthy AI

Another set of principles specific to AI was presented in 2019 by the High-Level Expert Group (HLEG) of the European Commission known as the *Ethics Guidelines for Trustworthy AI.* "According to the Guidelines, trustworthy AI should be: (1) lawful – respecting all applicable laws and regulations; (2) ethical – respecting ethical principles and values; (3) robust – both from a technical perspective while taking into account its social environment" (High-Level Expert Group on AI, 2019).

There are seven key requirements an AI system must comply with to be designated as trustworthy. These requirements are assessed against specific criteria to include a review of the following (paraphrased and summarized below):

- **Human Agency and Human Oversight**: AI systems are required to empower humans and ensure humans' fundamental rights. AI systems should permit individuals to make informed decisions and maintain proper human oversight through the following approaches: human-in-the-loop, human-on-the-loop, and human-in-command (where artifacts are taught to an AI by a human teacher).
  - Two of these three approaches above (i.e., human-in-the-loop and human-on-the-loop) were defined as categories of autonomy described by Bonnie Docherty in a 2012 Human Rights Watch report, *Losing Humanity: The Case against Killer Robots*. In this report, the following categories were detailed within the context of human control over autonomous weapons (i.e., killer robots):
    - *Human-in-the-Loop Weapons*: Robots that can select targets and deliver force only with a human command;
    - *Human-on-the-Loop Weapons*: Robots that can select targets and deliver force under the oversight of a human operator who can override the robots' actions; and
    - *Human-out-of-the-Loop Weapons*: Robots that are capable of selecting targets and delivering force without any human input or interaction.

    (Docherty, 2012)

- **Technical Robustness and Safety**: To mitigate the risk of harm from AI, AI systems need to be resilient, providing a fail-safe plan if something were to happen. AI systems need to be safe, accurate, and reliable, and the same decisions need to be reproduced under the same circumstances each time the AI system produces an output.
- **Privacy and Data Governance**: AI systems need to respect individual's privacy and ensure data protection. Data being used to train AI models needs to be of high quality, maintain integrity, and developers need to ensure they have a legitimate purpose to access the data (such as under authorized consent abiding by data governance regulations).
- **Transparency**: AI systems need to be transparent to include data, systems, and models. Output from an AI system should be able to be explained to affected stakeholders, and individuals need to be aware they are interacting with an AI system (such as notifying a user when they are talking with an AI chatbot). Individuals need to be made aware of the AI system's capabilities and/or limitations.
- **Diversity, Non-Discrimination, and Fairness**: AI systems should focus on diversity to ensure there is no unfair bias. AI systems need to be accessible

(even by individuals with disabilities) and include all relevant stakeholders throughout their life cycle.

- **Societal and Environmental Well-Being**: AI systems consider future generations and benefit everyone. Due to the consumption of power and other resources needed to maintain AI systems, the environment is an important consideration, as well as any impact AI may have on society.
- **Accountability**: Developing, deploying, and using AI must be done in a responsible manner, with developers, deployers, and users being accountable for the AI systems' output. AI systems need to be auditable to assess the algorithms, which can provide individuals with redress in case AI may do harm.

UNESCO Principles

The General Conference of the United Nations Educational, Scientific, and Cultural Organization (UNESCO) met for its 41st session in Paris from 9 November 2021 to 24 November 2021. UNESCO developed a set of recommendations aimed "to make AI systems work for the good of humanity, individuals, societies, and the environment and ecosystems, and to prevent harm" (UNESCO, 2022). The recommendations covered 11 policy areas to include ethical impact assessment, ethical governance and stewardship, data policy, development and international cooperation, environment and ecosystems, gender, culture, education and research, communication and information, economy and labor, and health and social well-being.

AI Action Summit (Paris Summit Declaration)

In a twist of events, the United States and the United Kingdom refused to sign the Paris Summit Declaration proposed at the AI Action Summit in Paris on 11 February 2025, which was attended by over 60 other countries. The declaration priorities included "ensuring AI is open, inclusive, transparent, ethical, safe, secure and trustworthy, taking into account international frameworks for all and making AI sustainable for people and the planet" (Milmo, 2025). In his speech to the delegation, the US Vice-President, JD Vance said, "We need international regulatory regimes that foster the creation of AI technology rather than strangle it, and we need our European friends, in particular, to look to this new frontier with optimism rather than trepidation" (Dan Milmo, 2025). He also indicated "excessive regulation of the AI sector could kill a transformative industry" (Dan Milmo, 2025). It appears the new US administration is looking for less regulations over AI to permit US companies to innovate with this new technology. The US aspires to become the leader in AI. As far as the United Kingdom's decision is concerned, UK representatives indicated that although they agreed with some of the declarations, they didn't feel it went far enough to answer national security challenges surrounding AI.

Asilomar AI Principles

During the Beneficial AI 2017 conference coordinated by the Future of Life Institute (FLI), the Asilomar AI Principles were developed as a set of 23 AI governance principles covering three fundamental issues: research issues, ethics and values, and longer-term issues. Under ethics and values, the principles touch on safety, failure transparency, judicial transparency, responsibility, value alignment, human values, personal privacy, liberty and privacy, shared benefit, shared prosperity, human control, non-subversion, and the AI arms race. Further details of these principles can be found at this source: https://futureoflife.org/open-letter/ai-principles/.

The Institute of Electrical and Electronics Engineers Initiatives on Ethics of Autonomous and Intelligent Systems

The Institute of Electrical and Electronics Engineers (IEEE) Standards Association (SA) identified "an urgent necessity for the establishment of stringent standards that not only uphold scientific integrity but also prioritize public safety" as autonomous and intelligent systems (AIS) are being deployed and integrated into critical infrastructure (IEEE SA, 2024). During the IEEE's Executive Committee in 2023, a renewed interest was being placed on safety first and safety by design principles. "Central to this conversation is the imperative for AIS technologies to be developed with a foundational commitment to sound ethical considerations and demonstrated safety-first principle" (IEEE SA, 2024). IEEE's initiative focuses on providing standards, toolkits, AI safety champions, and campaigns to promote their IEEE 7000 series resources and related certifications.

CNIL AI Action Plan

The French Data Protection Agency, known as the Commission Nationale Informatique & Libertés (CNIL), has published its action plan on AI. One of the main focuses of the CNIL is to regulate generative AI, and its action plan is structured around the following four objectives:

- Understanding the functioning of AI systems and their impacts for people;
- Enabling and guiding the development of AI that respects personal data;
- Federating and supporting innovative players in the AI ecosystem in France and Europe; and
- Audit and control AI systems and protect people.

(CNIL, 2023)

The CNIL is concerned with data protection involved in the design and operation of AI systems, including fairness and transparency, protection of publicly available data on the web, protection of data transmitted by users, consequences for the rights of individuals to their data, protection against bias and discrimination, and unprecedented security challenges.

Code of Conduct or Practice

AI ethics and principles need to be applied to the development of machine learning and AI use to mitigate potential issues. Organizations need to have an AI Code of Conduct covering the ethical use of AI as well as practices implemented to identify, analyze, and ultimately mitigate concerns surrounding AI procurement, development, and deployment.

There are several key ethical issues to address within an organization's AI Code of Conduct. One of these issues is the lawfulness of AI. First, is the development (or use) of the AI legal and can the organization comply with their regulatory (or contractual) obligations? Second, the organization needs to determine if the development (or use) of AI abides by the organization's existing policies and procedures. As discussed, bias is a major legal concern when it comes to the development (or use) of AI. Appropriate policies (and processes) need to be implemented to mitigate against this bias. Organizations should ensure AI is equitably designed with a team of diverse thinkers. When working with AI classified as higher risk, a diverse group of individuals within different demographics needs to be considered. Legal reviews should also be performed to ensure AI is being developed (and used) in an ethical manner.

AI systems are trained on a large amount of data, but *did the organization have permission to utilize this data in this way to train AI systems? Were individuals given a choice about the use of their personal information in training the machine learning models and was consent obtained for this use?* An organization's Code of Conduct may tie back to the Privacy Notice, disclosing how data is collected and used within the AI systems. In most cases, the use of personal information to train machine learning models must come by way of consent. This is according to several privacy regulations, such as the General Data Protection Regulation (GDPR), the California Consumer Privacy Act (CCPA), and other state and country privacy laws. Most of these privacy regulations also require individuals to have the right to access, modify, and delete their personal information, which includes their personal information used in training models. Organizations should consider implementing mechanisms to minimize data use and only use the minimum required data to improve machine learning models.

Another key ethical issue to consider is the impact the development (or use) of AI has on people's safety, as well as the impact AI can have on the world. Although AI technology might be able to solve problems and assist people in their daily lives, organizations need to ask *is the AI system safe? Can the AI system turn 'bad' and hurt people? Could the AI system meant for one purpose be used in a malicious manner for another nefarious use?* These are just some of the questions that need to be asked when developing, deploying, or using AI.

Ethical Challenges

Many organizations may talk about their ethical practices in dealing with AI; however, some of these organizations do not actually practice what they preach. Some of the reasons why ethics is a challenge in AI are the difficulties in quantifying ethical values, the lack of a cohesive definition of ethics, and the very nature of the complexity of some AI models not being able to be explained. To overcome these challenges, organizations may introduce institutional entrepreneurship where "new institutions arise when organized actors with sufficient resources see in them an opportunity to realize interests that they value highly" (Ali et al., 2023). To effect change, individuals or groups must become institutional entrepreneurs and utilize their interpersonal skills to garner support from cross-functional groups where they may lack leadership support. There are many factors such as little regulatory guidance, minimal research, priorities, and resource constraints leading to the lack of clarity, which tends to go against obtaining buy-in from leadership.

In most technology firms, "power lies with product and, regardless of whether or not ethics is siloed per se, the goal of product innovation supersedes goals related to responsible AI" (Ali et al., 2023). As opposed to referring to terms such as ethics or fairness, ethical entrepreneurs may leverage product quality as a motivating driver to integrate activities related to responsible AI. Many organizations may not have consistent processes in place, leading to individuals taking on individual responsibility, which may put them at risk in their careers. "While individual ethics entrepreneurs may act as catalysts for organizational change, we conclude that the meaningful implementation of ethical concerns within technology companies must grapple with questions of power and inertia in organizational contexts" (Ali et al., 2023).

The Federal Trade Commission

Transparency and explainability are other key ethical issues to consider when developing a Code of Conduct. The Federal Trade Commission (FTC) has issued some important guidance to organizations emphasizing "the use of AI tools should be transparent, explainable, fair, and empirically sound, while fostering accountability" (Smith, Using Artificial Intelligence and Algorithms, 2020). Per the FTC, being transparent means organizations should not deceive consumers about how they use AI systems (such as the use of AI models or embedded AI solutions). This also includes organizations being transparent about how they collected sensitive data or, in some cases, requiring the organization to provide an 'adverse action' notice where data obtained by other sources is used as the basis for making an automated decision, as in the case of providing credit. Organizations need to ensure adequate data governance is implemented over the quality and integrity of the data used in training machine learning models. The FTC further warns that an organization could face enforcement actions if it attempts to mislead consumers in its use of AI systems.

AI systems or systems using algorithmic decision-making technology need to be explained to consumers. The FTC warns that if a consumer is denied something of value based on algorithmic decision-making, the consumer needs to be specifically notified as to what data was used in the model and how the data was used to arrive at the decision. In basic terms, if an organization is going to use AI that would financially impact a consumer, the organization must notify the consumer and provide the opportunity for the consumer to correct information involved in the decision. Organizations need to consider the ability to incorporate human intervention in AI decisions when these decisions impact individuals' rights.

Additionally, AI system decisions need to be fair and not discriminate against certain protected classes. AI models must be validated and revalidated to ensure they work as intended. The FTC focuses on both the input and outputs of an AI system when reviewing illegal discrimination. The FTC suggests asking the following four key questions to avoid bias: "How representative is [the] dataset?; Does [the] data model account for biases?; How accurate are [the] predications based on big data?; [and] Does [the] reliance on big data raise ethical or fairness concerns?" (Smith, Using Artificial Intelligence and Algorithms, 2020)

Furthermore, the FTC recommends ensuring that data and models used in AI systems are robust and empirically sound. If the organization,

> compile[s] and sell[s] consumer information that is used or expected to be used for credit, employment, insurance, housing, or other similar decisions about consumers' eligibility for certain benefits and transactions, [the organization] may indeed by subject to the FCRA [Fair Credit Reporting Act].
>
> *(Smith, Using Artificial Intelligence and Algorithms, 2020)*

Even if the organization is not considered a consumer reporting agency, the organization may still have obligations to ensure that the data is accurate.

Finally, the FTC recommends considering the protection of the AI systems from unauthorized use and implementing an accountability mechanism. Organizations need to consider how their AI systems could be used (or abused) in a way they were not intended to be used, along with what mitigating controls can be implemented to prevent this misuse. These mitigating controls also include steps to protect against unauthorized access or disclosure of sensitive information, as well as the restriction on the ability to poison the datasets during training. The FTC recommends the use of independent standards (or independent experts) to assist in holding the organization accountable for the development (or use) of AI.

AI Pact Organisation's Commitments

The *AI Pact Organisation's Commitments* from the European Artificial Intelligence Office requests organizations to participate in an initiative to agree to three core commitments focusing primarily on transparency obligations for high-risk AI systems as paraphrased below [Source: https://ec.europa.eu/newsroom/dae/redirection/document/107430]:

- *AI Governance* – organizations should adopt a strategy over AI and work toward compliance with regulations such as the EU Artificial Intelligence (AI) Act.
- *AI Systems Mapping* – organizations should map AI systems based on whether the organization develops or deploys AI systems.
- *AI Awareness Training* – organizations should promote awareness of AI systems based on factors such as knowledge (or experience), along with consideration of use and individuals impacted.

For developers of AI systems, organizations should identify risks of AI systems throughout their entire life cycle. Datasets used for training, validation, and testing should be of high quality. Logging should be implemented to trace intended purposes. In addition, deployers should be informed on how to use AI systems along with the AI system's limitations and risks. High-risk AI systems must have human oversight and processes implemented to mitigate risks. Like the FTC recommendations, individuals should be informed that they are interacting with AI systems, and content generated by AI systems should be appropriately marked to provide for the clear distinction between AI content and human-generated content.

For deployers of AI systems, organizations should map known (or foreseeable) risks to the fundamental rights of individuals. Like developers, deployers need to ensure human oversight, and AI-generated content needs to be properly labeled. Individuals should also be made aware that they are interacting with AI systems and provided explanations on any decisions made by the AI systems. If AI systems are deployed within the workplace, workers need to be informed.

A Blueprint for Greece's AI Transformation

Many countries are following the examples set by the United States and the European Union as their countries adopt, develop, and deploy AI technologies. For instance, Greece released *A Blueprint for Greece's AI Transformation: High-Level Advisory Committee on Artificial Intelligence*. This blueprint provides a national AI strategy with the following guiding AI principles: respect for human dignity, human flourishing, pluralism, participation, transparency, oversight, adaptability, and international multilateral cooperation.

The blueprint further describes six flagship programs Greece intends to achieve: "become a model nation in data collection and governance, AI readiness, and AI strategy", "establish a world-class AI research and education institute", "develop a central AI education platform supporting teaching and learning, virtual collaboration, and hosting AI competitions", "foster the development of AI ecosystems around data, computation, and opportunities for investment, training, and mentoring", "develop the Greek language and culture data space", and "launch a global AI ethics forum and a global AI observatory for the democratic process" (High-Level Advisory Committee on Artificial Intelligence, 2024). In addition, the blueprint makes several recommendations to strengthen Greece's AI strategy.

The blueprint sets out 12 key guidelines regarding the feasibility and meaningfulness of AI, along with AI responsibility and trustworthiness. To maintain feasible and meaningful AI, the blueprint recommends ensuring that the problem being solved actually requires an AI system. An organization must ensure the project is feasible and if so, must train machine learning models on high-quality data. Organizations must define guidelines regarding access to the training data and ensure alignment of all stakeholders. A question an organization should ask is, *what does success mean?* Organizations need to define key performance indicators (KPIs), other model metrics, and/or determine return on investment. Finally, organizations need to ensure resources are available to support the deployment of an AI system.

To maintain responsible and trustworthy AI, the blueprint further recommends that AI systems are interpretable and can add value throughout their life cycle. Organizations need to be aware of risks and mitigate them as much as possible. AI systems need to comply with regulations and data governance requirements. AI systems also need to conform to ethical obligations. Finally, organizations need to ensure AI systems are environmentally sustainable.

Data Protection and Privacy

Data protection and privacy are primary concerns when working with AI systems, especially as it relates to the use of personal data in training machine learning models, as in the case of generative AI. Since regulations are still being developed, passed, and interpreted, this section will discuss some of the work being done to provide guidance to lawmakers, regulators, and organizations trying to navigate data privacy requirements. The European Union is leading the way in data privacy and AI regulations. This section will summarize some of these efforts, starting with recommendations for policymakers, explaining some of the concerns the General Data Protection Regulation (GDPR) has on AI systems, and finishing with some recent opinions from the European Data Protection Board (EDPB) on the processing of personal data in the context of AI models.

Centre for Information Policy Leadership

The Centre for Information Policy Leadership (CIPL) *Applying Data Protection Principles to Generative AI: Practical Approaches for Organizations and Regulators* provides 14 recommendations focused primarily on regulators when enforcing data protection requirements within generative AI models. These recommendations are paraphrased as follows:

1. Regulations should permit the lawful use of personal data in model training and should avoid interpretations of laws that are unduly restrictive in the use of personal data.
2. Since there are distinct phases of the AI life cycle, such as data collection, training, tuning, and deployment, data privacy rules need to apply separately within the context of the applicable phases of the life cycle.
3. Model training should be able to rely on 'legitimate interest' as a legal basis for processing publicly available personal data (such as for web scraping) or where personal data is already under an organization's control, if the interest doesn't outweigh fundamental rights. Risk-based mitigating controls must be implemented.
4. Regulations should recognize and permit the processing and retention of sensitive personal data for AI model training.
5. Regulations should encourage the use of privacy-enhancing and privacy-preserving technologies (PETs/PPTs).
6. The fairness principles should be incorporated in personal data processing to ensure model training is accurate and to minimize discrimination.
7. Regulations should rely on data minimization principles, but should not stand in the way of collecting or using data to create high-quality models.
8. Training general-purpose AI models should itself fall under a legitimate and permissible purpose if appropriate accountability measures are taken and safeguards are implemented. This is similar to point three above.
9. Principles related to purpose (or use limitations) should be flexible, and a distinction needs to be made between separate purposes of generative AI models versus those leveraging these models for specific applications.
10. Individual notification responsibilities regarding the use of personal data are placed on the entity closest to the individual from whom data was collected. Public disclosures should be made for full transparency by organizations where data is not directly collected by individuals.
11. Organizations should respect and provide the ability for individuals, particularly where personal data is involved, to request their input prompts and output responses not to be included in fine-tuning modeling.
12. The context and meaning of the generative AI should factor into transparency when meeting regulatory requirements; however, transparency should not be overprioritized over other factors such as security, usability, functionality, or creating undue burden.
13. Across the AI life cycle, regulators, developers, and deployers of generative AI systems should work together to define their duties and responsibilities with generative AI.

14. Organizations must implement a comprehensive, risk-based AI and data privacy program. Regulators should reward organizations for being accountable in improving their controls and AI practices (CIPL, 2024).

General Data Protection Regulation

The European Union's GDPR went into effect on 25 May 2018. The GDPR tends to be one of the 'gold standards' in the area of data protection and privacy. The GDPR imposes requirements on organizations collecting (or processing) personal data of EU citizens (or residents). Since AI systems utilize data, GDPR may apply to developers (and deployers) of AI systems under certain conditions. The GDPR applies to organizations offering goods or services (even if they are offered for free) to EU citizens (or residents). The GDPR also applies to organizations monitoring the behavior of EU citizens (or residents) where the activity is taking place in the EU. AI systems designed for pattern recognition and behavioral analysis will need to abide by the GDPR. Furthermore, the GDPR applies to processing of personal data by organizations NOT established in the EU through contractual obligations between controllers, processors, and sub-processors. The GDPR maintains a flow-down principle, bringing the entire supply chain of data processing within scope. In basic terms, the GDPR protects the fundamental rights and freedoms of individuals in the EU. More specifically, the GDPR protects EU citizens' (or residents') rights to protect their personal data.

The GDPR requires organizations to protect privacy and levies steep fines (or restrictions) for organizations not complying with the GDPR. The GDPR is based on the following principles, which are also applied to AI systems:

- **Lawfulness, Fairness, and Transparency**: Personal data should be processed lawfully, fairly, and in a transparent manner in relation to the data subject.
- **Purpose Limitation**: Personal data should be collected for specified, explicit, and legitimate purposes and should not be further processed in a manner that is incompatible with those purposes.
- **Data Minimization**: Personal data should be adequate, relevant, and limited to what is necessary in relation to the purposes for which they are processed.
- **Accuracy**: Personal data should be accurate and, where necessary, kept up to date; every reasonable step must be taken to ensure inaccurate personal data (having regard to the purposes for which they are processed) is erased or rectified (i.e., corrected) without delay.
- **Storage Limitation**: Personal data should be kept in a form that permits identification of data subjects, for no longer than is necessary for the purposes for which the personal data is processed.
- **Integrity and Confidentiality**: Personal data should be processed in a manner ensuring appropriate security of the personal data (including protection

against unauthorized or unlawful processing and against accidental loss, destruction or damage) using appropriate technical (or organizational) measures.

- **Accountability**: The organization should be responsible for and able to demonstrate compliance with the GDPR.

The GDPR covers 11 chapters and 99 articles across the following topic areas: General Provisions; Principles; Rights of the Data Subject; Controller and Processor; Transfers of Personal Data to Third Countries (or International Organizations); Independent Supervisory Authorities; Cooperation and Consistency; Remedies, Liability, and Penalties; Provisions Relating to Specific Processing Situations; Delegated Acts and Implementing Acts; and Final Provisions.

Two main roles applicable to the GDPR are controllers and processors. A controller is a natural (or legal) person, public authority, agency, or other body, which alone (or jointly with others), *determines* the purposes and *means* of the processing of personal data. A processor is a natural (or legal) person, public authority, agency, or other body that processes personal data on *behalf* of a controller.

Depending on the context of the articles, applicable, or context of the organization (whether they are a controller, processor, or both), some articles and requirements may not apply. For example, articles under Chapters 6 through 11 of the GDPR are related to the establishment of governmental bodies to enforce the GDPR (and/or the processes, activities, steps of these governmental authorities outside of the scope of a controller or processor).

When it comes to AI governance, the GDPR is applicable; however, traditional privacy principles become a concern. For instance, AI systems are built to infer certain outputs or predict outcomes, tending to go against the accuracy principle since AI results may not always be completely accurate. As it relates to providing notice, individuals must be permitted to provide their personal data freely and with informed consent. Individuals must also be provided with the ability to opt out of sharing their personal data. With the need for AI to learn on large datasets, personal data may have been ingested by the models without appropriate consent in violation of these personal rights. Furthermore, some AI systems are very complex and can't be explained. Individuals should have the right to know they are dealing with an AI system and ensure any personal data they share with the AI system is explicitly permitted.

Under most privacy regulations, individuals have the right to access or delete their personal data. This becomes a challenge for AI systems when these models learn from large datasets, which may not be able to be accessed by individuals. In addition, if a request is made to delete personal data, *how is this data deleted from the models?* Personal data may stay within the original training model, and as previously discussed, models are retrained through a dynamic process.

Article 22 – Automated Decision-Making

Although the GDPR was intended to cover all types of technology as the technology evolves, one area the GDPR directly intersects with AI systems is with requirements related to automated decision-making. Article 22 of the GDPR states: "The data subject shall have the right not to be subject to a decision based solely on automated processing, including profiling, which produces legal effects concerning him or her or similarly significantly affects him or her" (EU Commission, 2025).

Article 22 further states that the data controller (or in the case of AI systems, the developer or deployer depending on who has ultimate control over the processing of personal data) will provide safeguards to protect individuals' rights, freedoms, and legitimate interests. The data controller is required to provide the right to individuals to obtain human intervention and provide individuals with the ability to contest a decision. Some AI systems are complex, and decisions made may pose a challenge to human reviewers to explain. The operators of these AI systems need to understand the technology. AI algorithms should be well documented for them to be understood along with being explainable.

AI systems used for decision-making abilities impacting individuals need to ensure a redress process is in place for individuals to register a complaint. These processes need to include steps on how an individual can have a review performed by a human.

Article 35 – DPIA (New Technology in High-Risk Processing)

Another area the GDPR directly intersects with AI systems is with requirements related to data protection impact assessments (DPIAs). Article 35 of the GDPR states:

> Where a type of processing in particular using new technologies, and taking into account the nature, scope, context and purposes of the processing, is likely to result in a high risk to the rights and freedoms of natural persons, the controller shall, prior to the processing, carry out an assessment of the impact of the envisaged processing operations on the protection of personal data. A single assessment may address a set of similar processing operations that present similar high risks.
>
> *(EU Commission, 2025)*

Performing a DPIA on AI systems is understood to be best practice, there are only a few situations where DPIAs are required such as when processing occurs for

> (a) a systematic and extensive evaluation of personal aspects relating to natural persons which is based on automated processing, including profiling, and on which decisions are based that produce legal effects

concerning the natural person or similarly significantly affect the natural person; (b) processing on a large scale of special categories of data referred to in Article 9(1), or of personal data relating to criminal convictions and offences referred to in Article 10; or (c) a systematic monitoring of a publicly accessible area on a large scale.

(EU Commission, 2025)

Existing DPIAs may need to be updated to include threats posed by AI systems, or entirely new DPIAs will need to be performed on AI systems.

Although not required by the GDPR, AI conformity assessments may be required by other regulations and have also been understood to be best practices when it comes to demonstrating accountability over responsible AI. AI conformity assessments were discussed previously to describe how the AI system was developed, what type of data was used in training, details on how the AI models were trained, expected outcomes, and any potential limitations of the AI system. The successful completion of an AI conformity assessment ensures the AI system meets criteria and is continuously monitored. AI conformity assessments may require more technical documentation than DPIAs; however, they can be used to supplement the artifacts needed for DPIAs. DPIAs will be discussed in more detail later in this book.

Recital 26 – Pseudonymization and Anonymization of Data

An important concept to understand is the GDPR's applicability on data pseudonymization and anonymization. According to Recital 26 of the GDPR: "The principles of data protection should apply to any information concerning an identified or identifiable natural person" (EU Commission, 2025). Article 4(5) of the GDPR defines pseudonymization as replacing any information that could be used to identify an individual with other words (or values) known as pseudonyms. Once data is pseudonymized, it does not permit an individual to be directly identified; however, if additional information can be used to attribute the pseudonymized data to a natural person, GDPR applies. "Personal data which have undergone pseudonymisation, which could be attributed to a natural person by the use of additional information should be considered to be information on an identifiable natural person" (EU Commission, 2025).

The EDPB recently published guidelines on pseudonymization to comply with GDPR. The guidelines uphold the concept of the use of additional information, which can be attributed to pseudonymized data, and linking the data back to an individual is considered personal data.

Pseudonymisation can reduce risks and make it easier to use legitimate interests as a legal basis (Art. 6(1)(f) GDPR), if all other GDPR requirements are met. Likewise, pseudonymisation can aid in securing compatibility with the original purpose (Art. 6(4) GDPR). The guide-lines also explain how pseudonymisation can help organisations meet their obligations relating to the implementation of data protection principles (Art. 5 GDPR), data protection by design and default (Art. 25 GDPR) and security (Art. 32 GDPR).

(EDPB, 2025)

If data is fully anonymized, meaning the data can no longer identify a natural person considering costs, time required for identification, or other available technology in place for processing data, the GDPR does NOT apply to this data.

The principles of data protection should therefore not apply to anon-ymous information, namely information which does not relate to an identified or identifiable natural person or to personal data rendered anonymous in such a manner that the data subject is not or no longer identifiable.

(EU Commission, 2025)

There isn't necessarily one way to anonymize data, and anonymization may vary based on jurisdiction. A test to determine if data can identify an individual was suggested by the Article 29 Working Party on Data Protection (which has been replaced by the EDPB):

In general terms, a natural person can be considered as "identified" when, within a group of persons, he or she is "distinguished" from all other members of the group. Accordingly, the natural person is "iden-tifiable" when, although the person has not been identified yet, it is possible to do it…

(Guidance Note: Guidance on Anonymisation
and Pseudonymisation, 2019)

As it relates to AI, individuals may have their personal data unknowingly (or with-out consent) scraped from websites to help train AI models. This data may be aggre-gated with other data making it easy for someone to identify an individual. AI developers must consider how data is being sourced to train models. Model accu-racy may be impacted if data is pseudonymized (or anonymized) based on the use case of AI. Reducing the ability to identify individuals when a business case for AI requires such functionality could have a devastating effect on AI use. Running pseudonymization or anonymization techniques on large datasets may not be fea-sible, so developers may look to implement privacy-enhancing technologies, but this may not solve all issues with identifying individuals.

European Data Protection Board

An important opinion or interpretation was adopted by the EDPB, known as *Opinion 28/2024 on Certain Data Protection Aspects Related to the Processing of Personal Data in the Context of AI Models (Adopted 17 December 2024)*. The Irish Supervisory Authority requested the EDPB issue an opinion related to the processing of personal data by AI models. The request asked:

> (1) when and how an AI model can be considered as 'anonymous'; (2) how controllers can demonstrate the appropriateness of legitimate interest as a legal basis in the development and (3) deployment phases; and (4) what are the consequences of the unlawful processing of personal data in the development phase of an AI model on the subsequent processing or operation of the AI model.
>
> *(European Data Protection Board, 2024)*

As it relates to the first question, the EDPB states that personal data cannot, in all cases, be considered anonymous and therefore, supervisory authorities need to assess these claims on a case-by-case basis.

> For an AI model to be considered anonymous, both (1) the likelihood of direct (including probabilistic) extraction of personal data regarding individuals whose personal data were used to develop the model and (2) the likelihood of obtaining, intentionally or not, such personal data from queries, should be insignificant, taking into account 'all the means reasonably likely to be used' by the controller or another person.
>
> *(European Data Protection Board, 2024)*

The EDPB provides some methods a controller can use to demonstrate anonymity such as the limitation of collection to reduce identifiability.

For the second and third points, to demonstrate legitimate interest as an appropriate legal basis, the EDPB states the controller needs to identify the legal basis, and there isn't a hierarchy provided by the GDPR. The EDPB further reminds controllers of the three-step test when determining legitimate interest to include:

> (1) identifying the legitimate interest pursued by the controller or a third party; (2) analysing the necessity of the processing for the purposes of the legitimate interest(s) pursued (also referred to as "necessity test"); and (3) assessing that the legitimate interest(s) is (are) not overridden by the interests or fundamental rights and freedoms of the data subjects (also referred to as "balancing test").
>
> *(European Data Protection Board, 2024)*

Finally, regarding consequences, the EDPB reminds supervisory authorities of their "discretionary powers to assess the possible infringement(s) and choose appropriate, necessary, and proportionate measures, taking into account the circumstances of each individual case" (European Data Protection Board, 2024). The EDPB's opinion did not analyze some provisions, such as special categories of data processing, obligations of AI under automated decision-making (including profiling), processing based on compatibility, requirements for data protection impact assessment, and implementing data protection by design. The opinion was also narrowly scoped to cover the subset of AI models resulting from training such models with personal data.

The EDPB suggests some mitigating measures developers and deployers of generative AI systems could implement to ensure they abide by GDPR obligations. Technical measures could include performing pseudonymization of data to ensure personal data will not be able to identify individuals, masking personal data, or substituting personal data with 'fake' personal data in training sets. Specific to web scraping, measures to exclude certain data, certain data categories, certain websites with robots.txt, or imposing collection limitations could be implemented. Implementing mechanisms to permit individuals to exercise their rights is another measure. This could include observing time periods between collection and training, providing an unconditional 'opt-out' when data is collected, permitting exercise of the right to erasure, and permitting individuals to submit claims regarding regurgitation (or memorization) of their personal data. Transparency measures could include releasing communications about data collection and datasets utilized or running campaigns to inform individuals through frequently asked questions, labels, model cards, emails, or other alternative forms. Other technical transparency measures could include digitally watermarking outputs generated by general-purpose AI models or removing/suppressing personal data in outputs. Finally, ensuring appropriate documentation such as DPIAs involving the data protection officer, where applicable, can go a long way to demonstrate accountability over lawful processing of personal data.

As previously discussed, there are always concerns with the lawful use of personal data scraped from websites used in datasets. According to some preliminary consultation from the Information Commissioner's Office (ICO) of the United Kingdom, the lawful basis for training generative AI models utilizing scraped data could be legitimate interest if the following three concerns are addressed:

1. **Purpose Test**: Are the developers of the generative AI models able to frame the specific interest, at the time of collection, to train with the data? Developers may not know what their models will be used for and can't assume their models are going to be used for their intended purpose. "The key question is this: if you don't know what your model is going to be used for, how can you ensure its downstream use will respect data protection and people's rights and freedoms?" (ICO, 2024).

2. **Necessity Test**: Is the processing (i.e., web scraping) necessary to achieve the purpose identified under the purpose test? According to the ICO, due to the volume of data needed to train generative AI, it couldn't be trained on smaller datasets.

3. **Balancing Test**: What is the impact on individuals, and do the interests of the controller (i.e., AI developer) override the interests, rights, and freedoms of those individuals? The ICO opines that since web scraping is done without individuals being aware that their personal data is being processed, individuals can lose control over their personal data in knowing how their personal data is used, what purposes their personal data is being processed, or the ability to exercise their rights. The ICO states, "Invisible processing and AI related processing are both seen as high-risk activities that require a DPIA under ICO guidance" (ICO, 2024).

The ICO further identifies upstream and downstream risks and harms to individuals by having their personal data scraped for generative AI development. AI developers need to consider risk mitigation activities to minimize the harm of these risks. When AI developers deploy on their own platform, they have a lot more control over ensuring the generative model is used as stated, assessing and monitoring risks, and implementing appropriate measures. When generative AI models are deployed through an application programming interface (API), technical controls could be implemented on the API such as limiting (or filtering) queries for the intended purpose. The AI developers can also enforce limitations through contractual agreements. When generative AI models are used in an unlimited fashion, the developers don't know what the model will be used for or have any way to monitor the model. The ICO states, "contractual controls may mitigate this risk, though the developer would also need to evidence that any such controls are being complied with in practice" (ICO, 2024).

EU Digital Services Act

The EU Digital Services Act (DSA)

> regulates online intermediaries and platforms such as marketplaces, social networks, content-sharing platforms, app stores, and online travel and accommodation platforms. Its main goal is to prevent illegal and harmful activities online and the spread of disinformation. It ensures user safety, protects fundamental rights, and creates a fair and open online platform environment.
>
> *(EU Commission, 2025)*

The DSA requires businesses to use simpler mechanisms to flag illegal content on their platforms, as well as any goods infringing on individuals' rights (including property rights). Businesses may become 'trusted flaggers', enabling them to use priority procedures. The DSA provides for "enhanced obligations for marketplaces to apply dissuasive measures, such as 'know your business customer' policies, make reasonable efforts to perform random checks on products sold on their service, or adopt new technologies for product traceability" (EU Commission, 2025).

For AI systems, the DSA will call for transparency related to the type of ads presented to users and the 'logic' or profiling algorithms used in presenting these ads. If an AI system is recommending products (or services), these systems need to be transparent in explaining the impact of the information displayed. To ensure fair markets, gatekeeper systems will need to inform business users on expectations, provide clear applicable obligations, and define procedural rules to ensure quick decision-making.

These regulations are still to be tested when it comes to enforcement actions on AI systems since AI systems may not be 'directly' referenced in the laws; however, AI systems may still be impacted by the regulatory requirements due to the type of processing performed, as well as the use case. Regulatory requirements need to be considered throughout the AI systems' development life cycle. The issue with AI systems as it relates to regulations is that AI systems may perform a function currently covered by a regulation, but in a new way. AI systems can also perform entirely new functions, not addressed in current regulations. These AI system issues do not provide developers, deployers, and users with exceptions to the regulations where AI systems intersect, such as the case with data governance. Furthermore, consumer protection and safety rules may still apply to AI systems.

Product Safety and Liability Laws

AI systems may not be exempt from product safety or laws involving liability. AI developers, deployers, and possibly even users may still be held liable for harm caused by their AI systems.

> Product safety laws establish guidelines for products before they ever become available to the public, in the hope of preventing injuries from occurring at all…. If an injury does occur due to a dangerous or defective product, the law of products liability provides the injured party with a means to hold the manufacturer, distributor, or seller of the product liable.
>
> *(Justia, 2025)*

There are two paths liability laws tend to follow. The first is fault-based where knowledge, intention, recklessness, or negligence are considered when proving an action (or inaction) of a manufacturer, distributor, or seller of a product caused harm. Crimes, such as theft, rape, or murder, are fault-based since there is the physical conduct of the crime and the crime was done with knowledge or intent (i.e., *mens rea* or 'the guilty mind'). The second is strict liability where there isn't a need for intent, but rather just proving a product was defective and caused harm is good enough. Strict liability tends to be attached to lesser crimes such as speeding where a driver may get a ticket even though they didn't know they were speeding.

When it comes to liability laws related to software, there are still a lot of opportunities for improvement. Most of these liabilities are addressed within contracts between organizations or within a company's terms of use. Damages tend to be capped, agreements maintain indemnity clauses, and/or by using a certain piece of software, individuals give up their rights to class-action lawsuits, trial by jury, or may be forced to work through arbitration. The same is occurring with AI systems since these product liability laws are not well defined, and there is a lot of uncertainty in their applicability. Attributing who is at fault for outputs generated by AI or harm caused by autonomous systems may be hard to prove. Not only are AI systems complex and decisions leading up to any harm caused by an AI system hard to explain, but the court systems may have a hard time judging cases of liability based on current legislation or lack of legal precedent.

> Product liability law, including claims and defences, is governed by the laws of individual [US] states, meaning that there is no product liability law that applies to all [fifty] 50 states. Some states have crafted specific state statutory regimes that govern the requirements and limitations of products liability claims. But in most states, product liability claims arise under common law theories of negligence, warranty or strict liability, including specific products liability theories.
>
> *(Dechert LLP, 2023)*

Since there is limited guidance on where product safety and harm arise from AI systems, there is a lot of uncertainty in this area of law. Unfortunately, AI developers, deployers, and possibly users use AI 'at their own risk' since they could be exposed to litigation, having to pay complainants over claimed harm, and risks of utilizing personal data, proprietary data, or copyright infringement within learning model datasets.

Not only can individuals in the United States bring specific liability claims to court through the states' liability laws, but agencies can also refer cases to the Department of Justice (DOJ) for investigation. In an unusual situation, the FTC has referred a complaint to the DOJ. In a recent case against Snap, Inc., developers of the Snapchat application, Snap is accused of causing "risks and harms" to young users through their use of a chatbot (known as *My AI*). In a letter to the public dated 16 January 2025, the FTC notes it referred this complaint to the DOJ for investigation following a compliance order review from a settlement they had against Snap back in 2014 for violating Section 5(a) of the FTC Act, § 15

U.S.C. 45(a). The letter doesn't go into any further detail regarding the alleged complaint or investigation; suffice it to say, the FTC investigated other potential violations of the FTC Act, which they believed were violated (or were about to be violated). The FTC further goes on to say they don't normally make this type of referral public; however, they felt it necessary to report in the best interest of the public [Source: https://www.ftc.gov/legal-library/browse/cases-proceedings/public-statements/statement-federal-trade-commission-matter-snap-inc].

According to the new chair of the FTC, Andrew N. Ferguson, in a rebuttal letter dated 16 January 2025, Mr. Ferguson opposed the complaint against Snap and further goes on to say, "the complaint's application of Section 5 of the FTC Act is not only wrong as a matter of statutory interpretation, but is also in direct conflict with the guarantees of the First Amendment" (Ferguson, 2025). He further states he will release more details if the DOJ brings a complaint against Snap.

In the European Union, the liability framework consists of the Product Liability Directive 85/374/EEC (or the PLD) and other national liability rules. As opposed to fault-based or strict liability, the PLD combines these two claims, where a victim can be compensated if they can prove damages were caused by a defective product. In September 2022, the European Commission published a proposal to adapt non-contractual civil liability rules to ratification intelligence. This proposal is known as the Artificial Intelligence (AI) Liability Directive.

> The new rules intend to ensure that persons harmed by AI systems enjoy the same level of protection as persons harmed by other technologies in the EU. The AI liability directive would create a rebuttable 'presumption of causality', to ease the burden of proof for victims to establish damage caused by an AI system.
>
> *(European Parliament, 2023)*

The proposal is still being worked through since there are debates occurring on several key points such as the ability of the law to cross borders and for victims to receive damages from organizations outside of the EU. *Since the proposal ties in with other national laws, could the non-compliance with the EU AI Act, for instance, cause an organization to be liable for fault or negligence?* Thus, non-compliance of a regulation led to negligence, leading to harm where the courts could presume this harm existed through the presumption of causality. In addition, the proposal provides courts with the power to obtain evidence from providers of high-risk AI systems. This could include sensitive or proprietary technical documentation such as information on how the AI system was developed or what models were used. Being part of court filings, this information could find its way into the public domain. Note: During the writing of this book, the European Commission withdrew discussions around the EU AI Liability Directive due to the lack of agreement. According to the Commission, "No foreseeable agreement—the Commission will assess whether another proposal should be tabled or another type of approach should be chosen" (Andrews, 2025).

AI Specific Regulations (Existing/Emerging)

Several countries have passed, in the processing of passing, and/or updating existing laws to cover AI. A great resource to stay informed about some of these regulations is *White & Case – AI Watch Global Regulatory Tracker* (Visit: https://www.whitecase.com/insight-our-thinking/ai-watch-global-regulatory-tracker). The following are some of the more notable countries implementing specific AI regulations or having a major impact on AI development, deployment, and use.

US Laws

Currently, the United States does not have a comprehensive AI law, but utilizes other laws already in place to cover some of the aspects of new technology (i.e., AI systems). The following are some instances where existing regulations apply to AI systems in the United States:

EEOC and Title VII of the Civil Rights Act

The Equal Employment Opportunity Commission (EEOC) is a regulatory agency that investigates complaints and enforces compliance over Title VII of the Civil Rights Act of 1964 (Title VII) prohibiting discrimination against employees based on race, color, national origin, religion, and sex. The EEOC released guidance related to AI use (or as they term 'algorithmic decision-making tool') in the context of making hiring or selection decisions. The guidance provided different examples of software and applications used in employment to include: "automatic resume-screening software, hiring software, chatbot software for hiring and workflow, video interviewing software, analytics software, employee monitoring software, and worker management software" (EEOC, 2023).

The guidance states:

> If use of an algorithmic decision-making tool has an adverse impact on individuals of a particular race, color, religion, sex, or national origin, or on individuals with a particular combination of such characteristics (e.g., a combination of race and sex, such as for applicants who are Asian women), then use of the tool will violate Title VII unless the employer can show that such use is 'job related and consistent with business necessity' pursuant to Title VII.

(EEOC, 2023)

CFPB and the Equal Credit Opportunity Act

The Consumer Financial Protection Bureau (CFPB) is a regulatory agency that enforces the Equal Credit Opportunity Act requiring lenders to notify consumers of any adverse actions taken against the consumer related to credit offerings.

> The Equal Credit Opportunity Act (ECOA), implemented by Regulation B, makes it unlawful for any creditor to discriminate against any applicant with respect to any aspect of a credit transaction on the basis of race, color, religion, national origin, sex (including sexual orientation and gender identity), marital status, age (provided the applicant has the capacity to contract), because all or part of the applicant's income derives from any public assistance program, or because the applicant has in good faith exercised any right under the Consumer Credit Protection Act. ECOA and Regulation B require that, when taking adverse action against an applicant, a creditor must provide the applicant with a statement of reasons for the action taken. This statement of reasons must be 'specific' and indicate the 'principal reason(s) for the adverse action'; moreover, the specific reasons disclosed must 'relate to and accurately describe the factors actually considered or scored by a creditor'.
>
> *(CFPB, 2023b)*

The CFPB issued guidance regarding legal requirements for lenders when using AI (and other complex models). The guidance confirms that creditors must provide accurate and specific reasons for adverse decisions. In addition,

> creditors that simply select the closest factors from the checklist of sample reasons are not in compliance with the law if those reasons do not sufficiently reflect the actual reason for the action taken. Creditors must disclose the specific reasons, even if consumers may be surprised, upset, or angered to learn their credit applications were being graded on data that may not intuitively relate to their finances.
>
> *(CFPB, 2023a)*

FTC and The Fair Credit Reporting Act

The FTC is a regulatory agency that enforces several different laws related to antitrust and consumer protection. FTC has broad authority over enforcement matters and, more specifically, enforcement of Section 5 of the FTC Act related to unfair trade practices. The Fair Credit Reporting Act (FCRA) is a regulation under Title VI of the Consumer Credit Protection Act protecting information collected by consumer reporting agencies. "Under the FCRA, a vendor that assembles consumer information to automate decision-making about eligibility for credit, employment, insurance, housing, or similar benefits and transactions, may be a 'consumer reporting agency'" (Smith, Using Artificial Intelligence and Algorithms, 2020).

There are several requirements a consumer reporting agency must comply with, such as prohibiting information in a consumer report from being provided to anyone who is not authorized under the FCRA. In addition, consumer reporting agencies must investigate any disputed information and provide consumers with certain notices such as any adverse action taken. Additional regulations such as the Fair and Accurate Credit Transaction Act enhanced these consumer protection laws to ensure records are accurate and safeguards are in place to protect against identity theft. Although rulemaking authority was transferred over to the CFPB, the FTC still retained enforcement authority.

US Federal Reserve Bank and Standard SR 11-7

In April of 2021, the Board of Governors of the Federal Reserve System issued *SR 11-7: Guidance on Model Risk Management* standard. This standard explains:

> The Federal Reserve and Office of the Comptroller of the Currency (OCC) are issuing the attached *Supervisory Guidance on Model Risk Management*, which is intended for use by banking organizations and supervisors as they assess organizations' management of model risk. This guidance should be applied as appropriate to all banking organizations supervised by the Federal Reserve, taking into account each organization's size, nature, and complexity, as well as the extent and sophistication of its use of models.
>
> *(Board of Governors of the Federal Reserve System, 2011)*

The guidance describes "the key aspects of an effective model risk management framework, including robust model development, implementation, and use; effective validation; and sound governance, policies, and controls" (Board of Governors of the Federal Reserve System, 2011). As it relates to the guidance, "the term *model* refers to a quantitative method, system, or approach that applies statistical, economic, financial, or mathematical theories, techniques, and assumptions to process input data into quantitative estimates" (Board of Governors of the Federal Reserve System, 2011).

OSHA and Robots

The Occupational Safety and Health Administration (OSHA) is a regulatory agency under the US Department of Labor (DOL) with the "mission is to assure America's workers have safe and healthful working conditions free from unlawful retaliation"

(OSHA, 2025). As of this writing, there are no specific OSHA standards related to the robotics industry; however, OSHA has published guidance related to industrial robot systems and industrial robot system safety. The guidance discusses the hazards of robotic systems and the implementation of safeguards to include the following from least effective to most effective: protecting workers with personal protective equipment (PPE); administrative controls to change worker's behaviors; engineering controls to isolate workers from hazards; substation controls replacing a hazard with something safer; and total physical elimination of the hazard.

The guidance further states and refers to other standards provided by the American National Standards Institute (ANSI):

> Employers and the workers involved in developing robots should understand, design, and implement robot applications that comply with applicable safety regulations and standards. The safety standard for robots is Part-1 and Part-2 of American National Standards Institute (ANSI)/ Robotic Industries Association (RIA) R15.06-2012, *Industrial Robots and Robot Systems – Safety Consideration.* Among other things, ANSI/ RIA R15.06-2012 requires that relevant, safe operating and maintenance information be provided with the robot (Part 1) and the robot system/application (Part 2).

The guidance takes a risk approach requiring a risk assessment to be performed at each stage of a robot's application, such as design, manufacturing, integrating, operating, and maintaining. The risk assessment should be documented, and an example risk assessment along with risk reduction measures is provided in the guidance.

The FDA and AI-Enabled Devices

The Food and Drug Administration (FDA) is a regulatory agency "responsible for protecting the public health by ensuring the safety, efficacy, and security of human and veterinary drugs, biological products, and medical devices; and by ensuring the safety of our nation's food supply, cosmetics, and products that emit radiation" (FDA, 2024).

> On January 6, 2025, the FDA published the *Draft Guidance: Artificial Intelligence-Enabled Device Software Functions: Life cycle Management and Marketing Submission Recommendations.* This draft guidance proposes both life cycle considerations and specific recommendations to support marketing submissions for AI-enabled medical devices. The draft guidance highlights recommendations from other guidances in order to assist manufacturers with applying those recommendations to AI-enabled devices, as well as providing additional recommendations on topics of specific relevance for AI.
>
> *(FDA, 2025a)*

The FDA refers to the total product life cycle (TLPC) approach when it comes to AI-enabled devices and includes some of the following sections aligned with the TLPC:

- **Development** – Risk Assessment, Data Management, and Model Description and Development
- **Validation** – Data Management and Validation
- **Description of the Final Device** – Device Description, Model Description and Development, User Interface and Labeling, Public Submission Summary
- **Postmarket Management** – Device Performance Monitoring and Cybersecurity

(FDA, 2025b)

The CPSC

The US Consumer Product Safety Commission (CPSC) is a regulatory agency that "works to save lives and keep families safe by reducing the unreasonable risk of injuries and deaths associated with consumer products and fulfilling its vision to be the recognized global leader in consumer product safety" (CPSC, 2025). The CPSC issued a report in May 2021 outlining a proposed framework to evaluate the safety of AI and machine learning (ML), but has yet to create any specific standards. Per the report,

> Currently, there are no statutes that direct or authorize CPSC to regulate AI/ML applications specifically. However, the Consumer Product Safety Act and other statutes enforced by the Commission provide CPSC authority to regulate consumer products. (See, e.g., 15 U.S.C. §§ 20512089). Therefore, consumer products with AI/ML integrated into them are within the agency's statutory authority.

(CPSC, 2021)

The FTC and Section 5

As discussed earlier, the FTC maintains broad enforcement over Section 5 of the FTC Act (15 U.S.C. § 45) prohibiting "unfair or deceptive acts or practices in or affecting commerce". Most of the guidance offered up by the FTC comes by way of enforcement actions. In September 2024, the FTC announced its *Operation AI Comply* related to actions taken against organizations using AI in deceptive or unfair ways. According to the former FTC Chair Lina M. Khan,

> The FTC's enforcement actions make clear that there is no AI exemption from the laws on the books. By cracking down on unfair or deceptive

practices in these markets, FTC is ensuring that honest businesses and innovators can get a fair shot and consumers are being protected.

(FTC, 2024)

More recently, the FTC published additional guidance and warned: "Because there is no AI exemption from the laws on the books, firms deploying these AI systems and tools have an obligation to abide by existing laws, including the competition and consumer protection statutes that the FTC enforces" (Staff in the Office of Technology and the Division of Advertising Practices, 2025). The FTC further highlighted the need for organizations developing, maintaining, using, or deploying an AI-based product to consider the following:

- **Prevent Harm** – The FTC recommends organizations take steps to prevent harm before and after deploying AI to include assessing and mitigating harm from AI models as well as addressing use and impact of AI making decisions during deployment.
- **Prevent AI Impersonation** – The FTC recommends organizations implement "preventative measures to detect, deter, and halt AI-related impersonation, fraud, child sexual abuse material, and non-consensual intimate imagery" (Staff in the Office of Technology and the Division of Advertising Practices, 2025).
- **Avoid Deceptive Claims** – The FTC recommends organizations avoid any deceptive claims about their AI systems. The FTC warns organizations not to misrepresent the functionality around their AI systems or make promises about their AI systems that aren't true.
- **Implement Privacy and Security by Default** – The FTC not only highlights the need for generative AI to be trained on a large amount of data but also warns that this data could contain highly sensitive information. The FTC has a record of providing information to organizations regarding data security and privacy. The FTC also recommends that data security and privacy settings should be enabled by default. In addition, the FTC warns organizations not to quietly (or surreptitiously) change their terms of service to obtain data in an illegal manner.

HHS and HIPAA Security Rule NPRM

The Department of Health and Human Services (HHS) is a regulatory agency with rule-making authority over the Health Insurance Portability and Accountability Act of 1996 (HIPAA) and the Health Information Technology for Economic and Clinical Health Act of 2009 (HITECH Act). In 2003, HHS published the Security Rule requiring administrative, technical, and physical safeguards over electronic protected health information (ePHI). In 2013, HHS finalized an 'omnibus rule' enhancing the Security Rule requirements as well as compliance activities by the Office for Civil Rights (OCR), the enforcement arm of HHS. The author of this book also wrote *The Definitive Guide to Complying with the HIPAA/HITECH Privacy and Security Rules* published by CRC Press in 2013 to provide "a comprehensive manual to ensuring compliance with the implementation standards of the Privacy and Security Rules of HIPAA and provides recommendations based on other related regulations and industry best practices" (Routledge Taylor & Francis Group, 2025).

Recently, HHS published a Notice of Proposed Rulemaking (NPRM) to accept public comments on proposed modifications of the Security Rule. As it relates to AI, HHS has noted the benefits and opportunities AI presents, but also warns that "regulated entities must be prepared to identify, mitigate, and remediate such risks and vulnerabilities" (HHS, 2024). Additionally,

> the E.O. [Executive Order 11410 amending E.O. 11183 related to Safe, Secure, and Trustworthy Development and Use of Artificial Intelligence] required the Secretary of HHS, in consultation with the Secretary of Defense and the Secretary of Veterans Affairs, to establish an HHS AI Task Force to develop a strategic plan that includes policies and frameworks on responsible deployment and use of AI and AI-enabled technologies in the health and human services sector, including the incorporation of safety, privacy, and security standards into the software-development life cycle for the protection of personally identifiable information, such as measures to address AI-enhanced cybersecurity threats in the health and human services sector.
>
> *(HHS, 2024)*

Note: With the incoming administration of President Trump, Executive Order 11410 was rescinded, and he signed a new executive order: *Removing Barriers to American Leadership in Artificial Intelligence.* "It is the policy of the United States to sustain and enhance America's global AI dominance in order to promote human flourishing, economic competitiveness, and national security" (Trump, 2025). It is still too early to determine how the Trump administration is going to regulate AI or if the states are going to fill the gaps where federal regulations leave off.

The NPRM provides a specific section covering AI and more specifically, since AI could be trained on patient data and result in impermissible uses (or disclosures), HHS states "ePHI, including ePHI in AI training data, prediction models, and algorithm data that is maintained by a regulated entity for covered functions is protected by the HIPAA Rules and all applicable standards and specifications" (HHS, 2024). Furthermore, HHS expects "a regulated entity interested in using AI would include the use of such tools in its risk analyses and associated risk management activities". It is important to note that regulated entities under HIPAA include covered entities and business associates. Covered entities are healthcare providers, health plans, and healthcare clearinghouses. Business associates are organizations that create, receive, maintain, or transmit protected health information on the covered entities' behalf. There is also a 'flow-down' of requirements through contractual obligations and compliance assurance to subcontractors of business associates.

The NPRM clarifies the HHS's intent to ensure the HIPAA Security Rule covers not only electronic information systems that create, receive, maintain, or transmit ePHI, but also information systems "connected to or otherwise affect electronic information systems that do create, receive, maintain, or transmit ePHI" (HHS, 2024). HHS proposes to

> interpret an electronic information system as otherwise affecting the confidentiality, integrity, or availability of ePHI if it is insufficiently segregated physically and electronically from an electronic information system that creates, receives, maintains, or transmits ePHI or one that otherwise affects the confidentiality, integrity, or availability of ePHI.
>
> *(HHS, 2024)*

HHS' new terminology 'relevant electronic information systems' broadens the scope and applicability of the HIPAA Security Rule.

Finally, HHS is looking to answer the following questions from the public related to new technologies:

a. Whether the Department's understanding of how the Security Rule applies to new technologies involving ePHI is not comprehensive and if so, what issues should also be considered.
b. Whether there are technologies that currently or in the future may harm the security and privacy of ePHI in ways that the Security Rule could not mitigate without modification, and if so, what modifications would be required.
c. Whether there are additional policy or technical tools that the Department may use to address the security of ePHI in new technologies.

(HHS, 2024)

Algorithmic Accountability Act (Emerging)

A bill known as the Algorithmic Accountability Act of 2023 was introduced by US Senator Ron Wyden (D-OR), Senator Cory Booker (D-NJ), and Representative Yvette Clark (D-NY).

The Algorithmic Accountability Act of 2023 requires companies to assess the impacts of the AI systems they use and sell, creates new transparency about when and how such systems are used, and empowers consumers to make informed choices when they interact with AI systems.

(Wyden, 2023)

This bill requires companies to assess the impact of critical automated decision-making based on FTC regulations and guidelines around assessment and reporting. The bill places responsibilities on companies using this automation to make critical decisions and the companies developing the technology with requirements to report impact assessments to the FTC. The bill also requires the FTC to publish aggregate reports and trends for consumers to review, along with an allocation of resources to establish a Bureau of Technology to enforce the regulations. The bill received endorsement from several organizations, and it will be seen if further support is gained through the new Trump administration.

State Specific Laws

States within the United States are starting to pass laws regulating AI and/or automated decision-making algorithms. A great resource to stay informed about some of these regulations is the IAPP's *US State AI Governance Legislation Tracker* (Visit: https://iapp.org/resources/article/us-state-ai-governance-legislation-tracker/). The following are some of the states that have passed AI-related laws (or in the process and gaining traction on passing AI-relevant laws).

California

California Governor, Gavin Newsom, signed several bills into law in September 2023. These laws represent some of the most comprehensive regulations related to AI around the United States. Some of the most notable are the following:

- *Amendments to California Consumer Privacy Act (CCPA) (Assembly Bill 1008 and Senate Bill 1223)* – both laws work in tandem with Assembly Bill 1008, clarifying that personal information is covered by the CCPA, no matter what format it is in, to ensure the CCPA addresses AI systems. Senate Bill 1223 clarifies sensitive personal information to encompass consumers' neural data, which limits developers and deployers from using neural data within their AI systems.
- *Artificial Intelligence (Assembly Bill 2885)* – this law standardized the definition of "Artificial Intelligence" to mean "an engineered or machine-based system that varies in its level of autonomy and that can, for explicit or implicit

objectives, infer from the input it receives how to generate outputs that can influence physical or virtual environments" [CA Government Code Section 11546.45.5].

- *California AI Transparency Act (Senate Bill 942)* – this law requires AI systems, which are publicly accessible in California with more than 1 million monthly users, to disclose AI-generated content. The law requires AI detection tools, disclosures, and licensing processes to ensure compliance. The law also requires watermarking or embedding 'provenance data' in the content metadata.
- *Contracts against Public Policy: Personal and Professional Services: Digital Replicas Act (Assembly Bill 2602)* – with the rise of 'deep fakes', this law restricts the misappropriate use of AI images of actors and performers.
- *Defending Democracy from Deepfake Deception Act (Assembly Bill 2655)* – this law requires the identification and blocking of content deemed materially deceptive by online platforms during specific election periods.
- *Education Initiatives (Assembly Bill 2876 and Senate Bill 1288)* – these laws address AI literacy within the educational curriculum. Students need to know how AI works, AI limitations, and ethical considerations in the use of AI. California superintendents are required to form a working group to work on how AI is used in public education.
- *Generative AI: Training Data Transparency Act (Assembly Bill 2013)* – this law requires generative AI system developers to publish a summary of the datasets used for training.
- *Generative Artificial Intelligence Accountability Act (Senate Bill 896)* – within state agencies and departments, this act establishes oversight and accountability measures. This law requires the Office of Emergency Services (CalOES) to perform risk analysis of the potential risks of generative AI.
- *Health Care Services: Artificial Intelligence Act (Assembly Bill 3030)* – requires healthcare providers to notify patients when communications are generated by an AI system, along with instructions on how a patient can contact a human. Senate Bill 1120 also requires licensed physicians to review the use of AI tools in healthcare providers and insurance services.
- *Pornography (Assembly Bill 1831; Senate Bill 926; and Senate Bill 981)* – these laws expand child pornography laws to include AI-generated content, using AI-generated nude images for blackmail is illegal, and requires social media platforms to provide mechanisms for users to report deepfake nudes.
- *Robocalls (Assembly Bill 2905)* – this law requires the disclosure of voices by AI.
- *Use of Likeness: Digital Replica Act (Assembly Bill 1836)* – if an AI is used to create an unauthorized digital replica of a dead celebrity, this law creates a cause of action by beneficiaries of the deceased celebrity. This law requires AI deployers to obtain consent prior to producing a digital replica of a deceased personality.

Illinois Biometric Information Privacy Act

Illinois enacted the Biometric Information Privacy Act (BIPA), requiring private entities possessing biometric identifiers (or biometric information) to develop written, public policies on retention and destruction of this information. The law further restricts the collection, capture, purchase, or receipt of biometric information, along with the restriction to sell, lease, trade, or otherwise profit from biometric information. The law prohibits the disclosure, redisclosure, or dissemination of biometric information unless certain criteria are met. The law also requires protection over biometric information and provides for the right of action by individuals.

New York City Local Law 144

Along with the states, some local government agencies are also passing regulations to protect individuals from the adverse impacts of AI systems. The New York City Commissions passed Local Law 144 in 2021. This law, enforced by the New York City Department of Consumer and Worker Protection (DCWP), prohibits employers (and employment agencies) from using automated employment decision tools (AEDTs) in the city unless these tools have undergone a bias audit and require notification to applicants. The law covers AEDTs that substantially help assess or screen candidates at any point in the process of hiring or promotion. The bias audit must be performed by an impartial and independent auditor. The law also requires the bias audit to be performed annually and must publicly share results.

Texas Responsible AI Governance Act

Texas' House Bill 1709, known as the Texas Responsible AI Governance Act (TRAIGA) proposes regulations and requirements for reporting on the use of AI systems. The bill proposes to require developers of a high-risk AI system to protect consumers from risks of discrimination arising from AI systems using reasonable care and providing instructions to deployers on the AI systems' use, risks, limitations, types of data, governance measures, and principles to be used for the deployers' risk management policy. The bill also proposes requirements on the distributors and deployers of high-risk AI systems with the same due diligence of care and requires them to stop using these systems if they fall out of compliance with the regulations.

The bill defines a 'high-risk artificial intelligence system' as any AI system making or contributing to making a consequential decision. There are some exemptions to the term and example exceptions such as technology used for anti-malware, cybersecurity, firewalls, networking, spell-checking, etc. Natural language AI systems may also be exempt as a 'high-risk' AI system with some caveats. The bill calls for the attorney general to bring an action to restrain (or enjoin) a person in violation of the regulation, as well as any injunctive relief.

Virginia (Executive Order 30)

Virginia Governor, Glenn Youngkin, "issued Executive Order 30 on Artificial Intelligence (AI), which implements AI Education Guidelines for the classroom and AI Policy and Information Technology Standards that safeguard the state's databases while simultaneously protecting the individual data of all Virginians" (Office of the Governor, 2024). The AI Policy and Information Technology Standards are made available through the Virginia Information Technology Agency (VITA).

> The Standards set the technological requirements for the use of AI within government agencies and the approval process for AI initiatives to ensure the safe and ethical use of such initiatives. The Education Guidelines establish guiding principles for the use of AI at all education levels to ensure that our students will be prepared for the jobs of tomorrow without sacrificing any current learning opportunities. The Executive Order also calls for the development of standards for the use of AI by law enforcement personnel.
>
> *(Office of the Governor, 2024)*

EU AI Act

The European Union passed the European Artificial Intelligence Act (AI Act), which entered into force on 1 August 2024. One of the first regulations related specifically to AI, "the act aims to foster responsible artificial intelligence development and deployment in the EU" (Directorate-General for Communication, 2024). Under the EU AI Act, AI is defined as

> a software that is developed with one or more of the techniques and approaches listed in Annex I and can, for a given set of human-defined objectives, generate outputs such as content, predictions, recommendations, or decisions influencing the environments they interact with.

According to the FLI, there are four primary areas covered by the EU AI Act as follows:

1. There are four risk classifications of AI to include:
   a. **Unacceptable Risk** – these are AI systems that are prohibited from being used, such as subliminal manipulation resulting in physical/psychological harm, exploitation of children (or mentally disabled persons) resulting in physical/psychological harm, general-purpose social scoring, and remote biometric identification for law enforcement purposes in publicly accessible spaces (with some exceptions permitted for this use).

    b. **High Risk** – most of the EU AI act addresses this classification of risk, which includes AI systems as a safety product, or a component of a safety product, already regulated by EU safety laws such as medical devices and machinery, as well as eight stand-alone AI systems in the following fields:

        i. Biometric identification and categorization of natural persons

        ii. Management and operation of critical infrastructure

        iii. Education and vocational training

        iv. Recruitment: Employment and workers management, access to self-employment

        v. Access to and enjoyment of essential private services and public services/benefits

        vi. Law enforcement

        vii. Migration, asylum, and border control management

        viii. Administration of justice and democratic processes

    c. **Limited Risk** – this classification has less requirements than higher risk AI systems, such as transparency obligations, ensuring individuals are aware they are interacting with AI and know when content is generated by AI. Examples of limited risk AI systems include impersonation bots, biometric categorization systems, and emotional (text audio or visual) deep fakes.

    d. **Minimal Risk** – this classification has no mandatory obligations; however, codes of conduct are created to encourage voluntary application of requirements. Examples of minimal or no risk AI systems include AI-enabled videogames, spam filters, predictive resource optimization, or any other AI system not categorized as limited, high, or unacceptable risk classifications.

2. The EU AI Act defines AI stakeholders, and most of the regulations apply to providers (or developers) of high-risk AI systems. A provider is an entity that intends to develop AI systems to sell (or put in use) in the EU market. The provider can be located outside of the EU, but will still be obligated to meet the requirements of the regulation.

3. The EU AI Act applies to deployers (or persons deploying) an AI system in a professional capacity for users to use the AI system. Deployers have less obligations than providers under the regulations; however, deployers located outside of the EU where the AI system's output is used in the EU are also within the scope of the regulations.

4. The EU AI Act applies to general-purpose AI (GPAI). Providers of GPAI have certain obligations under the regulations to include providing technical documentation on how the GPAI works, instruction for users on how to use the GPAI, the GPAI must comply with Copyright Directive, and a summary must be published about the training content used. There are some exceptions for free and open licensing for GPAI model providers, where obligations only include copyright and training data summary requirements unless there is

a systemic risk. All GPAI model providers with systemic risk must perform a model evaluation of the GPAI, perform adversarial testing, ensure serious incidents are tracked and reported, and implement cybersecurity protection measures.

The EU AI Act requires providers of high-risk AI systems to implement a risk management system throughout the AI system's life cycle. The provider must also identify risks and appropriate mitigation measures. Providers are required to conduct data governance to ensure their training, validation, and testing datasets are relevant, as well as sufficiently represent the scoped population. Datasets used in training models must be free of errors and must be as complete as possible for the intended purpose.

Providers must create and maintain technical documentation to demonstrate compliance prior to the AI system being placed on the market. These compliance requirements include defining the purpose of the AI system, risk management information, required conformity assessments, documents on how the AI system was developed, describing the architecture of the AI system, and publishing training and model information.

High-risk AI systems must be designed to ensure record-keeping is enabled to automatically record events relevant to identifying national-level risks, as well as any substantial modifications throughout the AI system's life cycle. In addition, to meet transparency requirements, providers of high-risk AI systems must provide instructions for use to deployers to permit deployers in their compliance efforts. Providers must permit deployers of their high-risk AI systems to implement human oversight. Providers must also design their high-risk AI systems to achieve appropriate levels of accuracy, robustness, and cybersecurity. AI systems need to perform consistently, be regularly assessed, and be cyber resilient.

Providers of high-risk AI systems must establish a Quality Management System (QMS) to include regulatory compliance strategies, technical build specifications, and post-deployment monitoring plans. Providers of high-risk AI systems need to perform required conformity assessments depending on health, safety, and fundamental rights and may require obtaining a CE marking prior to placing on the market. From French, *conformité européenne*, meaning European conformity, an importer of goods or manufacturer may affix the CE marking to their commercial products if they conform to European health, safety, and environmental protection standards. Providers must conduct post-marketing monitoring and report any serious incidents, which could breach obligations to protect fundamental rights as well as collaborate with market surveillance authorities. The EU AI Act establishes an EU-wide database for high-risk AI systems, and these high-risk AI systems must be registered prior to being placed on the market.

Under the EU AI Act, a general-purpose AI system (GPAI) is an AI system based on a GPAI model having the capability to serve a variety of purposes directly or integrated into another AI system. A GPAI model is an AI model trained with a large amount of data using self-supervision at scale displaying significant generality. The GPAI model can perform a wide range of distinct tasks placed on the market directly or integrated into other AI systems. AI models used for research, development, and prototyping activities are NOT included in the GPAI model definition.

The EU AI Act requires all providers of GPAI models to create and maintain technical documentation, which includes the training/testing process and result evaluations. Documentation must be provided to downstream providers intending to integrate the GPAI model into their own AI systems to ensure these providers can maintain their compliance efforts by understanding the model's capabilities and limitations. GPAI model providers must implement a policy to respect the Copyright Directive, along with publishing summaries in sufficient detail to describe the content used for training in the model.

If a GPAI model uses a cumulative amount of computer processing greater than 10^{25} floating-point operations per second (FLOPS), it is considered systemic. The provider of the GPAI model must notify the EU Commission and can present arguments that the model does not present systemic risks. The EU Commission may decide the model has high impact capabilities, classifying it as systemic. If the GPAI model is determined to be systemic, the provider has four additional obligations under the EU AI Act:

1. The provider must perform model evaluations, which include performing and documenting adversarial testing to identify (and mitigate) any systemic risks.
2. The provider must assess and mitigate any possible systemic risks along with their sources.
3. The provider must track, document, and report serious incidents. Any possible corrective measures must also be reported to the AI Office (and any relevant national competent authorities without undue delay).
4. The provider must ensure adequate cybersecurity protection measures are implemented.

Providers can demonstrate compliance by adhering to the approved code of practices or through other approved alternative adequate means of compliance. As previously discussed, codes of practice tend to take an international approach and may not be limited to just the obligations listed above. Codes of practice will involve several stakeholders such as providers, national competent authorities, civil societies, industry, academia, and other AI stakeholders.

Although the EU AI Act concentrates on providers and deployers of AI systems, it also covers AI users. For instance, AI users must operate AI systems according to user instructions. AI users must monitor high-risk systems for possible risks and update providers/deployers regarding any serious incidents or malfunctioning AI systems. In addition, AI users must ensure these AI systems are using human oversight and automatically generating adequate logs. Finally, AI users are still obligated to cooperate with existing legal obligations (such as the GDPR) and cooperate with regulators as necessary.

Although the EU AI Act requires some AI providers to report on climate-related concerns, in a report titled *AI, Climate, and Transparency: Operationalizing and Improving the AI Act*, the authors argue that there are at least seven significant concerns with the requirements summarized and paraphrased below:

1. There is no explicit requirement to report energy consumption, only computational resources, for high-risk AI systems under Article 11, section 1.
2. Although there is an explicit requirement to report on energy consumption for general-purpose AI (GPAI) models, the requirement technically only covers the model development and not the inference phase.
3. Open-source (OS) GPAI models, except posing a systemic risk, are exempt from transparency obligations and do not require reporting of emergency consumption of these models.
4. There is some debate regarding fine-tuning with some ambiguity in minor changes of a GPAI, making the organization rise to a level of a provider (reference Recital 97), but reporting obligations are only scoped to the fine-tuning (reference Recital 109). Article 25, section 1b, contradicts this by indicating that only substantial modifications for high-risk AI systems make the organization a provider, in essence, exempting smaller organizations.
5. The EU AI Act doesn't account for greenhouse gas (GHG) reporting, which may have an impact on the environment through climate change.
6. Energy consumption is only reported to authorities and not to other providers or the public.
7. The EU AI Act also does not factor in toxic materials or water consumption, which play a role in operating datacenters (Alder et al., 2024).

The EU AI Act requires high-risk systems to be explainable. In a report titled *How Should AI Decisions Be Explained? Requirements for Explanations from the Perspective of European Law*, the authors suggest leveraging the standards provided by ISO/IEC CD TS 6254, along with the use of eXplainable Artificial Intelligence (XAI). Three areas of law were considered as the basis of the authors' opinions requiring XAI: fiduciary decisions, right to explanation, and safety and liability. A variety of audiences are captured within explanations to include the layperson, domain expert, and ML expert. Explanations are also recommended to cover the following areas: correctness, completeness, consistency, continuity, contrastivity, covariate complexity, compactness, compositionality, confidence, context, coherence, controllability, consilience, computations, coverage, counterability, and constancy (Fresz et al., 2024).

Australia (Emerging)

Currently, Australia does not have a comprehensive regulation related to AI; however, Australia has plans to strengthen existing laws. Australia published eight principles of ethical AI back in 2019 to include the following: human, societal, and environmental well-being; human-centered values; fairness; privacy protection and security; reliability and safety; transparency and explainability; contestability; and accountability.

Brazil (Emerging)

Brazil is proposing specific AI regulations under Bill No. 2,338/2023. This proposed regulation uses a risk-based approach defining excessive-risk AI systems and high-risk AI systems developed, implemented, and used within Brazil. "Brazil's Proposed AI Regulation aims to protect fundamental rights and ensures the implementation of secure and reliable systems for the benefit of the human person, the democratic regime, and scientific and technological development" (Freitas and Giacchetta, 2025).

Canada Artificial Intelligence and Data Act (Emerging)

> The proposed Artificial Intelligence and Data Act (AIDA), introduced as part of the Digital Charter Implementation Act, 2022, would set the foundation for the responsible design, development and deployment of AI systems that impact the lives of Canadians. The Act would ensure that AI systems deployed in Canada are safe and non-discriminatory and would hold businesses accountable for how they develop and use these technologies.
>
> *(Government of Canada, 2023)*

While the proposed act is being worked on, the Canadian Minister of Innovation, Science, and Industry, published *Voluntary Code of Conduct on the Responsible Development and Management of Advanced Generative AI Systems* providing voluntary standards for organizations to demonstrate responsible development and use of generative AI systems.

China (The AI Measures)

China has been working through AI-related regulations for several years and has issued its first administrative regulation on the management of generative AI services, effective 15 August 2023, known as the Interim AI Measures. There are other related laws, but "the AI Measures are formulated to promote a healthy development and regulated application of generative artificial intelligence, safeguard national security and social public interests, and protect the lawful rights and interests of citizens, legal persons and other organizations" (Yang and Li, 2024). Some of the key compliance requirements under the AI Measures include lawful use, data labeling rules, data training, content moderation, and reporting mechanism.

China's National Technical Committee 260 on Cybersecurity of SAC published its first version of the *AI Safety Governance Framework* in September 2024.

> Upholding a people-centered approach and adhering to the principle of developing AI for good, this framework has been formulated to implement the Global AI Governance Initiative and promote consensus and coordinated efforts on AI safety governance among governments, international organizations, companies, research institutes, civil organizations, and individuals, aiming to effectively prevent and defuse AI safety risks.
>
> *(Zhong Lun Law Firm, 2024)*

India (Advisories)

India does not have a comprehensive regulation; however, India's Ministry of Electronics and Information Technology issued two initial advisories on AI. The first advisory issued on 1 March 2024 advised "intermediaries or platforms to ensure compliance with their due diligence requirements under the Information Technology (Intermediary Guidelines and Digital Media Ethics Code)" (D'Souza, 2024). The advisory required generative AI systems to have explicit permission to be deployed. It also required a notification warning users of inaccuracies in AI content. The second advisory was issued on 15 March 2024, nullifying the mandate to require permission, but required generative AI to ensure it did not facilitate any unlawful content.

> Untested or unreliable AI models, or those in development, could only be made available to the public after proper labelling of the output as being inherently fallible or unreliable. The revised advisory maintained the ban on use for threatening the electoral process by intermediaries or platforms. It also expanded platforms' responsibility to ensure they did not facilitate such unlawful use.
>
> *(D'Souza, 2024)*

Japan (Proposed AI Bill and Hiroshima Principles)

Japan does not currently have any specific AI laws; however, a working group has proposed *The Basic Act on the Advancement of Responsible AI* (i.e., Proposed AI Bill) to regulate generative AI. The proposal looks for voluntary obligations based on regulated general frameworks, with the government enforcing non-compliance penalties on AI developers. On 19 April 2024, the Government of Japan published *AI Guidelines for Business Version 1.0*. In addition, the *Hiroshima International Guiding Principles for Organizations Developing Advanced AI Systems* (i.e., The Hiroshima

Principles) were also published. "The Hiroshima Principles identify several significant risks, including disinformation, copyright, cybersecurity, risks to health and safety, and societal risks such as the ways in which advanced AI systems can give rise to harmful bias and discrimination" (Albagli et al., 2024).

Singapore (AI Verify)

Singapore does not currently have any specific AI laws; however, Singapore boasts being one of the first Asian countries to issue an AI governance framework in 2019, known as the Model AI Governance Framework. *AI Verify*, developed by the Infocomm Media Development Authority of Singapore (IMDA), created an AI governance testing framework after consulting with the private sector. AI Verify validates AI systems against the following 11 governance principles: "transparency, explainability, repeatability/reproducibility, safety, security, robustness, fairness, data governance, accountability, human agency and oversight, inclusive growth, societal and environmental well-being" (PDPC, 2025).

South Africa (POPIA)

South Africa enacted the Protection of Personal Information Act (POPIA) on 1 July 2020. This regulation is similar to the GDPR and incorporates the FIPPs. The act intersects with AI systems when personal information is processed. The Thomson Reuters Foundation recently published the *AI Governance for Africa Toolkit Series* introducing AI governance principles as well as examining "emerging AI governance instruments and approaches on the continent [Africa], with a focus on Southern Africa – in particular, South Africa, Zambia, and Zimbabwe" (Thomson Reuters Foundation, 2025). "The aim of the toolkit is to empower journalists and civil society organisations to inform public discourse, drive policy and regulatory change and advocate for ethical and responsible AI deployment" (Thomson Reuters Foundation, 2025).

South Korea (AI Act)

The Republic of South Korea does not currently have specific regulations on AI and failed to pass comprehensive regulations in its most recent assembly. There are several outstanding bills and amendments in the works to include *the Act on Promotion of the AI Industry and Framework for Establishing Trustworthy AI* (AI Act), *Personal Information Protection Act*, *Fair Hiring Procedure Act*, and *Copyright Act*, just to name a few. Like other countries without specific AI regulations, South Korea created a non-binding guidance directive, *Secure Artificial Intelligence (AI) – Data Utilization: AI Privacy Risk Management Models*.

> The Model will guide AI developers and providers regarding managing AI privacy risks to ensure that they safely process personal data

in the course of providing AI services. The risk management process would involve (i) identifying the types and applications of the AI model and system, (ii) identifying and measuring privacy risks associated with each type and application of the AI model and system, and (iii) preparing measures to mitigate such risks.

(Kim & Chang, 2024)

Standards

Abiding by recognized standards is highly recommended, and standards are generally used to tie back policies (and procedures) to regulatory requirements.

ISO 42001

ISO/IEC 42001 is an international standard that specifies requirements for establishing, implementing, maintaining, and continually improving an Artificial Intelligence Management System (AIMS) within organizations. It is designed for entities providing or utilizing AI-based products or services, ensuring responsible development and use of AI systems.

(ISO, 2025b)

An organization is able to certify its AI management system against this standard and is one of the most respected standards to demonstrate responsible AI. This book goes into further detail on how this standard can be used, implemented, and the process to obtain certification from a practitioner perspective.

Microsoft

From years of experience developing software and now with the introduction of AI, Microsoft has published its *Responsible AI Standard*. This standard covers Microsoft's six AI principles, consisting of fairness, reliability and safety, privacy and security, inclusiveness, transparency, and accountability. Although version 2 of the Microsoft Responsible AI Standard was released on June 2022, this document is updated as new processes are considered in AI, and additional information on this standard can be found at this source: https://blogs.microsoft.com/wp-content/uploads/prod/sites/5/2022/06/Microsoft-Responsible-AI-Standard-v2-General-Requirements-3.pdf

HITRUST AI Security

"HITRUST® is an information protection standards organization and certifying body" (HITRUST, 2025). HITRUST® has been a leader in developing standards to certify organizations against the HITRUST˙ CSF (and other frameworks) across several industry verticals. HITRUST˙ has developed an AI Risk Management Assessment. "The AI Security Assessment and Certification for AI platforms and deployed systems, brings HITRUST's trusted approach to securing AI technologies with a comprehensive set of controls and assurances" (HITRUST, 2025).

Frameworks

Along with the regulations and standards, there are several other AI frameworks an organization could leverage to help them demonstrate trustworthy and responsible AI development, deployment, or use. These additional frameworks include the following:

- **US Government Accountability Office (GAO) AI Framework** – This framework was developed to help managers "Ensure accountability and responsible use of artificial intelligence (AI) in government programs and processes" (GAO, 2021).

    This framework is organized around four complementary principles, which address governance, data, performance, and monitoring. For each principle, the framework describes key practices for federal agencies and other entities that are considering, selecting, and implementing AI systems. Each practice includes a set of questions for entities, auditors, and third-party assessors to consider, as well as procedures for auditors and third- party assessors.

    (GAO, 2021)

- **US Department of Homeland Security (DHS) Roles and Responsibilities Framework for Artificial Intelligence in Critical Infrastructure** – This framework was developed in consultation with the Artificial Intelligence Safety and Security Board to propose actions organizations can take to bolster security concerns involving their roles/responsibilities over critical infrastructure services as it relates to the use of AI.
- **Institute of Internal Auditors (IIA) Artificial Intelligence Auditing Framework** – The Institute of Internal Auditors maintains an AI auditing framework to help organizations "understand risks and identify best practices and internal controls for AI" (IIA, 2025).
- **Trusted AI (TAI) Model** – The Holistic Information Security Practitioner Institute (HISPI) established *Project Cerebellum*. Their "mission is to be the brains behind the promotion and harmonization of best practices, standards, and frameworks for AI and related technologies" (HISPI, 2025). The HISPI Think Tank developed the Trusted AI (TAI) Model designed to be an open-source project with the vision to serve safe, secure, and trustworthy AI.

- **Cybersecurity Capability Maturity Model (C2M2)** – Although not directly an AI framework, the Office of Cybersecurity, Energy Security, and Emergency Response of the US Department of Energy published the C2M2 framework to address cybersecurity practices with information technology (IT) and operations technology (OT). The framework, or model, is intended to help establish new cybersecurity programs or improve existing programs.
- **STEEPLE** – STEEPLE is a strategic planning framework to help organizations assess external factors impacting operations. STEEPLE stands for the following: social, technological, economic, environmental, political, legal, and ethical. STEEPLE is similar to PESTLE, but also includes ethical factors, which makes this framework helpful in analyzing AI strategies. In a blog post on LinkedIn written by Zhicheng Weng, the author rearranges the factors and adapts the STEEPLE framework to SLE³PT. In the post, titled *SLE³PT: A Framework for Environment Analysis & Risk Assessment*, Mr. Weng details how this framework could be used in the technology sector and provides an example of the analysis to AI. Additional details can be found at this source: https://www.linkedin.com/pulse/slept-environment-risk-framework-zhicheng-weng-mltnc/

Guidelines

Guidelines are other important tools to demonstrate responsible AI. Some of these guidelines are issued by regulatory agencies to ensure regulations are appropriately implemented. Others are issued by groups to help organizations in need of assistance with complex compliance efforts. The following are some notable guidance related to AI:

- **AI Guide for Government** – IT Modernization Centers of Excellence developed an AI Guide for Government – A Living and Evolving Guide to the Application of Artificial Intelligence for the US Federal Government "intended to help government decision makers clearly see what AI means for their agencies and how to invest and build AI capabilities" (COE, 2025).
- **Responsible Use of AI Guide** – Amazon Web Services (AWS) published the Responsible Use of AI Guide to share recommendations on responsible AI across the AI life cycle, including design, development, deployment, and operation phases. According to the guide, "organizations build responsible AI capabilities through a programmatic approach with specific objectives, dedicated leaders, metrics, mechanisms, and resourcing" (AWS, 2025b).
- **CNIL's First Recommendations for GDPR-Compliant AI Systems** – The CNIL issued recommendations on how AI systems can be compliant with the GDPR on 19 June 2024. These recommendations focus on developing

privacy-enabled AI to apply the following GDPR principles: purpose; controllership; legal basis, minimization, and others.

- **AI Opportunities Action Plan: Government Response** – The Department for Science, Innovation, and Technology of the UK Government published the AI Opportunities Action Plan: Government Response policy paper on 13 January 2025. This plan lays out how Britain will become an AI superpower by making discoveries in AI and exporting them to the rest of the world. Although not direct guidance, per se, to organizations, the plan does provide some of the priority areas the UK government will be looking at in AI.

- **Department of Defense (DoD) Zero Trust Reference Architecture** – Although not a direct guide for AI, the Zero Trust Reference Architecture, prepared by the Defense Information System Agency (DISA) and National Security Agency (NSA) Zero Trust Engineering Team, can be used in the development and architecture of AI systems. "ZT [zero trust] is a cybersecurity strategy developing an architecture that requires authentication or verification before granting access to sensitive data or protected resources at a financial cost by reducing data loss and preventing data breaches" (DoD CIO, 2022).

> While straightforward in principle, the actual implementation and operationalization of ZT [zero trust] incorporates several areas which need to be smartly integrated and that include software defined networking, data tagging, behavioral analytics, access control, policy orchestration, encryption, automation, as well as end-to-end ICAM [identity, credential, and access management].
>
> *(DoD CIO, 2022)*

Integrated Management System

The primary goal and objective of an IMS is to develop and use responsible and trustworthy AI systems. Regulations applicable to the organization will define some of the criteria or requirements along with contractual obligations pertaining to the context of the AI systems provided to consumers (or other organizations). Standards play a significant role in developing AI governance and compliance efforts. There are several different standards that may apply to AI; however, this author will focus on the management system standards provided by the International Organization for Standardization (ISO) and the International Electrotechnical Commission (IEC). The ISO/IEC standards are recognized across the world and provide a foundation for an effective IMS.

AI systems cross several domains. For this reason, this author highly recommends an organization develop and implement an IMS. The IMS should include the following standards: ISO/IEC 27001:2022 – Information Security Management

System (ISMS), ISO/IEC 27701:2019 – Privacy Information Management System (PIMS), ISO/IEC 9001:2015 – QMS, and ISO/IEC 42001:2023 – AI Management Systems (AIMS). This book will go into detail on how these standards relate to each other and are woven together to create the IMS; however, the focus will be specific to the AIMS and AI-related areas.

When standards align with regulations and contractual obligations, they form the basis of an organization's AI governance efforts. One of the deliverables of AI governance activities is the AI Governance Policy. This policy aligns with executive management's intent for the organization to develop and use responsible and trustworthy AI systems.

The NIST provides several frameworks and guidance, which are very helpful in developing the IMS. As previously mentioned, AI systems need to be based on risks. Leveraging these frameworks provides for the integration of risk management into the IMS. This author uses the NIST Risk Management Framework (RMF) and, more specifically, the NIST AI RMF when it comes to identifying risks related to AI deployment and use. The NIST Cybersecurity Framework (CsF) and the NIST Privacy Framework (PrF) can be used to incorporate controls to mitigate identified risks.

In addition, this author uses the *NIST Special Publication (SP) 800-53, Security and Privacy Controls for Information Systems and Organizations,* an extensive list of controls an organization could implement to mitigate (or minimize) the risks associated with diverse types of technology including AI. NIST SP 800-53 also includes controls around people and processes. This author utilizes the 'families' or categorical groups of controls to organize policies and procedures. As of this writing, NIST SP 800-53 is at revision 5 and is continually updated.

NIST 800-53r5 includes the following 20 families: Access Control (AC); Awareness and Training (AT); Audit and Accountability (AU); Assessment, Authorization and Monitoring (CA); Configuration Management (CM); Contingency Planning (CP); Identification and Authentication (IA); Incident Response (IR); Maintenance (MA); Media Protection (MP); Physical and Environmental Protection (PE); Planning (PL); Program Management (PM); Personnel Security (PS); PII Processing and Transparency (PT); Risk Assessment (RA); System and Services Acquisition (SA); System and Communications Protection (SC); System and Information Integrity (SI); and Supply Chain Risk Management (SR).

To demonstrate accountability, an organization should obtain independent verification or validation (also known as certification). Within the ISO/IEC certification process, an organization will need to perform an internal audit, which will function as a 'gap' review prior to certification. If the organization successfully completes the internal audit and is determined to be ready for a certification, the certification process will occur in two phases. Phase 1 of the certification will identify the scope and context of the certification. The auditor will review some evidence to determine the adequacy of the evidence provided such as performing reviews to ensure policies and procedures are available. Policies and procedures are mapped accordingly to the controls implemented to mitigate risks. These controls are defined within a Statement of Applicability (SoA), which will be discussed further in this book.

If the organization successfully completes Phase 1, Phase 2 of the certification will start. Phase 2 will involve more scrutiny of the policies and procedures, as well as require evidence to be provided to the auditors to ensure these policies/procedures are sufficiently implemented. Evidence might be adequate (or the right evidence), but the evidence must also be sufficient (or enough of the right type of evidence). For instance, an organization might have the right policies and procedures implemented, but the organization must also have enough evidence in place to demonstrate these policies and procedures are actually taking place as written. Controls need to be implemented in an effective way to ensure they meet the criteria of the standards being assessed.

ISO/IEC certifications are valid for three years. The second and third years are called surveillance audits, and the organization must provide evidence to demonstrate continued improvements in the management system. As a note, there are very few certifying bodies (i.e., organizations that perform certification audits against management system standards) that may be able to do all four of these recommended certifications (i.e., ISMS, PIMS, QMS, AIMS). Most certifying bodies might not be able to perform a QMS audit since this tends to be a little bit more

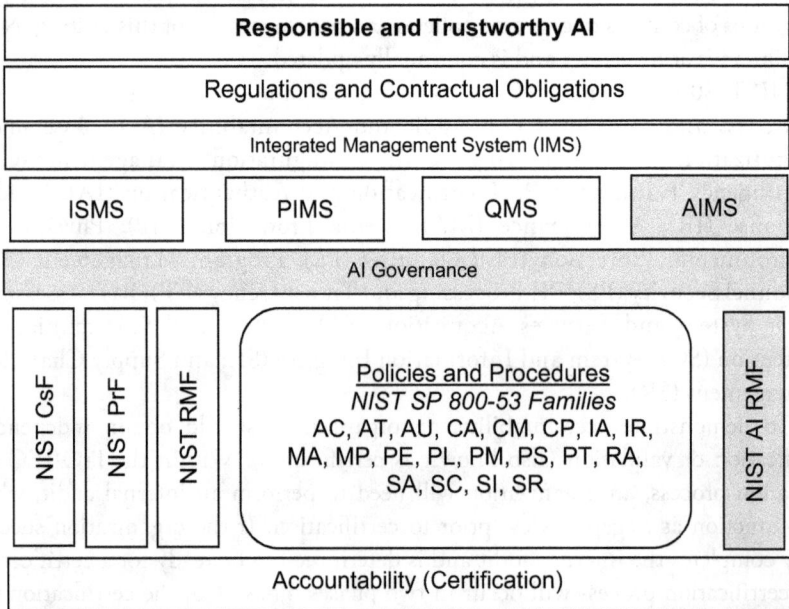

Figure 3.1   Example of an Integrated Management Framework.

specialized; however, quality is important in maintaining a successful AI management system. Some practitioners may argue that an organization should start their IMS journey with a QMS in place first.

The figure below shows the relationship between the distinct factors making up a comprehensive Integration Management Framework (IMF). This IMF, when implemented, will provide a good baseline to deploy and use responsible and trustworthy AI. There is still a lot more work to be done; however, this figure provides an overview of an IMS. This book focuses primarily on the highlighted items of this figure (Figure 3.1).

Chapter 4

AI Risk Management

Thou should not make a machine in the likeness of a human mind.

–Dune: Prophecy (Foerster, 2024)

Any management system implemented must be based on risks. Responsible AI is centered around effective risk management processes. This chapter will discuss some of the AI risks or concerns an organization needs to be aware of and factor into its decisions. There are several concerns from environmental, human rights, intellectual property, regulatory, safety, and other issues that need to be addressed when developing, deploying, and using AI. This chapter discusses different risk management strategies and delves into performing a system impact assessment, a data protection impact assessment, and a fundamental rights impact assessment. How risks are identified, managed, treated, and tracked is discussed at the end of this chapter.

AI Concerns

There are several areas of concern when developing, deploying, and using AI systems. These concerns may present themselves as individual (or privacy related) concerns, group (or society related) concerns, environmental concerns, or organizational concerns. As summarized in the pre-amble of the Whitehouse's *Blueprint for an AI Bill of Rights*:

> Among the great challenges posed to democracy today is the use of technology, data, and automated systems in ways that threaten the rights of the American public. Too often, these tools are used to limit our opportunities and prevent our access to critical resources or services.

90

DOI: 10.1201/9781003624073-4

These problems are well documented. In America and around the world, systems supposed to help with patient care have proven unsafe, ineffective, or biased. Algorithms used in hiring and credit decisions have been found to reflect and reproduce existing unwanted inequities or embed new harmful bias and discrimination. Unchecked social media data collection has been used to threaten people's opportunities, undermine their privacy, or pervasively track their activity—often without their knowledge or consent.

(Whitehouse, 2024)

Accountability Concerns

A major concern regarding AI is who will be responsible for any damage caused by AI. *Who is ultimately responsible for the content (or possible actions taken) from the output generated from AI?* Developers, deployers, and users of AI systems need to consider the ramifications over their AI systems to possibly include pecuniary and non-pecuniary damages. Pecuniary damages are measured financially such as costs associated with damage from a personal injury lawsuit. These costs could include medical fees, loss wages, property damages, or future monetary damages in earnings. Non-pecuniary damages are those that are not quantified by money. These could include emotional distress, physical pain (or suffering), and physical/mental impairments.

Environmental Concerns

Training machine learning models requires a lot of resources and energy. The energy consumption needed for AI systems could have a direct impact on the environment. The concerns over the environmental impact of the deployment and use of AI systems are being considered by governments and regulatory authorities. Organizations must factor in these environmental impacts as part of their due diligence when considering the deployment of AI systems.

Group or Socioeconomic Inequality Concerns

Not only individuals but also groups of individuals can be impacted by the deployment or use of AI systems. The use of AI systems to perform mass surveillance or analysis on a population could lead to discrimination against a group of individuals. This surveillance or analysis could lead to profiling a certain group of individuals and could limit their ability to assemble. Restricting the right to assemble by a group of individuals could lead to racial or social tensions.

AI systems could impact the democratic process by distributing misinformation created by an AI system. A common use case seen with AI is to provide recommendations on products or services matching an individual's profile. If this profiling use case is expanded more broadly to a group of individuals with the same ideals, providing misinformation generated by AI systems could alter the reality of a situation. The use of deepfakes to alter video, audio, or other images could incite discord or hate, leading to safety concerns for a particular group of individuals.

Another major concern is the fear that AI may take over jobs. "Studies suggest that up to 30% of U.S. jobs could be impacted by AI and automation in some capacity over the next decade" (Gaper, 2025). Although some jobs may be eliminated by AI, there may be other new roles and opportunities. Still, individuals need to understand how AI may impact their own situations and be ready to learn new skills or pivot into other industries to ensure their career success.

Human Rights Concerns

Government and other organizations realize that, with all the benefits of AI, there are risks of harm, especially when it comes to AI unintentionally infringing on human rights. In a resolution adopted by the General Assembly of the United Nations on 21 March 2024, all 193 member states affirmed and emphasized "that human rights and fundamental freedoms must be respected, protected and promoted throughout the life cycle of artificial intelligence systems" (United Nations, 2024). Furthermore, the resolution

> calls upon all Member States and, where applicable, other stakeholders to refrain from or cease the use of artificial intelligence systems that are impossible to operate in compliance with international human rights law or that pose undue risks to the enjoyment of human rights.
>
> *(United Nations, 2024)*

Will AI ever be granted human rights or personhood? This is an ongoing debate between scholars where one group believes AI may need certain rights, especially when they decide their own actions. Another group believes providing human rights status to AI diminishes the value of being human and believes AI will never rise to the state of being human (or being self-aware).

Individual or Privacy Concerns

Individuals may be directly impacted by the deployment or use of AI systems. Individual concerns may involve the AI system's violation of civil rights or liberties, privacy, economic opportunities, or physical and psychological safety. Within AI systems, personal data may persist longer than expected (or go against one of the principal privacy rights, which is 'to be forgotten'), and data may be repurposed for other reasons than what the purpose was for the data to be originally collected.

Personal data, when aggregated in datasets, may be collected from unintended individuals or collected without consent in the first place. Individuals may not have the ability to 'opt-out' of the collection or maintain their right to delete their personal data from a dataset. The nature of the processing of personal data may not be appropriately explained, and over time, models could be trained on AI-generated data.

In their legal research paper titled *Privacy Harms*, well-known legal scholars Danielle Keats Citron, from the University of Virginia School of Law, and Daniel J. Solove, George Washington University Law School, provide a taxonomy of privacy harm breaking these down into multiple categories and subcategories. These privacy harms include some of the following: physical, reputational, relationship, economic discrimination, psychological (such as emotional distress/disturbance), and autonomy (such as manipulation, social norms, and chilling effects). Additional details can be found, and their paper can be downloaded from this source: https://papers.ssrn.com/sol3/papers.cfm?abstract_id=3782222.

The resulting output of AI systems is only as good as the data being inputted or learned; this may cause AI systems to be biased. Bias may come in the form of implicit, sampling, or temporal. When AI systems discriminate against a particular individual (or group of individuals), implicit bias has been introduced into the AI system. If there is more data about a particular subset of individuals and the results start to favor this subset over others, this is known as sampling bias. An AI system may also see temporal bias where a model works as expected initially, but over time, it stops working as well. This can be seen in overfitting where a machine learning model works well with training data, but not as well as new data is introduced. AI systems may also show bias to outliers where the data is outside of the training data.

With biased machine learning models, individuals could be subject to discrimination by the AI systems in use. Individuals could face employment and hiring decisions based on the use of a biased AI system. For instance, when AI is used to review resumes, the AI system could automatically reject individuals or groups of individuals. This discriminatory hiring practice could lead to an impact on an individual's job opportunities and economic loss. As previously mentioned, discrimination may have already been seen in the areas of insurance or other social benefits as in the case of the lawsuit against United Healthcare. The use of AI in determining credit scores could lead to discrimination causing individuals to be charged higher interest rates or be denied credit to purchase a house, vehicle, or other items. AI could be used to evaluate college applications leading to discrimination in the opportunity to obtain higher education.

Bias and fairness tend to be tied to privacy, and the use of AI systems can introduce privacy concerns. Training data could include personal or sensitive information. This personal or sensitive data could then be shared in the output to individuals who should not see this information. The use of this data being trained by models may have required consent for use, making the machine learning model illegal (or any derivative model produced illegally – 'fruit of the poisonous tree'). Training data should be cleaned to ensure personal information is not present, and personal data should be de-identified. Unfortunately, the use of multiple datasets combined (or aggregated) could potentially re-identify an individual negating the efforts of any de-identification activities. Since AI systems do well at identifying patterns, initial scrubbed datasets could eventually contain personal or sensitive information when the AI systems are actually deployed. However, when AI systems start making inferences, machine learning models may become inaccurate or state information about individuals which is not true.

Intellectual Property Rights Concerns

Copyrights over content produced by AI systems have raised some concerns and discussions. In fact, the US Copyright Office had received several registrations for copyrights of material generated by AI. The Copyright Office published a policy on 16 March 2023, titled *Copyright Registration Guidance: Works Containing Material Generated by Artificial Intelligence*. In this guidance, the Copyright Office noted "copyright can protect only material that is the product of human creativity. Most fundamentally, the term 'author', which is used in both the Constitution and the Copyright Act, excludes non-humans" (Copyright Office, 2023).

The guidance further states that submissions for copyright will be reviewed on a case-by-case basis when the content of the registration contains both human-authored and uncopyrighted material (such as content generated by AI). The question that needs to be answered is

> whether the 'work' is basically one of human authorship, with the computer [or other device] merely being an assisting instrument, or whether the traditional elements of authorship in the work (literary, artistic, or musical expression or elements of selection, arrangement, etc.) were actually conceived and executed not by man but by a machine.
>
> *(Copyright Office, 2023)*

The guidance further states, "in the case of works containing AI-generated material, the Office will consider whether the AI contributions are the result of 'mechanical reproduction' or instead of an author's 'own original mental conception, to which [the author] gave visible form'" (Copyright Office, 2023). An example of a submission received by the Copyright Office was of a graphic novel where text was combined with images generated by an AI service (i.e., Midjourney). The Copyright Office concluded the 'text' was a copyrightable work; however, the images created by the AI system were NOT copyright protected.

Another aspect of content produced by AI is the possibility of AI creating something new where a patent is requested. Under the case (*Thaler v. Vidal, 43 F.4th 1207, 12109 Fed.Cir. 2022*), the US Court of Appeals of the Federal Circuit denied a petition for a patent and determined ONLY humans can be named as an inventor on a patent (cert. denied, No. 22-919 (US 24 April 2023). This is further substantiated by the US Patent and Trademark Office's *Guidance on Use of Artificial Intelligence-Based Tools in Practice Before the United States Patent and Trademark Office*. This notice, published on 11 April 2024, states the current rules in place to protect against potential AI risks by reminding individuals of their requirements of full disclosure when it comes to submitting patent applications. Patent seekers must disclose all aspects of their requests, including any AI involvement, and must certify all matters of truth by signing the application.

The European Patent Office (EPO) follows the United States in denying two previous patent applications attempting to designate AI as an inventor (see EP 18275163 and EP 18275174) for additional details). The EPO took the stand that an inventor needs to be a 'legal personality'; however, different jurisdictions may interpret intellectual property rights, copyrights, trademarks, and patents differently. *What about AI systems creating similar, but not identical works? Are these differences able to be detected and could intellectual property rights be enforced?*

What about AI systems scraping copyright information from websites to train AI models? This may be decided by a court case filed by several news organizations including The New York Times, The New York Daily News, and the Center for Investigative Reporting against OpenAI. These organizations claim OpenAI used millions of copyrighted works without consent or payment. OpenAI argues the information has been protected by 'fair use' rules. "That is a doctrine in American law that allows copyrighted material to be used for things like educational, research or commentary purposes" (Allyn, 2025). There are some caveats to pass the fair use test such as "the work in question has to have transformed the copyrighted work into something new, and the new work cannot compete with the original in the same marketplace, among other factors" (Allyn, 2025). This lawsuit may have major impacts in holding OpenAI liable for billions of dollars in damages as well as possibly requiring the datasets to be destroyed. OpenAI would then need to train models from authorized datasets only.

Under the copyright protection of the European Union, a database can be protected under two different protection rights. The first is copyright protection guaranteeing exclusive rights if the database is created by original intellectual property. Copyright protects the structure of the database, but not necessarily its content. *Sui generis*, interpreted as meaning "in a class by itself" or 'unique', protects the content of the database. To utilize sui generis rights, an individual needs to show that the database content was created through substantial investment in money, resources, or humans. Sui generis provides automatic protection for 15 years starting from date of creation or the first date the database was made publicly available.

Justice Concerns

According to the National Center for State Courts,

> AI has the potential to streamline tasks within the courts, increase efficiency and allowing staff to work on higher level tasks. AI also has the potential to be used to help create resources for self-represented

litigants, expanding access to justice. But like any technology, AI is not infallible or without risks.

(NCSC, 2024)

Since AI may hallucinate or provide inaccurate information, these documents need to be carefully reviewed by humans to uphold their integrity. A perfect example of this risk is where a lawyer was sanctioned by a US District Judge in New York for filing a brief that included six fake case citations generated by ChatGPT. "The judge found the lawyers acted in bad faith and made 'acts of conscious avoidance and false and misleading statements to the court'" (Merken, 2023). The lawyers and the law firm were fined a total of $5,000.

Lack of Human Oversight Concerns

AI, by its very nature, is autonomous; however, AI cannot be permitted to make certain decisions without human oversight. Many factors need to be considered when human involvement is required such as the jurisdictions AI operates in, the type of data being processed, the content of the processing, and whether output (i.e., decisions) have a substantial impact on individuals. If a process is fully automated, such as may be the case with a loan application, *does the process maintain an alternative option of review or the ability to challenge the decision?* For instance, law enforcement agencies, such as the US Customs and Border Protection (CBP), may use biometric systems to verify identities; however, these agencies may also be required to have an alternative way to process identities by manually reviewing passports or other documentation by law enforcement officers. Although these alternatives might be in place, some human rights advocates have argued that they are not made transparent to individuals and leave the burden to the individual to exercise their rights.

According to an article published in the *International Journal of Organizational Analysis*, "many decision rules are rational but opaque, and many others are irrational but transparent".

> The authors show that opacity is asymmetric as different organizational actors possess different degrees of knowledge about how the decision rules work. Organizational actors often opacify the decision rules to increase their power (based on asymmetric knowledge). Opacity also presents a significant impact on organizational accountability, as transparent organizations are more reputable.
>
> *(Mastrogiorgio and Lattanzi, 2022)*

Organizations need to consider their processes for human reviews and ensure they are adequate. Guardrails need to be implemented to cover automated decision-making. Individuals assigned to review AI decisions must be trained on the use of AI and how AI came to the decision, and they must be given authority to override AI as necessary.

Organizational Concerns

One of the major concerns faced by any organization is its reputation. An organization's reputation is hard to achieve, and if trust is lost, it is even harder to gain back. If an organization uses an AI system found to be untrustworthy, the organization could be faced with a lot of negative press. The organization could also be facing litigation costs in the form of damages or remediation if the organization were found to deploy AI in an unethical (or illegal) manner. By the very nature of operating a business, risks are present, but the deployment and use of AI can increase these risks exponentially. Organizations that do not fully understand requirements, perform a gap review, and monitor concerns through the AI system's life cycle could face several legal, economic, and reputational concerns.

Organizations need to understand how AI is going to be used in their environment and understand the role AI is going to play within the organization. Organizations need to set (and enforce) standards on the deployment and use of AI. Organizations need to ensure their staff are aware of the rules and establish appropriate management systems to adequately address AI concerns. The deployment and use of AI will tend to involve many different stakeholders across the organization, requiring an effective governance structure to be implemented.

Regulatory Concerns

As discussed extensively thus far throughout this book, meeting obligations of AI regulations is going to get more complex as new laws go into effect at the local, state, national, and international levels. As regulators prioritize AI governance and require more accountability from developers, deployers, and users, these regulatory concerns will increase. There are a lot of unknowns when it comes to AI, and AI is a new technology, charting new paths through the regulatory 'mine field'. As organizations find out what AI may be able to do, regulations will follow when there are indications that AI and the organizations developing, deploying, or using AI are not playing by the rules.

Reputational Concerns

AI can introduce risks to an organization's reputation. Since businesses are built on trust, it could take some time to build, but one simple act such as using AI in an unethical manner could destroy trust in a minute. For instance, according to the United Kingdom's Information Commissioner's Office (ICO), "If you don't provide people with explanations of AI-assisted decisions you make about them, you risk being left behind by organisations that do, and getting singled out as unethical and uncaring toward your customers and citizens" (ICO, 2025).

Safety Concerns

According to the Center for AI Safety, catastrophic AI risks can be grouped into four categories: malicious use, AI race, organizational risks, and rogue AIs. Under malicious use, individuals could use AI to cause large-scale harm, such as using AI to create a bioweapon or mass surveillance. Attempting to become the world's super-power in AI could lead to unsafe AI development or turning control over to AI systems (such as the use of 'Skynet' in the *Terminator* movies). Organizations could prioritize profit over safety, leading to accidents. Losing control over AI in cases where AI is unable to be turned off or carries out deceptive acts is another major concern.

Security Concerns

There are several concerns regarding security over AI. Here is a non-exhaustive list of some of the top security concerns to take into consideration when developing, deploying, or using AI:

- *Adversarial Attacks* – this is when an attacker makes small changes to the input to manipulate the output (or to bypass guardrails established). Another variant of an adversarial attack is to use one AI system to attack another AI system.
- *Concentration of Power* – this can occur where it takes a lot of resources to train and manage AI systems, where the data used to train these systems is controlled by a small number of companies. This type of concentration of power over AI could impact individual freedom and control over an individual's personal data.
- *Data Leakage* – where content from AI outputs contains sensitive information such as personal data or trade secrets. Another variation of this attack is where outputs are analyzed for patterns to infer certain sensitive information, which may be in the dataset.
- *Data Poisoning* – this is when data training sets are modified with 'bad' data to manipulate the output (i.e., basically AI model 'hacking'). Another variant of the data poisoning attack is to implant malicious backdoors into the training model through model poisoning directly into the AI model (as opposed to the datasets).
- *Deep Fakes* – this is an example of AI systems creating realistic images, videos, texts, or audio recordings of real people. Enhanced social engineering attacks can occur with deep fakes convincing individuals to do something they may not normally do through the ability to authenticate an authorized individual (such as the Chief Executive Officer).
- *Evasion Attacks* – this is when an attacker manipulates inputs to bypass an AI-based security detection system. An offshoot of this type of attack could be seen in data within a development environment (or sandbox) being accessed. Sometimes, data stored in development environments may not be as strongly protected as in production environments.
- *Filter Bubbles* – this is when AI systems do not actually provide any meaning-ful content, but rather, repeat back what was just told to them.

- *Hallucinations* – this is when generative AI models produce outputs that are not within the source datasets or create, what appears to be, factually incorrect outputs. This can create a false sense of security when a user relies on the AI system to be accurate and factual in its response.
- *Model Inversion* – this is when an attacker of the AI system wants to determine the model used in its creation by running repeated queries to analyze the outcome. Another variant of a model inversion type attack is model stealing, where multiple queries are made to an AI system. An attacker may be able to 'reverse engineer' the model to build another competing AI model (or to uncover flaws in the original model).
- *Transfer Learning* – this is when attackers target the base model in a pre-trained model, creating bias that is inherited by any future fine-tuning process.

Social Manipulation Concerns

In 2019, Li Bicheng published a paper describing

> a plan for using artificial intelligence to flood the internet with fake social media accounts. They would look real. They would sound real. And they could nudge public opinion without anyone really noticing. His coauthor was a member of the Chinese military's political warfare unit.
>
> *(Irving, 2024)*

In another RAND research paper, the authors indicated the manipulation of social media "would pose a direct threat to democratic societies around the world" (Irving, 2024).

AI Risk Management Strategy

To minimize some of these AI concerns, an effective risk management strategy must be implemented. An existing risk management strategy could be leveraged to incorporate new AI risks, or a completely new risk management strategy could be implemented to mitigate AI-specific risks. Remember, just by operating a business, the organization will be undertaking risks. Risk management is essential since it provides executive management with the information needed to make decisions based on calculated risks (or subjective perceived risks). Most frameworks, standards, or regulations tend to be risk-based, and having an effective risk management strategy in place is a necessity. Risks are directed by the activity of an organization or, in the case of AI systems, the context under which the AI systems operate.

When establishing a risk management strategy, all stakeholders need to be involved. Organizations need to have executive support over risk management activities and decisions. This could be accomplished by establishing a Risk Management

Committee to include the appropriate stakeholders as well as executives. Risk Management Committees should be established through a formal charter describing the intent of the committee, individuals participating in the committee, the roles and responsibilities of committee members, reporting structures, deliverables or outputs from committee meetings, and the frequency with which the committee will meet. The Risk Management Committee should operate on a consensus where all participants can openly express their opinions on matters brought to the committee's attention. Risk tolerance levels are generally determined by the Risk Management Committee, and risk management activities are driven by these risk tolerance levels. For instance, the organization should allocate risk management resources to the most material issues to ensure effective risk management through mapping, measuring, and prioritizing risks.

NIST 800-37 (revision 2) – *Risk Management Framework for Information Systems and Organizations: A System Life Cycle Approach for Security and Privacy* is a sound starting point to establish an organization's risk management system. As it relates to specific risks involving AI systems, an organization should consider integrating specific AI risks into the existing risk management system such as leveraging the National Institute of Standards and Technology (NIST) AI Risk Management Framework (AI RMF), which will be discussed in more detail later in this book.

To understand risks, the organization must have a good understanding of the AI systems under review. This understanding can come from regular impact assessments performed throughout the entire AI life cycle to determine potential impact and likelihood utilizing a defined rating scale. In some cases, the scale will be qualitative such as very low, low, moderate, high, or very high risks. This approach tends to be a little easier and less time-consuming than attempting to determine quantitative (or actual monetary values) since this may sometimes be hard to calculate. One of the important points when using qualitative measures is to have formal definitions to keep the subjectivity out of the rating scale. Risk evaluations should be able to be recreated repeatedly; this is one sign of an effective risk management system being in place. Again, risks are based on the organization's tolerance, and risk levels may change over the life cycle of an AI system. Other factors such as performance, data security, and privacy may also influence risk tolerance decisions.

Along with the Risk Committee Charter, an organization should develop formal risk management policies. This is required by many standards and is also good practice to follow. The Risk Management Policy should pay special attention to (and address) high-risk AI systems, which are defined by regulations. These high-risk AI systems need to be identified and analyzed for any known (or foreseeable) risks. Estimations and evaluations of risks from high-risk AI systems need to be identified according to the system's intended purpose and under conditions of misuse. Other possible risks from analysis performed (or obtained by other sources) need to be considered, and suitable risk management measures need to be adopted to lower risks to acceptable levels. In addition, third-party AI service providers can introduce risks to the organization and need to be considered for full coverage. Not all risks can be eliminated, and the purpose of risk management is to lower risks to an acceptable level based on the organization's risk tolerance.

An effective risk management strategy will be agnostic to regulations, operations, or technology. The risk management strategy should be flexible to easily integrate all types of risks without having to 're-invent the wheel'. The strategy should be interoperable across many different systems, especially in the case of complex AI systems. In fact, Article 9 of the EU AI Act requires the establishment and implementation of a risk management process according to the purpose of the AI system.

The following is an example of a risk management strategy the organization may want to implement. The organization should start by identifying the purpose of a proposed AI system. Ask questions about what the AI system is supposed to accomplish and why. The organization should determine the resources needed for the AI system such as infrastructure, data, technology, human skills, and budget. Determine if the expected outcome of the project could be accomplished in other ways. *What are the cost and benefits?* This analysis will help in creating a business case for the project. *What are the expected outcomes and can these be measured using key performance indicators (or some other metric)? Who is ultimately responsible for this project?*

After the resource requirements and business case are developed, the next step in creating an AI risk management strategy is to perform impact assessments. These impact assessments will be discussed in more detail later in this book, but they could include fundamental rights impact assessment, system impact assessment, data protection impact assessment, and privacy impact assessment. Each of these assessments reviews and analyzes the AI project from different perspectives. The issues identified within these assessments will identify gaps that will need to be addressed during the risk assessment process. Regulations, standards, and frameworks can be leveraged during this impact assessment phase and utilized as baseline checklists to ensure full coverage of all aspects of the AI system. Any gaps identified during this step should be considered a risk to be analyzed as part of the risk assessment. In addition, the organization should record and maintain risk items within a risk registry.

Risks are initially assigned an inherent risk score. This risk score is a factor of the possibility (or likelihood) that something 'bad' will happen and the impact (or severity) of the event, if it were to occur. If the organization previously used formal standards or frameworks as part of the effort to recognize risks, these standards or frameworks generally maintain recommended controls to implement. The organization should determine what controls are in place and map these to associated risks. The organization should also determine how effective these controls are in mitigating identified risks.

Based on this analysis, residual risks are calculated. For instance, if a risk was determined to be inherently critical, but the organization has certain controls in place that effectively mitigate these risks, the residual risks may then be assigned a lower residual risk score. These residual risks will be prioritized, and risk treatment

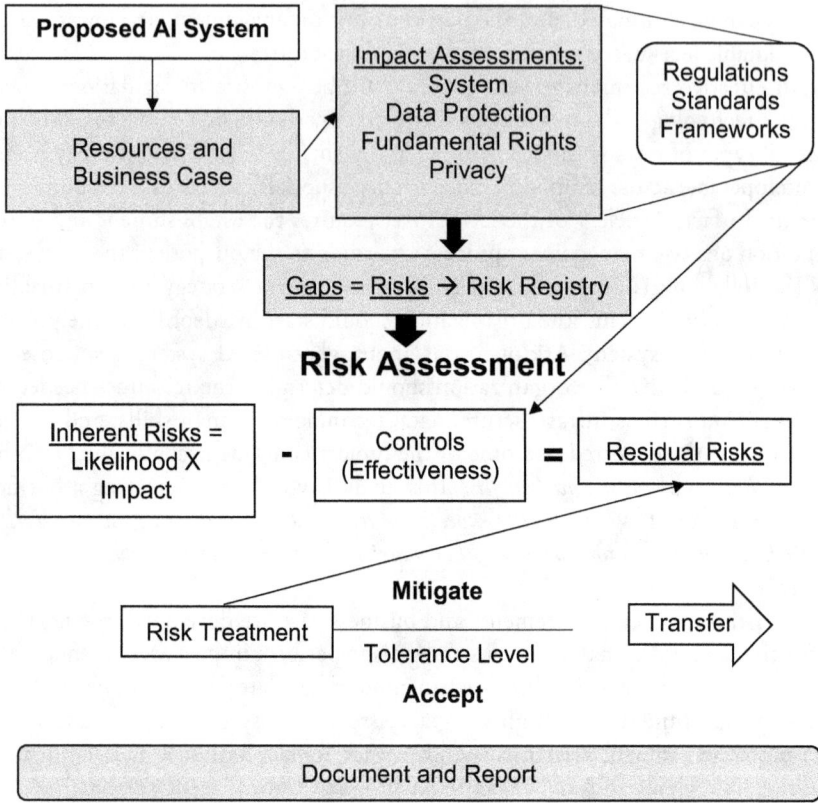

Figure 4.1   Risk Management Strategy Example.

determinations will be made. Risks could be accepted, transferred, mitigated, or ignored. *As a special note, this author would strongly recommend NOT ignoring identified risks.* If the residual risk score is lower than acceptable thresholds, then the risk may be accepted. If the residual risk score is higher than acceptable thresholds, then the risk should be mitigated. Risks can also be transferred to third parties or covered by insurance, but ultimately, the organization may still maintain some liability (or responsibility) over these risks (Figure 4.1).

To minimize risks (or responsibilities over risks), the organization could consider minimizing its scope of control over AI.

Data Governance

Since AI systems are built on data, a special consideration (or subset) of the risk management strategy specific to AI is data governance. Data governance ensures controls are in place to keep data secure, but also makes it available when needed. Some consider data as valuable as gold, and in technology (as well as business), data drives the world. An effective data strategy covers the collection of data, cleansing of data (or the removal of unnecessary data elements), and data labeling (to include tagging or annotating).

Data governance consists of curating data, understanding data context, and protecting data.

> Data curation is the process of creating, organizing and maintaining datasets so they can be accessed and used by people looking for information. It involves collecting, structuring, indexing and cataloging data for users in an organization, group or the general public.
>
> *(Pratt, 2025)*

> Data context refers to the background information and relevant details that surround and describe a dataset. In databases, this data context is stored in the form of metadata. The metadata provides users with a deeper understanding—citing the meaning and implications of the dataset.
>
> *(Crocker, 2023)*

"Data protection is the process of protecting sensitive information from damage, loss, or corruption" (Imperva, 2025).

As previously discussed, data can come in several different formats such as structured data, unstructured data, static data (or data that doesn't change), or dynamic data (where data changes on a constant basis). To use data in training models for AI, data scientists must figure out what data is required, how much data is needed, how the data will be collected and stored, and where this data can be found (such as through pre-trained models, internal, or external). Data also must be of high quality to make the AI models usable. Data must be prepared (or wrangled). Similar to the four 'C's of diamonds: color, clarity, cut, and carat weight; there are five 'V's considered in data wrangling: volume, velocity, variety, veracity (or trustworthiness), and value.

The EU AI Act requires certain data governance activities for high-risk AI systems under Article 10, with the use of training, validation, and testing to meet quality criteria.

> Training, validation and testing datasets shall be relevant, sufficiently representative, and to the best extent possible, free of errors and complete in view of the intended purpose. They shall have the appropriate statistical properties, including, where applicable, as regards the persons or groups of persons in relation to whom the high-risk AI system is intended to be used.
>
> *(EU Council, 2025)*

Article 10 also provides guidance on data governance and management practices related to high-risk AI systems, including the following: relevant design choices; data collection processes; data-preparation processing (such as labeling, cleaning, updating, and aggregating); assumption formulation; dataset availability, quantity, and suitability assessments; bias determinations and measures to detect, prevent, and mitigate bias; and gap identification.

Data management includes privacy and security over data use as well as threats from data dependency. Data management also includes transparency or the ability to explain data provenance (i.e., where the data came from). Data needs to be representative of the domain, and data needs to be accurate. Organizations will need to consider logging capabilities when designing or developing high-risk AI systems throughout the AI system's life cycle. Data management activities need to be documented, and the documents need to be accessible as well as retained according to applicable regulations.

An important area to consider when it comes to data governance is the assignment of responsibilities over the data. Segregation of duties needs to be considered to ensure there are checks and balances over data. The organization will generally consider two roles when it comes to data: the data owners and the data stewards. Data owners are usually executive-level staff members who approve data policies. These policies may be driven by regulations, contractual obligations, or ensuring only authorized individuals (or functions) have access to the appropriate data. Data owners may draft policies, implement policies, and enforce these policies on the workforce. Data stewards are the front-line managers. They are involved in normal operating processes and know what data is needed by different individuals or departments. Data stewards carry out the actual policies approved by data owners. They may assign roles to users based on the approved policies.

Risk Registry

As mentioned earlier, the risk registry is where an organization records risks, documents risk scores, prioritizes risk activities, and tracks risk mitigation. Risk statements are designed to translate identified gaps into areas of concern the organization needs to address. A risk statement tends to be written to describe having a lack of something (or failure to do something) causing harm to the organization. For example, the lack of understanding of AI regulatory requirements can lead to fines, penalties, loss of business, loss of reputation, and loss of trust. For tracking purposes, the originating source for the identification of a risk should be maintained. For instance, if the organization performed an assessment and identified certain non-conformities, the source of these gaps being identified from the assessment should be noted.

Risks should be associated with assets (or a category of assets). Assets could include specific technical assets (such as servers), operational/resource assets (such as people), or data assets. Inherent risk ratings are assigned as a factor between inherent probabilities of a threat actor exploiting a potential vulnerability and inherent impact rating. As discussed, controls are assigned to risks and an evaluation of these controls' effectiveness needs to be performed. Residual risk ratings are determined, and a course of action needs to be planned. The course of action needs to be described and assigned to an individual (or group of individuals). If an estimated time of completion is known, it should also be recorded in the risk registry. Actions taken can be to further mitigate, accept, or transfer the risks as previously discussed. A status of the actions taken should be recorded such as not started, in progress, completed, or blocked by another action.

Risks need to be reported to executive-level members through the Risk Manage ment Committee. This committee should meet at least quarterly and report on previous risk activities such as any new risks identified, progress of current risks, and recommendations on how to handle risks. The committee should be authorized to approve risk activities accordingly.

ISO 31000:2018 Risk Management – Guidelines

"ISO 31000 is an international standard that provides principles and guidelines for risk management. It outlines a comprehensive approach to identifying, analyzing, evaluating, treating, monitoring and communicating risks across an organization" (ISO, 2025a). "The [eight] 8 Principles of ISO 31000 are: integrity [and] ethical behavior; continual improvement; risk culture; integration; stakeholder engagement; structure [and] comprehensive approach; inclusive risk management; and dynamic [and] responsive" (Hammer, 2024). ISO 3100 clauses, like other ISO standards, focus on leadership, integration, design, implementation, evaluation, and improvement. The ISO 31000 Risk Management Guidelines are not intended to eliminate risk, but to identify risks, evaluate risk occurrences along with determining severity, and implement mitigation strategies to minimize risks.

ISO 23894:2023 AI Guidance on Risk Management

Leveraging the risk management guidelines provided by ISO 31000, ISO 23894 specifically addresses AI risks. Some of the specific areas covered under ISO 23894 related to AI include accountability (including verification and validation), AI expertise, availability and quality of training/testing data (including unrepresented data, bias such as automation bias or over-reliance on AI, and data poisoning), environmental impact, fairness, maintainability (including transferring models from one environment to another), privacy, robustness (including redundancy, safely failing, or load balancing), safety, security (including ML-type attacks such as adversarial attacks and model stealing), and transparency and explainability. Other sources of risk covered under ISO 23894 include complexity (or uncertainty) of AI environments, lack of transparency/explainability, automation levels, machine learning risk sources (such as model training risks of overfitting, underfitting, or drift), system hardware (such as AI infrastructure concerning memory, computing, network, storage, and other resources), system life cycle, and technology readiness.

NIST AI RMF

The NIST AI RMF provides a risk management structure to assist organizations in managing risks introduced by AI. The NIST AI RMF is split into two parts. The first part covers framing AI risks to intended audiences by analyzing or outlining characteristics of trustworthy AI systems. These characteristics include "valid and reliable, safe, secure and resilient, accountable and transparent, explainable and interpretable, privacy enhanced, and fair with their harmful biases managed" (NIST, 2023).

The second part of the NIST AI RMF covers the framework's core functions in implementing safeguards to address AI risks to include govern, map, measure, and manage. "While GOVERN applies to all stages of organizations' AI risk management processes and procedures, the MAP, MEASURE, and MANAGE functions can be applied in AI system-specific contexts and at specific stages of the AI life cycle" (NIST, 2023). The following is more details on the core functions:

Govern

The NIST AI RMF recommends ensuring policies and processes are in place covering AI risks. This includes ensuring these policies and processes map, measure, and manage AI risks. Policies and processes need to be transparent and implemented effectively. Appropriate teams and individuals should be empowered and responsible for managing AI risks. These individuals should be held responsible and trained to map, measure, and manage AI risks to implement an effective accountability structure. To adequately map, measure, and manage AI risks through the AI system's life cycle, diversity, equity, inclusion, and accessibility should be prioritized. In addition, AI risks should be communicated, and teams should be committed to a culture of communicating AI risks. Stakeholders should be fully engaged in the AI risk management process. Finally, AI risks may come from third-party software and data within the supply chain. These third-party risks should be addressed in policies and procedures.

Map

As it relates to AI, the specific AI context needs to be established and understood. AI systems need to be classified (under their own context) to assist in determining the applicable regulatory requirements that need to be applied. In comparison with the status quo, AI capabilities, usage, goals, and expectations need to be understood. In addition, risks and benefits should be mapped to third-party software (and data). Furthermore, impacts related to individuals, groups, organizations, and society need to be assessed.

Measure

To determine the success (or failure) of an AI project, the AI systems need to be measured. Organizations need to identify and apply appropriate methods and metrics. AI systems should be evaluated based on their trustworthy characteristics as discussed previously. Risks need to be tracked over time, and processes to capture feedback need to be implemented.

Manage

Output from activities within the mapping and measuring processes needs to be managed. AI risks identified within impact assessments also need to be prioritized, responded to, and managed. Strategic objectives need to maximize benefits and minimize any negative impacts. This can be accomplished through planning, preparing, implementing, documenting, and being informed by stakeholder inputs. In addition, organizations need to manage risks from third-party entities. Processes are assessed, and key steps to manage risks include testing, evaluating, verifying, and validating these risks. All these activities, responses, and measurements must be documented and regularly monitored.

ARIA

The National Institute of Standards and Technology developed the *NIST Assessing Risks and Impacts of AI (ARIA) Pilot Evaluation Plan.*

> ARIA (Assessing Risks and Impacts of AI) is a NIST AI Innovation Lab (NAIIL) program for improving AI risk and impact assessment. ARIA evaluation outcomes may improve AI technology, and build up the tools, measurement methods, and metrics necessary for AI risk and impact assessments. These outcomes can enable organizations to improve the trustworthiness of their AI applications, and make more informed decisions when acquiring or deploying AI technology.
>
> *(NIST, 2024)*

The first pilot effort to identify risks and impacts of AI focused on risks associated with generative AI and large language models (LLMs). The outcome of evaluating AI through people's engagement with LLMs, the context of outputs, and resulting feedback is intended to enhance understanding of the success and failure of LLMs. The pilot program reviewed three scenarios based on the 12 risks found in the *NIST AI 600-1 Artificial Intelligence Risk Management Framework: Generative Artificial Intelligence Profile.*

NIST AI 600-1 – NIST Trustworthy and Responsible AI

The *NIST AI 600-1 – Generative Artificial Intelligence Profile*

> is an implementation of the AI RMF functions, categories, and subcategories for a specific setting, application, or technology – in this case, Generative AI (GAI) – based on the requirements, risk tolerance, and resources of the Framework user. AI RMF profiles assist organizations in deciding how to best manage AI risks in a manner that is well-aligned with their goals, considers legal/regulatory requirements and best practices, and reflects risk management priorities.
>
> *(NIST, 2024)*

This profile includes the following 12 specific generative AI risks: chemical, biological, radiological, or nuclear (CBRN) information (or capabilities; confabulation (or hallucinations); dangerous, violent, or hateful content; data privacy; environment impacts; harmful bias (or homogenization); human–AI configuration; information integrity; information security; intellectual property; obscene, degrading, and/or abusive content; and value chain (and component integration).

HUDERIA

Human Rights, Democracy, and the Rule of Law Impact Assessment (HUDERIA) methodology is a risk and impact assessment tool provided by the Council of Europe for AI systems.

> The HUDERIA Methodology is specifically tailored to protect and promote human rights, democracy and the rule of law. It can be used by both public and private actors to help identify and address risks and impacts to human rights, democracy and the rule of law throughout the life cycle of AI systems.
>
> *(Council of Europe, 2024)*

The HUDERIA Methodology maintains four elements: Context-Based Risk Analysis (COBRA); Stakeholder Engagement Process (SEP); Risk and Impact Assessment (RIA); and Mitigation Plan (MP).

COBRA

The COBRA "assists in the identification of different risk factors – characteristics or properties of an AI system and its context that affect the probability of adverse impacts on human rights, democracy, and the rule of law" (Council of Europe,

2024). The four steps of the COBRA phase are preliminary scoping, risk factor analysis, mapping of potential impacts, and triage.

SEP

The SEP ensures the appropriate stakeholders are considered in the process to improve the next RIA step. "The SEP involves five key steps: Stakeholder Analysis, Positionality Reflection, Establishment of Engagement Objectives, Determination of Engagement Method, and Implementation" (Council of Europe, 2024).

RIA

"The purpose of the Risk and Impact Assessment is to provide detailed evaluations of the potential and actual impacts which the activities within the life cycle of an AI system could have on human rights, democracy and the rule of law" (Council of Europe, 2024). The RIA phase includes two steps: focusing on identifying potential impacts and assessing "risk variables of scale, scope, reversibility and probability of potential or actual impacts identified takes place" (Council of Europe, 2024).

MP

The final element of the HUDERIA Methodology is establishing an MP to remediate risks identified in the previous phases. The HUDERIA Methodology defines four possible options to mitigate risks from most to least preferred: avoid, mitigate, restore, and compensate.

HUDERIA Principles

The HUDERIA Methodology covers several principles related to AI system activities throughout the AI life cycle to include the following: human dignity and individual autonomy, transparency and oversight, accountability and responsibility, equality and non-discrimination, privacy and personal data protection, reliability, and safe innovation.

Committee of Sponsoring Organizations Enterprise Risk Management Framework

Organized in 1985, the Committee of Sponsoring Organizations (COSO) was set out with a mission "to help organizations improve performance by developing thought leadership that enhances internal control, risk management, governance, and fraud deterrence" (COSO, 2025a). COSO is sponsored jointly by five major professional associations headquartered in the United States: the American Accounting Association (AAA), the American Institute of Certified Public Accountants (AICPA), Financial Executives International (FEI), the Institute of Internal Auditors (IIA), and the National Association of Accountants, now known as Institute of Management Accountants (IMA).

(COSO, 2025b)

COSO has released (and updated over the years) the *Enterprise Risk Management [ERM] – Integrated Framework*. The COSO ERM has gained popularity in use by sponsoring associations (and other private/public organizations) to improve risk management processes.

GenAI Risk Assessment (California)

California is one of the states leading the rest when it comes to regulating AI and providing guidance to organizations in the development, deployment, and use of AI. More specifically, California has provided guidance on conducting risk assessments on generative AI used by the State of California. Use cases for generative AI include content generation (such as text, image, video), chatbots, data analysis, explanations and tutoring, personalized content, search and recommendations, software code generation, summarization, and synthetic data generation. Risk assessment guidance from California suggests organizations consider the benefits (and risks) of deploying generative AI technology such as risks of data breach and risks of unexpected outputs. Some other risks of using generative AI include bias, hallucination, harmful (or inappropriate) material, lack of human-in-the-loop, automation bias, security vulnerabilities, inability to explain rationale/decisions (i.e., blackbox), and privacy re-identification risks.

The California risk guidance identifies three risk levels of generative AI: high risk (where data loss could cause a severe impact), moderate risk (where data loss could cause a serious impact), and low risk (where data loss could cause a limited adverse impact). The risk assessment guide first considers questions related to the use case of the generative AI. Based on certain criteria, the generative AI is assigned one of the three risk levels. If the risk level is rated as moderate or high, the risk assessment then looks at mandatory quality, security, and safety controls.

There are several controls required to be implemented to mitigate risks of moderate and high generative AI systems in use by California state agencies to include, but not limited to, data loss prevention, compliance with other federal standards such as NIST 800-53 and FIPS, compliance with state-defined standards such as SIMM 5300-A and SAM section 5300.5, multi-factor authentication, and training. Additional details of the generative AI include vendor information, transparency, human oversight and monitoring, equity assurance, and FIPS 199 categorization level determination.

System Impact Assessment

According to the NIST AI RMF, AI impact assessments are tasks performed by an organization, which "include assessing and evaluating requirements for AI system accountability, combating harmful bias, examining impacts of AI systems, product safety, liability, and security, among others" (NIST, 2023). AI impact assessments are required for AI governance and include many stakeholders to provide the needed perspectives (and expertise) in evaluating the different aspects AI can impact. AI impact assessments might be used interchangeably with AI risk assessments under certain regulations; however, some believe (like the author of this book) an impact assessment and a risk assessment are different.

The Future of Privacy Forum issued a report titled *AI Governance Behind the Scenes: Emerging Practices for AI Impact Assessments* in December 2024. The authors of this report researched over 60 companies and determined "organizations typically take four common steps when conducting AI impact assessments, including: (1) initiating an AI impact assessment; (2) gathering model and system information; (3) assessing risks and benefits; and (4) identifying and testing risk management strategies" (Berrick, 2024).

The report indicates there may be certain criteria triggering an AI impact assessment to be performed. These triggers may vary in different factors such as regulatory requirements, context of the AI, or the industry the AI is going to be deployed. These trigger points may also take place at different times throughout the AI system's life cycle such as within the development and/or within the deployment phase. Since AI primarily relies on its models, organizations must understand these models and how the AI systems work to perform an effective impact assessment. The impact assessment should include the benefits of the AI system as well as the risks. This is where risk management integrates with a system impact assessment. Finally, based on the analysis performed, an organization will implement risk management strategies to make a 'go' or 'no-go' decision about the AI system. This decision may take place at different phases of the AI system life cycle.

As part of an AI system impact assessment, it is highly recommended that an Algorithmic Impact Assessment (AIA) is performed. According to an article within the *Journal of Online Trust and Safety* titled *Algorithmic Impact Assessments at Scale: Practitioners' Challenges and Needs*, an "Algorithmic Impact Assessments (AIAs) are tools that are often suggested for systematic evaluation of potential societal impacts and are a technique often included within a suite of tools used for algorithmic auditing" (Ashar et al., 2024). Involving the responsible development of algorithmic systems, there are several gaps in the assessment of these systems, as well as no standardization across assessment methodologies.

The report indicated

> Algorithmic Impact Assessments on platform systems were designed to enable teams to (1) check baseline compliance with central requirements such as infrastructure tool usage and data restrictions; (2) proactively

find potential algorithmic issues before they significantly impact users or creators; (3) adequately plan and address problems identified; (4) manage risk and harms for highest-priority surfaces and users; and (5) inform product and platform strategy.

(Ashar et al., 2024)

There are three categories of concerns organizations face when trying to assess algorithms: technical and methods, infrastructure and operations, and resourcing and prioritization. The report provides some recommendations to mitigate these concerns as well as a suggested template to perform an AIA.

Another resource available to help identify the impact AI systems may have on society is a tool developed by Simon Mylius and Jamie Bernardi for *Scalable AI Safety Incident Classification*. Utilizing the casual and domain taxonomies provided by the Massachusetts Institute of Technology (MIT) AI Risk Repository, the developers of this tool classified incidents in an AI Incident Database, then assigned scores based on the Center for Security and Emerging Technology (CSET) AI Harm Taxonomy along with another scale to reflect impact ratings.

This project is intended as a proof of concept to explore the potential capabilities and limitations of a scalable incident analysis process, investigating the hypothesis that it could address the needs of policymakers by providing quantitative information on which to base policy decisions.

(Mylius and Bernardi, 2024)

The CSET published a paper *Adding Structure to AI Harm: An Introduction to CSET's AI Harm Framework* in July 2023. In this report, the authors defined AI harm occurring "when an entity experienced a harm event or harm issue that can be directly linked to a consequence of the behavior of an AI system" (Hoffman and Frase, 2023). This framework breaks harms into two categories: tangible harm and intangible harm. Tangible harm is observable, verifiable, and definitive harm such as physical health/safety, infrastructure damage, property damage, financial loss, environmental damage, additional definitions, or other tangible harms. Intangible

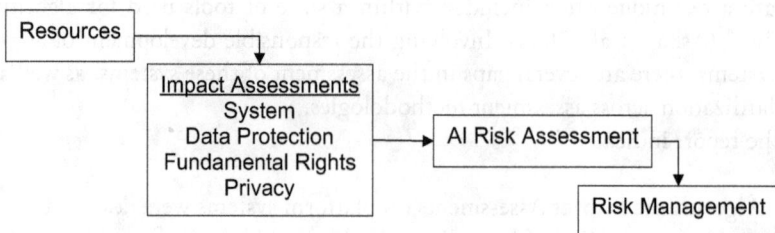

Figure 4.2 AI System Impact Assessment Example.

harm is harm not directly observed such as detrimental content, differential treatment, human or civil rights, democratic norms, privacy, and other intangible harms (Figure 4.2).

Microsoft Responsible AI Impact Assessment Guide

As part of Microsoft's Responsible AI Standard, Microsoft released a *Responsible AI Impact Assessment Guide and Template* to the public in June 2022. The guide directs organizations through a process to perform a Responsible AI Impact Assessment, and the template can be used to document the activities performed as well as responses obtained. Microsoft's Responsible AI Impact Assessment is split into five sections. The first section reviews the system information to provide a complete system profile. The assessment determines the AI system life cycle stage, which includes planning and analysis, design, development, testing, implementation and deployment, maintenance, and retirement. This section further provides a system description along with the system purpose and features (both existing and planned). The section ends with determining geographic areas and languages along with the deployment mode and intended uses.

Section 2 goes into specific details for each intended use listed in Section 1. The information obtained in this section relates to conducting a purpose fitness assessment along with identifying stakeholders and potential benefits as well as harm. Stakeholders are identified for different goal-driven requirements such as human oversight, decision-making, communication, and disclosures, where applicable. Considerations over fairness are assessed to include quality, resource allocation, and minimization of adverse outputs concerning stereotyping, demeaning, and erasing. Determinations are then made for technological readiness and task complexity along with human roles and the deployment environment.

Section 3 covers adverse impacts of the AI system to include restricted or unsupported uses, known limitations, potential impact of failure/misuses, and sensitive uses. Section 4 covers data requirements as well as plans to use any existing dataset assessed against the quantity of the data and suitability of the data for the specific use case.

Section 5 provides a summary of potential harm along with some preliminary mitigation efforts. This section also determines applicable goals related to accountability, transparency, fairness, reliability and safety, privacy and security, and inclusiveness. The party responsible for the assessment ends this section by signing off on the Responsible AI Impact Assessment. The assessment guide and assessment template can be found at the following sources, respectively:

- https://blogs.microsoft.com/wp-content/uploads/prod/sites/5/2022/06/Microsoft-RAI-Impact-Assessment-Guide.pdf
- https://blogs.microsoft.com/wp-content/uploads/prod/sites/5/2022/06/Microsoft-RAI-Impact-Assessment-Template.pdf

ISO 42005 AI Impact Assessment

The International Standards Organization (ISO) published guidance on how to perform an AI system impact assessment. Like Microsoft's Responsible AI Impact Assessment, *ISO 42005 – Information Technology – Artificial Intelligence – AI System Impact Assessment* starts with a section describing the AI system, features, purpose, intended use, and unintended use. This first section includes the AI system architecture such as network diagrams and flow-charts as well as technical requirements (or specifications). This section also includes any demonstrations and proof of concepts.

The next section covers data information and quality. For each dataset used for the AI system, several pieces of information should be captured such as the dataset name, version, size, and owner. Other areas to consider include dataset access rights, content description, purpose, and details on how the data was collected (and from whom). Additional notes on any bias and documenting quality characteristics round out this section.

Information on the algorithms used (or developed) by the organization for use in the AI system as well as the models used (or developed) is covered in the next section. When it comes to algorithms, the AI system impact assessment needs to identify suitability, origins, validity, real-world use/performance, data requirements, and susceptibility to undesired outcomes. The AIA needs to cover all data issues and document decisions made in the algorithm's use by stakeholders.

For model information, the assessment documents the training, testing, and validation data along with the training parameters. Steps taken to ensure samples are not reused in training and other steps related to training multiple models need to be addressed. A determination of the criteria selected along with the metrics used for performance evaluation is important to capture. The evaluation should include a determination of its adequacy on production data, ensure no bias or harm is created, and confirm that the output data does not contain sensitive information. The model should also be evaluated for robustness (and resiliency) as well as the steps taken to prevent data drift. Finally, the impact of continuous learning needs to be assessed as well as the process in place for retraining the models in use. The output in this step can be used for model cards or fact sheets. 'What-ifs', also known as counterfactual explanations (CFEs), could also be documented to assist in explaining why an output was made based on different inputs.

Microsoft and ISO align identically on detailing the deployment environment within the AI system impact assessment to include geographical area as well as language. A determination of the complexity of the deployment as well as any constraints should be identified. Furthermore, relevant interested parties need to be determined along with actual (and potential) benefits and harm for each interested party needs to be evaluated. Areas of concern related to the benefit/harm evaluation include the following:

- **Accountability** – objectives include oversight of significant adverse impacts, fitness for purpose, data governance, and human oversight.

- **Transparency and Explainability** – objectives include explainability, communication, performance, go/no-go decision, and disclosures.
- **Fairness and Discrimination** – objectives include service quality, opportunity allocation, stereotyping minimization, and accessibility.
- **Privacy and Security** – objectives include privacy protection and system security related to compliance with legal requirements.
- **Reliability** – objectives include failures, remediations, monitoring, feedback, evaluation, and system compromises.
- **Safety** – objectives include safety concerns, changes, and false positives/negatives.
- **Environmental Impact** – objectives include both direct and indirect environmental impacts.

Again, for each interested party, the impact of AI system failures, misuse, or abuse needs to be determined. The final section of the AI system impact assessment includes a description of the monitoring, measurement, analysis, and evaluation in place to determine success.

Data Protection Impact Assessment

A data protection impact assessment (DPIA) and privacy impact assessment (PIA) may be referred to interchangeably. For the context of this book, the DPIA and PIA will be described as two separate assessments; however, an organization may find it helpful to combine activities for both under one assessment report. The following is a suggested combined DPIA leveraging the following sources and modifying them to meet AI system requirements:

- **Information Commissioner's Office – Sample DPIA Template** – Source: https://ico.org.uk/media2/migrated/2553993/dpia-template.docx
- **FedRAMP Privacy Impact Assessment Template** – Source: https://www.fedramp.gov/assets/resources/documents/rev4/REV_4_SSP-A04-FedRAMP-PIA-Template.docx
- **Office of the Australian Information Commissioner Privacy Impact Assessment Tool**–Source:https://www.oaic.gov.au/privacy/privacy-guidance-for-organisations-and-government-agencies/privacy-impact-assessments/privacy-impact-assessment-tool

Like many other assessments, the DPIA starts out with an introduction of the organization and points of contact. The DPIA moves into identifying the different regulations applicable to the organization. This is important to ensure the AI system is evaluated against the applicable regulations and they are noted accordingly. Next, the DPIA requires the AI system to be described in detail to include data flow diagrams (and/or network diagrams). The output from the system impact assessment can be very helpful in completing the AI system description within the DPIA.

The DPIA must include the type of data in scope as well as the reason why the DPIA was needed in the first place such as describing the objectives, the processing involved, and the individuals involved. Like system impact assessments, certain impact areas need to be evaluated to include fairness, accountability, transparency and explainability, reliability, security and privacy, safety and health, financial consequences, accessibility, robustness and redundancy, and human rights. Societal impacts and human oversight also need to be addressed. These impacts are reviewed from the perspective of data protection.

The next section of the DPIA covers the nature of processing such as how data is collected, used, stored, and/or deleted. This assessment will be a little more involved than the previous system impact assessment since the DPIA will also look at the scope, context, and purpose of processing data (from a data protection perspective). Several stakeholders or interested parties may need to be consulted to assist in the evaluation of data processing. A review of the lawful basis used for processing to include necessity and proportionality is required. As it relates to processing personal data, an organization must have a legal right to process such data. The DPIA may include a PIA or a PIA may be a separate report as previously mentioned. Finally, the DPIA needs to be reviewed and approved by management as well as include consultation by the data protection officer (DPO).

Privacy Impact Assessment (Privacy Risk Assessment)

To better understand the impact of an AI system if data were to be compromised, privacy risk threat modeling should be performed. This privacy risk threat model establishes the context for DPIA and AI conformity assessments. Identifying concerns or privacy risks through modeling enables organizations to focus resources on direct mitigation activities. There are several sources available for organizations needing assistance in performing a privacy impact assessment to include the PIA open-source software offered by the CNIL located here: https://www.cnil.fr/en/open-source-pia-software-helps-carry-out-data-protection-impact-assessment

The PIA identifies and analyzes the impact an AI system has on privacy. The PIA determines the risk of privacy impacts on individuals and whether these impacts are necessary (or avoidable). The PIA will also consider any existing factors to mitigate negative impact and how privacy impacts the broader goals of a project. Of course, there is a review of compliance with privacy laws and how individuals may control their own personal information along with the alignment of community expectations when it comes to AI systems use.

The PIA is not intended to eliminate all privacy risks; however, it is meant to identify privacy risks associated with the AI system, the seriousness of these risks, and consideration of possible mitigations to minimize harm caused by these risks. Risks can be identified impacting individual rights, potential violations, breaches, or reputational concerns. For each privacy risk identified, mitigating controls need to be considered. The NIST 800-53 Controls and utilizing privacy-enhancing technologies (PETs) could be a sound practice to minimize privacy-related risks.

Fundamental Rights Impact Assessment

A new assessment introduced by the EU AI Act under Article 27 is the Fundamental Rights Impact Assessment (FRIA). "At its simplest, an FRIA is an assessment of the potential impact of an AI system on the rights of any individual that might be affected by the operation of that system" (Ajoodha and Browne, 2025). FRIAs are required for bodies governed by public law and private providers of public services of high-risk AI systems (as identified in Annex III) involved in the following areas: biometrics; critical infrastructure; education and vocational training; employment, workers management, and access to self-employment; access to (and enjoyment of) essential privacy services and public services/benefits; law enforcement; migration, asylum, and border control management; and administration of justice and democratic processes. Other deployers involved in creditworthiness assessment (and credit scoring) as well as life/health insurance risk assessment (and individual pricing) must also perform a FRIA.

Compared to DPIA, the FRIA may encompass a wider range of fundamental rights, but can complement the DPIA when it comes to data privacy and security measures. According to The EU Charter, there are 50 protected rights across six domains: dignity, freedom, equality, solidarity, citizen's rights, and justice.

AI Risk Assessment

With any new technology comes risks, and AI is no different. Performing a contextual risk assessment on AI development, deployment, and use is essential for effective AI governance. As previously discussed, risks are scored (or assigned values) as a factor of probability and impact. The author of this book likes to use a five-point scale for each of these factors as provided in the following example:

Probability

- *Very High* – Five points – Very probably, and the event will occur more than ten times over a target period (or once in 0% to 5% of the target period).
- *High* – Four points – Highly likely, and the event will occur five to ten times over a target period (or once in 5% to 25% of the target period).
- *Moderate* – Three points – Somewhat likely, and the event will occur three to five times over a target period (or once in 25% to 50% of the target period).

- *Low* – Two points – Unlikely, and the event will occur or may only occur one to three times over a target period (or once in 50% to 70% of the target period).
- *Very Low* – One point – Highly unlikely (or highly improbable), and the event will occur or it may only occur once to two times over a target period (or once in 75% to 100% of the target period).

These definitions are subjective and can be easily modified to fit the organization's risk profile. The target period is generally one year, but could be modified to be shorter (like every month) or longer (like every two years). Since AI is a new technology, there may not be a lot of data collected on AI risks so the likelihood of an event occurring may not be fully understood. Some assumptions might be made on the likelihood, and the probability scores may be adjusted over time to account for better data on AI risks being obtained.

Impact

- *Very High* – Five points – Very high (or critical impact) or above 90% of a set monetary value in acceptable loss.
- *High* – Four points – High impact or between 75% and 89% of a set monetary value in acceptable loss.
- *Moderate* – Three points – Some impact or between 50% and 74% of a set monetary value in acceptable loss.
- *Low* – Two points – Minimal impact or between 25% and 49% of a set monetary value in acceptable loss.
- *Very Low* – One point – Marginal (or no impact) or less than 24% of a set monetary value in acceptable loss.

The monetary value is determined by the organization's risk threshold. For instance, the organization may be good at taking a $100,000 hit since they have insurance to cover most of their losses, then the monetary value may be set to this $100,000 threshold. Again, these definitions may be a little subjective and should be modified to meet the organization's needs.

Risk Scoring

By multiplying the point value of the probability assigned and the impact value assigned, a risk factor is determined. The following is an example scale of risk score assignment:

- *Critical* risk score assignment – if the risk factor is between 20 and 25.
- *High* risk score assignment – if the risk factor is between 11 and 19.
- *Moderate* risk score assignment – if the risk factor is between 6 and 10.

		Impact				
		Very Low	**Low**	**Moderate**	**High**	**Very High**
Probability	**Very Low**	Obs	Obs	Low	Low	Low
	Low	Obs	Low	Moderate	Moderate	Moderate
	Moderate	Low	Moderate	Moderate	High	High
	High	Low	Moderate	High	High	Critical
	Very High	Low	Moderate	High	Critical	Critical

Figure 4.3   Risk Scores.

- *Low* risk score assignment – if the risk factor is between 3 and 5.
- *Observational* risk score assignment – if the risk factor is between 1 and 2 (Figure 4.3).

Generally, any risk score above Moderate should be assigned a mitigation plan. Determining risks and mitigation efforts is a team exercise and should include all decision makers as well as stakeholders. Communication of risks and mitigation strategies is paramount to an effective risk management strategy. Some risks of AI, although acceptable by an organization, may be too risky as defined by certain regulations (like the EU AI Act) and could be considered unacceptable (or prohibited).

AI risk assessments should be integrated with other risk management activities; however, AI systems may come with more areas of risk to evaluate. For instance, AI systems are complex, and to conduct a comprehensive AI risk assessment, the assessor may need to think 'out of the box'. This could include reviewing outlier use cases, unknown data, or specific AI attacks, such as attempting to circumvent guardrails in place to protect against malicious inputs. Performing adversarial testing and developing AI threat models may be good practices to identify AI risks.

AI Risk Treatment Plan

Once AI risks are identified, a determination must be made on how these risks will be treated. AI systems are complex, and there can be several layers or steps to mitigate AI risks within different levels such as the infrastructure, the module, the user interface (UI) (or API), or at the user level. To implement certain mitigation strategies, there might be trade-offs between security (and privacy) as well as functionality. For instance, if there are risks of disclosing sensitive information, guardrails may need to be introduced to ensure outputs do not disclose this sensitive information, or training models may not include this sensitive information within training. Limiting information, however, could have an impact on the accuracy of the inferences, depending on the purpose of the AI.

When AI risk mitigation strategies are finally determined, deployment of these solutions needs to be considered. *Will deploying remediation solutions adversely impact the use? Will they have any impact on functionality or availability of the AI system?* All risk and risk mitigation activities need to be documented and tracked. Organizations will want to determine how risks are being mitigated over time and what risk mitigation strategies work the best for specific use cases. Organizations will also want to track any trends that might be captured by risk monitoring activities. If risks are identified as systemic, then procedures implemented should be reviewed to determine if these processes are operating effectively. Determining the root cause of risks may shed light on process issues that have not been identified previously.

Risks and Bias

Identified risks may also point to specific tests that should be performed on the models themselves. AI systems are unique from other types of technology in that their algorithms need to be continuously monitored, tested, and validated to ensure they are meeting expectations (and they don't become biased). In addition, different models may require different testing or one type of test may be better suited for a specific model. Tests for safety, bias, accuracy, robustness/reliability, privacy, and interpretability should be conducted based on the use case of the AI system. Performing adversarial testing may uncover AI risks when testing outputs by providing malicious inputs, identifying outlier cases, ensuring repeatability of results, or testing for data not part of the original dataset. These tests need to be documented as well to include any changes made and the results of the output.

Specific AI Risks

The MIT created a 'living' database, known as the *MIT AI Risk Repository*, of over 1,000 AI-specific risks categorized by domains. The AI Risk Repository maintains three parts: the AI Risk Database (over 1,000 risks from 56 different frameworks), Casual Taxonomy of AI Risks (such as how, when, and why), and Domain Taxonomy of AI Risks (to include 7 domains and 23 subdomains). The Casual Taxonomy includes three categories and three levels per category: Entity (includes risks from AI, human, or other), Intent (includes intentional, unintentional, or other outcomes), and Timing (includes pre-deployment, post-deployment, and other). The Domain Taxonomy includes: discrimination and toxicity; privacy and security; misinformation; malicious actors and misuse; human–computer interaction; socioeconomic and environmental harms; and AI system safety, failures, and limitations. The MIT AI Risk Repository can be found here: https://airisk.mit.edu/. It is available for free to copy as well as use.

General-Purpose AI Systemic Risks

According to the *Second Draft of the GPAI Code of Conduct*, general-purpose AI may have several types of systemic risks. General-purpose AI systems could be used to discover vulnerabilities or develop exploits related to cyber offensive capabilities. These AI systems could arm individuals with knowledge on how to develop, design, acquire, or use chemical, biological, radiological, and nuclear (CBRN) weapons. General-purpose AI systems are complex and may be hard to explain, leading to a loss of control if they are used autonomously. General-purpose AI systems may be used to manipulate humans in generating substantial amounts of misinformation such as in the case of politics, human rights, or attempting to circumvent the media's trust. As previously discussed, bias and discrimination are systemic risks with general-purpose AI systems. Finally, since these AI systems may be used to develop other systems, the offspring of these systems may also inherit systemic risks.

Financial

The US Department of the Treasury issued a report in March 2024 titled *Managing Artificial Intelligence-Specific Cybersecurity Risks in the Financial Services Sector*. According to the report,

> The financial services sector is highly diverse and includes thousands of financial institutions, including depository institutions, providers of investment products, insurance companies, other credit and financing organizations, and the providers of the critical financial utilities and services that support these functions.
>
> *(US Department of the Treasury, 2024)*

In the financial industry, there is a major focus on cybersecurity and fraud. The report indicates many financial institutions use AI systems to detect fraud and mitigate cybersecurity risks; however, these institutions are under a lot of regulatory requirements, which makes them move slower in the adoption of AI when it comes to protecting their sensitive data. Attacks on this data are a major concern. The processing of data to detect anomalies is also a concern since this data may contain highly sensitive information such as financial records, personal data, or transaction histories.

The financial industry also faces attacks from several different threats such as social engineering, malware, discovery of vulnerabilities, and disinformation. These attacks become more difficult to prevent when advanced AI systems are used. Threats to AI systems themselves include data poisoning, data leakage, evasion, and model extraction. In addition, since financial institutions may utilize third parties to assist them with their AI infrastructures, third-party risks increase as these institutions become more reliant on services offered by these third parties. To mitigate some of these risks, "Interviewed financial institutions stated that they are embedding AI-specific risk management within their enterprise risk management programs, which vertically integrates AI-specific risk management within broader risk management practices" (US Department of the Treasury, 2024).

Healthcare

The US Department of Health and Human Services (HHS) issued a strategic plan in January 2025, titled *Strategic Pan for the Use of Artificial Intelligence in Health, Human Services, and Public Health*. According to the strategic plan, "HHS's vision is to be a global leader in innovating and adopting responsible AI to achieve unparalleled advances in the health and well-being of all Americans" (HHS, 2025). The strategic plan covers five primary domains including: medical research and discovery; medical product development, safety, and effectiveness; healthcare delivery; human services delivery; and public health. The plan also includes two additional domains: cybersecurity and critical infrastructure protection as well as internal operations.

There are several AI risks identified in the strategic plan, and here are some notable ones:

- Data breaches, privacy issues, biosecurity vulnerabilities, and bias within medical research and discovery due to the personal and confidential data involved.
- Bias and patient safety within medical product development, safety, and effectiveness.
- Re-identification of individuals and models providing incorrect answers in a confident manner (i.e., confabulation), resulting in unintended consequences in healthcare delivery, especially if healthcare professionals are relying 'blindly' on AI outputs.
- Third-party risks impacting data privacy, explainability, and accountability when making decisions as well as bias within human services delivery.
- Harm of spreading misinformation or disinformation impacting public health.

Government

The US Government is taking AI very seriously as previously discussed. Since most of the US critical infrastructure is owned, controlled, or maintained by private companies, these companies will be directly impacted by AI strategies (and requirements) issued by the government. Cybersecurity has always been a major concern for vendors selling products or services to government entities. These vendors have been contractually obligated to meet certain security requirements as part of receiving government contracts.

The Department of Defense (DoD), for instance, has increased its review and enforcement of security obligations of vendors under its Cybersecurity Maturity Model Certification (CMMC) program. AI systems used by these vendors may come under the scope of these requirements if they process federal contract information (FCI) or Controlled Unclassified Information (CUI). These requirements may also eventually extend to all government contracts as opposed to just the DoD.

An interesting point of reference for the CMMC program specifically is the forethought of AI technology being used to perform an audit. According to the *CMMC Code of Professional Conduct*, members of the ecosystem must use AI (and other emerging technologies) in a responsible and ethical manner when conducting CMMC activities. For instance, the use of AI (or other automated assessment technology) should be avoided that renders authority (or autonomy) to an auditor or makes the auditor subservient to the AI system when conducting an assessment. In addition, assessors should avoid AI systems (and algorithms) that are biased in the preparation or conduct of an assessment. Customer data is prohibited from being provided on an Internet-accessible AI application. Finally, technology employment should be transparent as well as data privacy and security need to be upheld.

AI Risk Mitigation Controls

There are several AI risk mitigation controls an organization can implement. Since AI is technology (or consists of technology components), a lot of the controls in place for other technologies can be applied to AI systems. This author likes to utilize a standard control set and primarily uses NIST 800-53 to identify, track, and implement controls necessary to mitigate AI risks. As part of an integrated management system, most of these controls are relevant to AI in some form or fashion. At a high-level, the family of controls include the following: access control; awareness an training; audit and accountability; assessment, authorization, and monitoring; configuration management; contingency planning; identification and authentication; incident response; maintenance; media protection; physical and environmental protection; planning; program management; risk assessment; system and services acquisition; system and communication protection; system and information integrity; and supply chain risk management. Specific controls related to AI will be further discussed in the next chapter.

Chapter 5

Artificial Intelligence Management System (AIMS)

> *AI systems are not autonomous, rational, or able to discern anything without extensive, computationally intensive training with large datasets or predefined rules and rewards. In fact, artificial intelligence as we know it depends entirely on a much wider set of political and social structures. And due to the capital required to build AI at scale and the ways of seeing that it optimizes AI systems are ultimately designed to serve existing dominant interests. In this sense, artificial intelligence is a registry of power.*
>
> *(Crawford, 2021)*

One of the best authoritative sources to assist in the establishment, implementation, maintenance, continual improvement, and documentation of an Artificial Intelligence Management System (AIMS) is the ISO 42001 standard. The AIMS should be integrated with other management systems like security, privacy, and quality, as well as including all required processes and interactions according to the standard. This chapter is dedicated to the process of implementing an AIMS.

Responsible AI Context and AI Governance

An organization must design a responsible AI governance program around its specific use or context. Guiding principles of AI governance are set by organizational values. These values are operationalized to form the organization's AI governance

                                    DOI: 10.1201/9781003624073-5

framework. Several considerations are made concerning the jurisdiction of the AI system to capture regulatory requirements, along with the risk tolerance levels previously discussed.

The organization can utilize its AI governance framework as a competitive advantage to ensure its trustworthiness with its customers. An AI governance framework is generally based on ethical principles related to AI such as fairness, transparency, accountability, oversight, and accuracy. This framework should address how the organization develops, acquires, deploys, and uses AI within its product or service offered to customers, as well as internally as part of ongoing administration or operations.

The AI governance framework must have buy-in from stakeholders and must be prioritized by executive management. An organization may face some challenges regarding changes being made, guardrails being established, or cultural obstacles. Some organizations such as startups want to move fast to get ahead of the competition, and establishing a governance framework could be perceived as a hindrance if it is not presented correctly (or there is no support from senior leadership).

Developing and approving an AIMS Policy and AI Governance Policy are recommended practices in documenting the importance of a strong management structure when working with AI. The AIMS Policy is intended to assist the organization in developing, providing, and using AI systems in a responsible manner to pursue the organization's objectives, meet requirements, comply with obligations (such as regulatory, customers, and other interested parties), and meet expectations. Determining external (and internal) issues relevant to the AIMS, along with a determination over changes needed, must be considered when evaluating the context of AI.

The context of AI is identified and considered through the evaluation of the intended purposes of the AI systems developed, deployed, or used by the organization. The organization's roles with respect to AI systems, the interested parties, and their relevant requirements must be determined. To assist in establishing the scope of the AIMS, the organization needs to determine the AI systems' boundaries and applicability. The AIMS' scope must be documented and determines other activities of the AIMS such as leadership, planning, support, operation, performance, evaluation, improvement, controls, and objectives.

The scope should describe the organization's structure, identify business processes, identify asset owners, identify decision-making processes, describe locations (or physical infrastructure), and define boundaries according to the network, operating systems, applications, databases, and processes. The scope statement should also be simple, understandable, and concise according to the size, nature, and complexity of the organization.

AI Literacy

Becoming familiar with AI is essential, and AI stakeholders need to understand both the technology (i.e., how AI works) and human dimensions (i.e., what is the impact on individuals from a privacy and related perspective) of AI. In a paper titled *Generative AI Literacy: Twelve Defining Competencies*, the authors introduce "a competency-based model for generative artificial intelligence (AI) literacy covering essential skills and knowledge areas necessary to interact with generative AI" (Annapureddy et al., 2024). The authors describe the following 12 competencies of Generative AI Literacy as paraphrased and summarized:

1. **AI Literacy Basics** – baseline AI concepts and familiarity with generative AI.
2. **Generative AI Models Knowledge** – peripheral understanding of generative AI workings.
3. **Capacity/Limitations Knowledge of Generative AI Tools** – proficiency to assess capabilities and constraints of generative AI tools.
4. **Generative AI Tools Use Skills** – practical proficiency to use tools in diverse context.
5. **AI-Generated Content Detection** – ability to discern AI-generated content.
6. **Generative AI Tools Output Assessment** – ability to assess quality, relevance, and bias of output.
7. **Prompt Engineering** – skill in working with generative AI tools to tailor personal outputs.
8. **Fine-Tuning** – ability to customize and optimize generative AI models.
9. **Generative AI Context** – knowledge to assess the appropriateness of generative AI tools across different situations, organizations, and professions.
10. **Ethical Implications** – makes individuals aware of the responsibility of AI through ethical considerations.
11. **Legal Aspects** – address legal aspects of AI, ensuring AI operates within legal frameworks.
12. **Continuous Learner** – developing a mindset of continuous learning to stay up to date on generative AI technologies, methods, and ethics.

AI training is important for stakeholders to understand the AI's purpose, limitations, and security/privacy controls. Employees need to be trained on the permissible (or prohibited) use of AI to ensure sensitive information is not shared in an unauthorized manner with AI systems. As a cautionary example, "multiple employees of Samsung's Korea-based semiconductor business plugged lines of confidential code into ChatGPT, effectively leaking corporate secrets that could be included in the chatbot's future responses to other people around the world" (Forlini, 2023). Not only can employees share sensitive information against confidentiality policies, but it may be hard to remove such information from the training models of AI once it has been ingested.

AI Governance Strategy

To build out a successful AI governance strategy, organizations should utilize existing governance structures already implemented and enhance these structures to use for AI. AI can impact several stakeholders and it is important to build communications with key stakeholders to further advance AI governance within an organization. The organization should choose the best model to fit their environment from the following options: centralized governance structure, decentralized governance structure, or federated (i.e., hybrid) governance structure.

A centralized governance structure is a top-down model where executive management (or committee made up of senior management) makes AI governance decisions. Under a decentralized governance structure, each team is responsible for AI governance specific to their own requirements. For the best of both options, the federated governance structure utilizes a global AI Governance Committee, but permits each team to manage AI governance practices at its level.

One of the first steps in establishing an AI governance structure is to understand the organization's roles. For instance, is the organization a developer (an organization that develops an AI system or utilizes models to train an AI system), a distributor (an organization that makes an AI system available to others), or a deployer/user (an organization that uses an AI system under its authority)? An organization may be classified as one (or more) of these roles and will need to account for different regulatory obligations mandated for each of these roles.

The next step is to establish internal roles responsible for AI governance activities. This could include establishing an Office for Responsible AI, establishing an AI Governance Committee, designating a Chief AI Officer, assigning a Chief Privacy Officer (or Data Protection Officer), assigning a Chief Information Security Officer, and/or assigning a Chief Ethics Officer (or Chief Compliance Officer) as senior executive members responsible for AI governance. AI governance support must be driven by senior leadership with input from other teams. Executive management needs to be made aware of regulatory requirements as well as stay in sync with AI's impact within their industry. The organization could then designate roles and responsibilities to carry out AI governance decisions to line managers such as AI Steering Committees, AI Project Managers, AI Researchers/Data Scientists, or AI/ML Engineers (and other non-AI engineers).

The organization must perform an inventory of AI to ensure they have a holistic perspective of where AI touches its operations. A central inventory should be developed identifying all AI applications and machine learning models (or algorithms). Specific individuals or teams should be assigned the responsibility to maintain the AI inventory list. The organization should ensure its risk management strategies address all these applications (or models) identified on the AI inventory. Risk assessments should be leveraged to establish the organization's AI risk tolerance profile. The organization should also ensure policies and processes are in place to mitigate any risks identified, including third-party vendor risks.

AI governance must be considered a discipline, and incentives need to be designed to ensure AI projects are implemented safely (and effectively). AI terminology should be standardized across the organization. Individuals need to be trained in AI to ensure they understand their roles and responsibilities related to AI. Key performance indicators need to be established to measure the success (or failure) of an AI project. These measures should also be utilized to identify the maturity levels of AI and permit the ability to correct deficiencies or change the course of action to improve AI systems. AI governance is about changing behaviors and influencing individuals to ensure AI is developed, deployed, and used in a responsible manner.

AI Governance Policy

As suggested, an AI Governance Policy should be drafted and approved by the organization's senior management. This AI Governance Policy should start by providing the purpose (or intent) of responsible AI governance as well as a statement regarding management's commitment to responsible AI governance. For example, the purpose of responsible AI governance is to promote human-centric and trustworthy AI while ensuring a high level of protection over health, safety, and fundamental rights, including democracy, rule of law, and environmental protection against the harmful effects of AI systems.

Executive Management should be committed to providing direction and support for AI systems according to business requirements. Some of these requirements may include rules for selling, deploying, using, and developing AI systems (or general-purpose AI models) as well as transparency over AI. Other requirements may include specific requirements for AI systems, such as high-risk AI systems, prohibition of certain AI practices, or obligations over the operations of AI systems. The organization may also be under rules for monitoring AI systems after deployment, ensuring governance, enforcement, or other measures supporting innovation. The organization should establish accountability to uphold its responsible approach for the implementation, operation, and management of AI systems.

Human Oversight Policy

The organization should develop and approve a Human Oversight Policy. This policy basically states that the organization will design and develop AI systems, especially high-risk AI systems, to include an interface to permit an individual to oversee the AI system when it is in use. As discussed previously, human oversight aims to minimize risks to health, safety, and fundamental rights emerging from the use of AI systems. Human oversight ensures the AI system is used as intended, and if unexpected behavior occurs, humans are in place to stop it. Human oversight capabilities should be built into the AI system, where possible, and/or implemented by the user after being identified by the organization.

Not only does the AI system need to integrate human oversight, but individuals assigned to oversee AI systems have certain responsibilities. Individuals with human oversight responsibilities must fully understand the capabilities and limitations of the AI systems. These individuals must be able to identify anomalies or unexpected issues and address these issues accordingly. These individuals must also remain aware of the tendencies to over-rely on the output produced by AI systems creating automation biases, especially when outputs made by the AI system are acted upon. Human oversight includes the ability to correctly interpret AI systems' outputs based on the AI system content and available tools. Human oversight also provides for the ability to disregard, override, or reverse the output of an AI System. Finally, individuals with oversight responsibilities must be able to intervene (or interrupt) an AI system through a 'stop' button (or other process).

Some regulations, like the EU AI Act, require AI systems considered high-risk (and that provide 'real-time' and 'post' remote biometric identification) to be verified by at least two individuals before any actions are taken on the output from the AI system.

Responsible AI Leadership

As said before, and it cannot be said enough, responsible AI needs demonstrable leadership from executive management. Executive management needs to be committed to the AIMS by ensuring AI objectives are established and enforced through the AI Governance Policy. Of course, AI objectives need to be driven by the organization's strategic decisions, but remember that requirements over AI need to be integrated into business processes. Resources must be allocated to ensure these requirements are implemented. Responsible AI leadership includes ensuring AI objectives are achieved and the effectiveness of the AIMS is communicated, as well as conforming to AI requirements. Responsible AI leadership also requires directing and supporting staff contributing to the effectiveness of AI, as well as continuously improving AI processes. Finally, executive management needs to support other relevant roles as they apply to their responsibilities related to AI.

The AI Governance Policy should document executive management's intent to carry out responsible AI actions, including the purpose of the AI systems, framework for setting objectives, commitment to meet requirements, and commitment to improve the AIMS. Controls should be implemented based on the governance policy, and the policy must be documented and available to staff (or others) as needed.

To ensure responsible AI leadership is carried out, relevant roles with assigned responsibilities and authorities need to be assigned. Staff members assigned to these roles need to be notified and understand their responsibilities. The AIMS should conform to standards, regulations, and other related frameworks, as well as performance results need to be reported to executive management for continued support (or direction).

AI Business Case

One way to get 'buy-in' for an AI project is to complete an AI Business Case. A business case is a document describing many factors to justify, in this case, an AI project. A business case contains several elements (or sections) such as the following:

- **Environment** – this section provides justification for the project to include economic, commercial, and/or competitive information. This section also provides details of the opportunities provided by AI.
- **Purpose and Objectives** – this section provides details about the project vision, general (and strategic) objectives, specific (and tactical) objectives, and operational objectives (including technical, economic, and temporal objectives).
- **Project Summary** – this section contains a summary of the project content to include the name or project reference, origins of the project, environment, and status of the AI project.
- **Expected Benefits** – this section explains the intended outcomes, financial benefits, financial scenarios, cost, return on investment (ROI), risks (to include the costs of not acting), and projected risks (such as for the AI project itself, for profit, and/or for business operations).
- **Preliminary Scope** – this section provides a scope of the AI project to include action framework, perimeter, boundaries, and prerequisites as applicable.
- **Critical Success Factors** – this section defines what makes the AI project a success, including material and human resources in the context of the organization.
- **Preliminary Project Plan** – this section defines the project approach, phases, reports, and deliverables expected.
- **Deadlines and Milestones** – this section provides for project activities (or modifications), technical distribution, and project planning.
- **Roles and Responsibilities** – this section covers the functions, roles, and assignments of resources to cover the AI project.
- **Resources** – this section defines the needed resources, such as staff members, funding, and other related elements, to complete a successful AI project.
- **Budget** – this section documents the financial plans, including AI cost controls.
- **Constraints** – this section defines any expected problems along with solutions. This section also covers assumptions, identified (or assessed) options, magnitude (and scale), and ratings pertaining to the complexity of the AI project.
- **Facilitation Plan** – this section covers how the project plan will be facilitated.
- **Communication** – this section determines who needs to know what and when about the AI project. This section also covers the media types, the target audience, and any internal or external promotions needed for the AI project.
- **Project Monitoring** – this section covers indicators, dashboards, reporting, project reviews, and traceability over monitoring of the AI project.

AI Governance Committee Charter

Responsible AI needs support from executive management. To obtain this support, an organization should consider establishing an AI Governance Committee. The AI Governance Committee is membered by senior leaders to oversee responsible

AI and the AI governance program development as well as the implementation of AI within the organization. The AI Governance Committee is responsible to integrate AI governance into the existing corporate structure to prevent risks from 'shadow' AI (or AI systems not officially approved by the organization) and ensure clear decision-making authority. The AI Governance Committee can be established through an AI Governance Committee Charter as discussed earlier. The charter should explain the objectives, mission, members, interested parties, and frequency of meetings.

The objective of the AI Governance Committee is to align the AIMS with the organization's business objectives and strategy. The mission of the AI Governance Committee is to set the objectives and strategy of the AIMS and validate the roles/responsibilities of interested parties, as well as the AI policies of the AIMS. The mission of the AI Governance Committee is also to approve criteria for risk tolerance and approve the risk treatment plan. The committee must implement the AIMS and provide resources to implement and maintain the AIMS.

The AI Governance Committee Charter documents the members as well as roles each are given when it comes to the committee's operations. The organization should consider related AI policies, AI objectives, and identified risks when assigning roles/responsibilities to ensure all relevant areas are covered. The organization should also prioritize how the roles/responsibilities are assigned.

The charter should identify other interested parties related to AI systems to include the following: providers (such as platform, product, or service providers), producers (or developers), customers (or users), partners (such as system integrators, data providers, evaluators, and auditors), subjects (or data subjects), and relevant authorities (such as regulators or policymakers). The AI Governance Committee Charter should also appoint an AI coordinator responsible for the strategic integration and management of AI; overseeing the planning, execution, and monitoring of AI projects; and communicating and coordinating with interested parties.

The AI Governance Committee Charter needs to define the frequency of meetings held by the committee, including conducting meetings when certain AI project milestones are completed. Meetings could also occur after risk analysis reports are completed to decide (and approve) risk treatment plans.

If the AI system relates to people, the organization may want to establish an Institutional Review Board (IRB) responsible for any ethical review applications, reviews, and/or approvals. The IRB may be required by regulations for industries such as healthcare.

Key Stakeholders of AI

Chief AI Officer

One of the key stakeholders of AI is the Chief AI Officer (CAIO). The CAIO is appointed (or designated) by executive management with the responsibility for oversight of AI systems, including overall implementation, maintenance, and enforcement of related AI policies, procedures, and practices. The CAIO should be an executive (or senior leader), and an organization may consider having the CAIO report up through the Chief Executive Officer (CEO). The CAIO is expected to collaborate cross-functionally with other executives, the AI Governance Committee, and any applicable IRBs. The CAIO should ultimately be responsible for any decisions of the AI, aware of intended uses (and limitations), and accountable for the ethical considerations during the entire AI life cycle.

The CAIO is responsible for developing principles and policies, as well as implementing guardrails to govern AI systems aligned to the organization's missions and values. The CAIO may leverage existing frameworks in order to identify high-risk AI use cases, which may need enhanced reviews. The CAIO is also responsible for security, privacy, quality, development, performance, supplier relationships, and safety when it comes to AI. More specifically, the CAIO must ensure AI performs adequately based on defined risk tolerance levels obtained through collaboration with senior leaders. The CAIO supports AI risk management efforts and integrates a risk prevention mindset throughout the AI life cycle. The CAIO identifies gaps in AI skills and makes recommendations (or takes actions) to ensure necessary skills, training, knowledge, and resources are appropriately considered, along with assigning AI responsibilities accordingly to staff members. Furthermore, the CAIO identifies (and tracks) risks related to AI and ensures risk management standards are implemented for system operations, along with oversight tasks. The CAIO establishes procedures to address AI responsibilities for human oversight and defines AI configurations according to the organization's risk tolerance. AI systems' explanation, interpretation, and transparency fall under the purview of the CAIO, along with establishing an impact assessment process. The CAIO is expected to manage risks, make public disclosures of incidents, and delegate authority over AI systems as necessary.

When it comes to managing reports of AI concerns, the CAIO is the point of contact to receive reports of issues regarding AI, including concerns that the AI system no longer meets ethical criteria. The CAIO assumes the responsibility to investigate and remedy the issue, if possible, or retains the authority to modify, limit, or stop the use of the AI system.

The CAIO must be knowledgeable in AI regulations and stay up to date on recent developments related to new legal cases involving AI, enforcement actions, regulations, standards, guidelines, contractual obligations, and other issues involving AI.

Other Key AI Stakeholders

Other key AI stakeholders include members of the board of directors (conduct oversight and fiduciary responsibilities); executive business leaders (assist in aligning AI to business objectives); IT leaders such as CISOs, CTOs, CIOs, or heads of AI departments or operations (may generally lead AI implementation); compliance, legal, governance, ethics, and privacy officers (assist in regulatory compliance); AI project managers (assume responsibility to manage AI projects); AI subject matter experts such as AI software engineers (and other AI designers, developers, researchers, managers, acquirers, and deployers); AI data scientists (responsible for AI models, data, and algorithms); AI risk managers (assist in managing AI risks); AI risk owners (maintain overall AI risk management responsibilities and monitoring of AI after deployment); trainers (train users on AI); quality assurance (perform tests to ensure quality of outputs); auditors (perform assessments, testing, and evaluations of AI systems); policy and document managers or analysts (ensure AI documents are developed and managed); marketing or AI public relations (manage communications with the public); and customers (users of AI).

The organization needs to determine the assignment of different responsibilities when it comes to using and monitoring AI systems as in the case of identifying and documenting AI risks. The organization may utilize a diverse team of stakeholders throughout the AI system's life cycle to engage in decisions made related to AI as well as assisting in mapping, managing, and measuring AI risks. A diverse group is needed to provide perspectives from different demographics, disciplines, experiences, expertise, opinions, and backgrounds to provide comprehensive feedback on AI. Since AI systems cross several different domains, obtaining a diverse perspective, not only technical but also non-technical, is important to capture any unintended consequences of bias from AI systems. Furthermore, the organization may need to consult with external parties if it lacks the necessary diversity, such as equity, inclusion, and accessibility, from internal teams.

Acceptable Use Policy

According to the *Second Draft of the General-Purpose AI Code of Practice*, "An Acceptable Use Policy (AUP) is defined as guidelines to users on what is and is not considered acceptable use" (Code of Practice Plenary Participants, 2024). The AUP should include, at a minimum, the following: the AUP's purpose and scope; intended uses and users of the AI system; listing of acceptable use activities along with unacceptable (or prohibited) uses; security measures users must adhere to when using the AI system; monitoring and privacy; process in handling misuse such as warning, suspension, or termination of use; and acknowledgment requiring understanding and agreement to comply with the AUP.

Copyright Policy

Organizations must consider how they may (or may not) use copyrighted material within AI systems. Organizations should document and approve a policy related to copyright material, abiding by all related laws. When utilizing third-party datasets, the organization should ensure due diligence is performed by executing contracts to confirm that the datasets used in the development of an AI model do not violate any copyright laws. Furthermore, the organization should address the output of an AI system and any copyright protections that may be applied to this output.

Issues arise when organizations scrape websites for text and data (also known as data mining) to obtain the datasets needed to train their large language models. These large language models create the foundational models used as generative AI models for more specific tasks. Organizations can demonstrate responsible AI by respecting the Robot Exclusion Protocol (or *robots.txt*) instructions provided by many websites. Organizations can also be transparent about their crawling activities by providing the names of the crawlers along with their robots.txt features.

Organizations can respect rights reservations provided in other means, utilizing industry standard tools, and collaborate on developing interoperable machine-readable standards over rights reservations. Organizations should further exclude pirated websites from crawling activities. A single point of contact to handle complaints should be designated for individuals to claim copyrights or file complaints concerning the use of their work. Finally, organizations should document sources and authorizations of data used in training, testing, and validating general-purpose AI models.

AI copyright laws are still being debated. This author recommends consulting an attorney with expertise in copyright matters for all related copyright concerns. From the US Copyright Office:

> We recommend that Congress establish a federal right that protects all individuals during their lifetimes from the knowing distribution of unauthorized digital replicas. The right should be licensable, subject to guardrails, but not assignable, with effective remedies including monetary damages and injunctive relief. Traditional rules of secondary liability should apply, but with an appropriately conditioned safe harbor for OSPs [online service providers]. The law should contain explicit First Amendment accommodation. Finally, in recognition of well-developed state rights of publicity, we recommend against full preemption of state laws.
>
> *(United States Copyright Office, 2024)*

The US Copyright Office under a report titled *Copyright and Artificial Intelligence Part 2: Copyrightability* circa January 2025, makes the following conclusion and recommendations [Source: https://www.copyright.gov/ai/Copyright-and-Artificial-Intelligence-Part-2-Copyrightability-Report.pdf]:

- *Human Authored Works ARE Copyrightable*: "Human authors are entitled to copyright in their works of authorship that are perceptible in AI-generated outputs, as well as the creative selection, coordination, or arrangement of material

	Human Authored	NO Human Involvement
NO AI Assistance (or AI Only)	**Copyrightable (NO AI Assistance)**	**NOT Copyrightable (If AI only)**
Some AI Assistance (or Unedited Content/ Prompts Only)	**Copyrightable (with Some AI Assistance)**	**NOT Copyrightable (If AI content is unedited OR prompts with unedited content)**

Figure 5.1   Copyrightability.

in the outputs, or creative modifications of the outputs" (US Copyright Office, 2025). "Whether human contributions to AI-generated outputs are sufficient to constitute authorship must be analyzed on a case-by-case basis" (US Copyright Office, 2025).

- *Human Authored Works Assisted by AI (or Includes AI-Generated Content) ARE Copyrightable*: "The use of AI tools to assist rather than stand in for human creativity does not affect the availability of copyright protection for the output" (US Copyright Office, 2025). "Copyright protects the original expression in a work created by a human author, even if the work also includes AI-generated material" (US Copyright Office, 2025).
- *Unedited AI-Generated Output IS NOT Copyrightable*: "Copyright does not extend to purely AI-generated material, or material where there is insufficient human control over the expressive elements" (US Copyright Office, 2025).
- *Prompts Alone Along with Unedited AI-Generated Outputs ARE NOT Copyrightable*: "Based on the functioning of current generally available technology, prompts do not alone provide sufficient control" (US Copyright Office, 2025) (Figure 5.1).

AI Safety Standards

The Governance Institute of Australia and the National Artificial Intelligence Centre published a *White Paper on AI Governance: Leadership Insights and the Voluntary AI Safety Standard in Practice* laying out ten guardrails as summarized and paraphrased below [source: https://www.governanceinstitute.com.au/app/uploads/2024/09/GovInst-AI-Whitepaper.pdf]:

1. **Accountability Process** – develop to include internal governance capabilities such as assigning an overall AI owner, AI strategy, and AI training.
2. **Risk Management Process** – assess AI's impact and risks, as well as develop effective risk mitigation strategies.

3. **Data Governance Measures** – implement measures for data management, privacy, and cybersecurity to include data quality, data provenance, and identify cyber vulnerabilities.
4. **Test and Monitor AI Models** – AI models need to be tested before deployment and monitored after being deployed for any changes.
5. **Human Oversight** – enable mechanisms to permit human control and intervention as needed within AI systems.
6. **Transparency with Users** – disclose the use of AI to users to ensure they can make informed decisions when interacting with AI-generated content.
7. **Complaint Process** – provide the ability for users to challenge AI outputs or file complaints on contested outcomes.
8. **Transparency with Other Organizations** – disclose information about models and systems to other organizations in the supply change for them to address risks.
9. **Record Management** – maintain records to demonstrate compliance such as inventories and AI documentation.
10. **Evaluate Needs** – identify bias, ensure accessibility, and focus on stakeholder needs when it comes to safety, diversity, inclusion, and fairness.

Responsible AI Planning

The adage from Benjamin Franklin, "if you fail to plan, you are planning to fail", still holds true to this day. In a report titled *The Root Causes of Failure for Artificial Intelligence Projects and How They Can Success: Avoiding the Anti-Patterns of AI*, the authors interviewed 65 data scientists and engineers. "By some estimates, more than [eighty] 80 percent of AI projects fail—twice the rate of failure for information technology projects that do not involve AI" (Ryseff et al., 2024). The authors attributed this to five root causes: misunderstanding (or miscommunication), lack of data (or ineffective training models), focus not on solving 'real' problems, inadequate infrastructure, and AI applied to problems too difficult to solve. To establish an effective AI governance program, it is imperative to properly plan AI project tasks.

AI Governance Plan (ISO 42001 Plan)

To implement responsible AI, it must start early within the software development life cycle. This starts with having a solid AI governance program in place. Following the steps to implement an AIMS will establish the framework for governance activities and demonstrate responsible AI.

One of the first actions an organization must take to implement an effective AIMS is to become knowledgeable regarding AI regulations and standards. Regulations should drive organization policies. Procedures are the actual

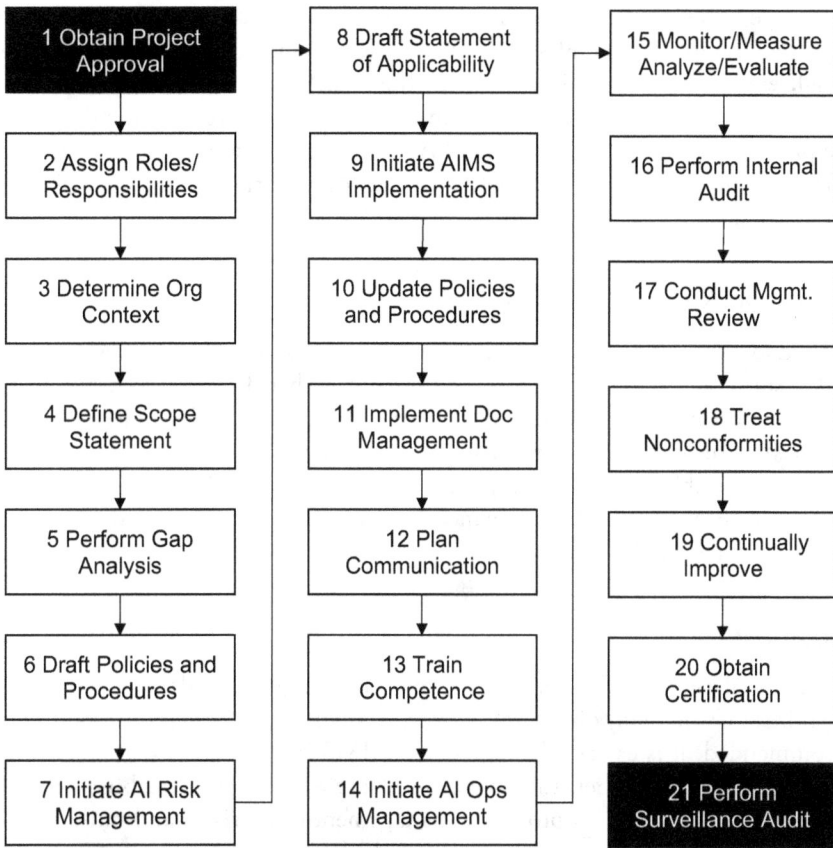

Figure 5.2 AI Governance Plan.

step-by-step processes to carry out the policies. Standards assist in tying the policies and procedures together through guidelines and criteria. In the case of certifications, these standards must be met to meet the criteria for the certification. Again, it is essential for executive management to support the management and governance systems. Presenting a business case is one way to obtain executive-level support. As previously discussed, executive management should designate an AIMS project manager and involve other interested parties as applicable (Figure 5.2).

Project Approval

Once support has been obtained from executive management, the AIMS needs to be planned and implemented. Some resources may need to be allocated to the AIMS such as people, data, equipment, finance, suppliers, and other assets. The AIMS project plan should be drafted by the AIMS project manager describing the scope, objectives, approach to achieve these objectives, responsibilities, expected results, deliverables, and specific requirements such as organization, social, environmental, and regulatory. The AIMS project should be approved by management and could be communicated through a presentation describing the project proposal, the alignment of AI with organizational strategy, feedback from stakeholders, ROI (or benefits such as competitive advantage), plans to manage risks, and final approval.

Roles and Responsibilities

Related to roles and responsibilities, the organization should define an AI structure and ensure there is an assigned AI coordinator (either delegated as a role to the AIMS project manager or assigned to another individual). Roles and responsibilities need to be assigned to certain stakeholders as well as the AIMS project team needs to be established with appropriate role assignments. If the AIMS 'committee' reports up through the AI Governance Committee, as recommended, then these assignments need to be defined.

Organizational Context

Members of the AIMS project team must have a good understanding of the organization's mission, objectives, values, strategies, and policies. As previously recommended, it is easier to integrate the AIMS into already existing management systems. Remember, the objectives of the AIMS are to establish effective management processes, improve the management of AI risks, and build a competitive advantage over the development, deployment, and use of AI to build trust with customers as well as demonstrate responsible AI. Since AI may expand across the entire organization, establishing a preliminary scope over the AIMS is important to document and communicate to management. The scope should describe system capabilities, management responsibilities, and obligations to maintain trustworthy AI systems.

An analysis should be carried out covering the internal and external environment. One of the methods to accomplish this analysis is by following the Strengths, Weaknesses, Opportunities, and Threats (SWOT) Analysis. Strengths and Weaknesses originate internally, while Opportunities and Threats originate externally. Of course, Strengths and Opportunities are helpful while Weaknesses and Threats are harmful. Demonstrating this is a 2 x 2 matrix that can help identify issues the organization may not be aware of. Similar frameworks include Strengths, Opportunities, Assets, and Risks (SOAR) and Needs, Opportunities, Improvements, Strengths, and Exceptions (NOISE) (Figure 5.3).

Another analysis method to assess major external factors, which can impact the competitive advantage of an organization, is Political, Economic, Social, and

	Positive	Negative
Internally	Strengths	Weaknesses
Externally	Opportunities	Threats

Figure 5.3   SWOT.

Technological (PEST) analysis. PEST can help with external factors, while SWOT looks at both internal and external. Another similar analysis covering external factors, but goes broadly into environmental areas, is Porter's Five Forces. This analysis includes competitive rivalry, supplier power, buyer power, threat of substitution, and threat of new entry.

To complete the understanding of the organization and its context, the organization needs to identify processes (or activities), interested parties, and business requirements. Some questions to ask in identifying processes are *what products (or services) does the organization offer, what are some of the assets, and what processes are needed for the organization to achieve its objectives?* Organizational context needs to include the requirements and expectations from interested parties. For example, *what do customers of the organization expect from the product or service offered?* Different organizations have different internal (and external), mandatory (or voluntary), standards, regulations, contractual obligations, and policies.

Scope Statement

After completing the organizational context analysis, the organization should be in a better position to develop the AIMS scope statement. This scope statement will address organizational, system, and physical boundaries along with processes, departments, and stakeholders of the AIMS. The scope statement doesn't have to be complicated, but should be concise and detailed enough to cover the entire scope of the AIMS. The scope statement is published on the final AIMS certification.

Gap Analysis

The organization needs to take an inventory of all AI systems. Once an inventory has been performed, the organization should perform a gap analysis to determine its current state against expected objectives. The analysis can be conducted through observations, interviews, reviews of documents, questionnaire surveys, or even tools like scanning tools to help identify AI technology. Objectives were previously set by leadership and should follow regulations, standards, and/or established frameworks. The gap analysis should identify maturity targets, and maturity ratings can be determined utilizing the Capability Maturity Model Integration (CMMI) as follows:

- **Nonexistent (or Incomplete)** – total absence of identifiable processes.
- **Initial** – processes are implemented on a case-by-case basis without any formal method.
- **Managed** – nonstandard processes are in place, but they are not formal.
- **Defined** – processes are well documented and communicated to stakeholders.
- **Quantitatively Managed** – processes are monitored and can be measured.
- **Optimized** – processes are optimized, and there is a focus on continual improvement.

The results from the gap analysis are presented to executive management through a gap analysis report. The report should contain, at a minimum, an introduction, baseline of current processes, framework, identification of gaps, recommendations, and summary of results.

Policies

An effective AIMS is established by policies. A policy should be drafted to address AI, specifically as discussed in previous sections of this book. Policies should be standardized according to the organization's document management process. The document management process may be a part of the organization's Quality Management System (QMS). Policies should contain a header section with titles of responsible parties, approvals, and departments impacted by the policy. A policy statement should include purpose, scope, and effective date. Some policies may include definitions, or the organization may choose to develop a central glossary to include all related terms and acronyms.

The body of the policy should contain context, rationale, details, processes, responsibilities, and alternatives available in case a certain policy isn't able to be fully implemented. Policies should also contain behavior expected from users as well as consequences for not abiding by the policy (i.e., sanctions). If policies are generated electronically, a reporting mechanism may already be in place with assigned contact information. If there are any related documents or regulatory footnotes, these should be included in the policy for easy referencing and mapping. The policy should identify when it will be reviewed (or last amended) and should abide by the organization's distribution plan, along with acknowledgment requirements. The policy should end with a log regarding any revisions (or changes) made.

All policies need to be approved, published, and disseminated to affected staff members through approved distribution channels such as an organization's Intranet, document management solution, hard copy printout, or as part of onboarding activities. A list should be maintained or reminders should be issued to review policies as necessary (or at least annually).

AI Risk Management

A risk should be identified for any gaps noted in the previous gap analysis. An entire chapter of this book was dedicated to AI risk management. This is the part in the AIMS plan where an AI risk assessment is performed. Risks are identified, and an analysis is performed on the likelihood, along with the impact a threat can exploit a vulnerability to cause harm. The risks are evaluated and prioritized. Risk treatments are determined, and plans of action are approved to mitigate risks. Risk activities are communicated, documented, and reported as part of the organization's risk management processes. Risks are continually monitored, updated, reviewed, and reported.

Statement of Applicability

To mitigate risks to acceptable levels, controls are implemented. A SoA can be developed to identify controls, the organization can implement to mitigate risks. Controls can be selected from many different sources, and the SoA is used to document the applicability of the control, provide a brief description, provide justification for implementing (or not implementing) a control, provide other documented information, and identify who in the organization is responsible for the control. Selected controls need to be justified and identified to mitigate a risk. Excluded controls also need to be justified, along with an explanation of why the controls are not applicable under the context of the AI risks. The SoA must be completed to obtain certification and must be approved by management.

AIMS Implementation Plan

After selecting the controls needed to mitigate risks, the controls must be appropriately designed for the AI system and implemented. Fully understanding the AI system and determining the AI landscape within the organization are needed to properly implement controls. After reviewing the list of AI systems and intended objectives, the organization needs to ensure that the functionalities of the AI system are understood. The organization will also want to determine how the AI system interacts with other systems (or integrations) as well as any limitations (or constraints) associated with the AI system. Controls are meant to protect data, and the organization needs to assess data used in (or flowing through) the AI system.

To implement controls, the organization needs to allocate appropriate resources and conduct any applicable cost analysis. The organization may determine it does not make sense to spend thousands of dollars on protecting a system that may be worth only a couple of hundred. Implementing some solutions may be complex. The organization needs to ensure that the resources allocated are competent to sufficiently implement the solution. A schedule needs to be established to track implementation activities such as a project tracker along with documentation such as instructions, technical configurations, processes, or procedures related to the implemented control. Detailed tasks should be identified along with responsible individuals, as well as the results of the implemented activities that need to be recorded. A description of the control should be developed since this will help with documentation and may be required by some frameworks (or standards).

Update Policies and Procedures

All policies and procedures should be updated to include new processes developed by implemented controls. Remember, AI governance and the AIMS should be integrated with other management systems such as the Information Security Management System (ISMS), the Privacy Information Management System (PIMS), and the QMS. The policies and procedures related to the ISMS, PIMS, and QMS should also be reviewed and updated to capture the new control processes integrated by the AIMS.

Document Management

When developing management systems, a lot of documentation is created. The organization must ensure it manages these documents appropriately. Establishing an effective document management system assists in complying with regulations, consistent communication and traceability, effective evaluation, improved process alignments, and demonstrates conformity during audits. The organization could group documents into the following levels:

1. **Level 1 – Governance (or Policies)** – these documents include policies, SoA, scope statements, or other high-level strategic documents where executive management is directing the course of the organization.
2. **Level 2 – Processes (or Procedures)** – these documents include procedures, control descriptions, or other related instructions describing who, what, when, where, why, and how.
3. **Level 3 – Records** – these documents are the actual activities occurring such as audit logs, evidence, or other proof of tasks performed.

Communication

The organization should develop a communication plan. This communication plan should abide by the principles of transparency, appropriateness, credibility (and reputation), responsiveness, and clarity. The communication plan should answer the questions around what, when, with whom, and how to communicate. The communication plan should establish objectives such as communicating with interested parties the importance of an AIMS, complying with AI policies, AIMS performance, and responsibilities. Interested parties may include employees, customers, investors, suppliers, media, and the public.

Executive management should develop a communication strategy that considers objectives, expectations, concerns, effective sources, influences, and latest developments. The communication strategy should consider the audience, purpose, perceptions, content, techniques, timing, and responsible parties. There are several communication channels to choose from, such as emails, reports, websites, interviews, surveys, presentations, and other forms. Like other aspects of the AIMS, the communication process needs to be evaluated to determine its effectiveness.

Competence

The organization needs to ensure they have competent employees to perform their assigned tasks. A competency assessment may be needed to determine if there are gaps in the workforce related to specific AI knowledge or to meet the organization's AI strategic objectives. Training programs should be designed based on the needs, which may include the following: AI policy awareness training; AI risk training to cover threats of attacks on the AI system or models; data modeling training to ensure bias is minimized along with appropriate data collection techniques, training on the use of AI to cover explainability and transparency; training on maintaining documentation; training related to AI maintenance activities; and other related AI training as needed. Training needs to be performed, documented, and evaluated for effectiveness.

AI Operations Management

The organization needs to manage operations involving AI systems. Managing AI systems could follow existing change management processes. These change management processes may start by submitting a change request. Most organizations utilize a ticketing solution to capture these changes, but change management could be tracked in other ways, such as through email, a form, or a spreadsheet. The change request needs to be reviewed for quality, specific changes, and resource allocation, and a decision needs to be made on whether the change should be approved or not. This could be an iterative process with additional follow-up from the approver to the requester to answer concerns that might arise from the review. Once the change is approved, it needs to be planned and implemented. Changes need to be tested, verified as successfully completed, and recorded. Changes should also be measured to ensure they meet their objectives.

To manage AI operations effectively, it is important to confirm a smooth transition when implementing AI solutions to ensure no business interruptions (or at least minimal interruptions where it is unavoidable to deploy AI). Performance of AI needs to be monitored, and any identified improvements need to be considered or acted upon. Again, documentation is key to demonstrating responsible AI, and AI projects must have the necessary resources to continue operations such as budget, tools, and competent personnel.

Monitor, Measure, Analyze, and Evaluate

Although similar, monitoring, measurement, analysis, and evaluation have different meanings. Monitoring is the process of observing to determine levels of performance. An example of monitoring would be collecting logs. Measurement determines values by setting objectives, selecting criteria, establishing performance indicators, and determining if objectives are met. An example of measurement would be determining the amount of downtime for a system within a certain period (or threshold). If the system goes off-line for a period greater than a certain threshold, an alert should be generated.

Analysis is understanding the system better to enable making improvements. An example of analysis could be the determination of a root cause to a system issue. Evaluation determines the effectiveness of a system. An example of evaluation could be the testing of the system to ensure it meets expectations (or a set of criteria).

Management should define the objectives that need to be monitored and measured. Certain standards may need to be met, and performance indicators of a system may need to be established. Examples of some performance indicators related to AI could be the number of false positives from outputs or the number of AI risks identified (and the number of days it takes to mitigate these vulnerabilities). The use of dashboards could help in recording activities related to monitoring and reporting these results to management to make decisions based on the data provided.

Internal Audit

Performing internal audits is important to understand the effectiveness of the organization's AIMS. Internal audits are also required to be performed prior to any certification under the ISO standards. An internal audit should be conducted by an independent and qualified individual (or team). Independence is important since the auditors should NOT have any role in the implementation of controls. Internal audits could be conducted by individuals within the organization, but do not have implementation roles or conducted by third-party auditors, which are completely independent of the organization with no advisory roles.

The objectives of an internal audit are to evaluate the following: AI objectives, governance, risk management, control effectiveness, AI life cycle management, measurement, continual improvement, and coordination with external auditors as needed. An internal audit operates under an audit charter explaining the scope, audit activities, responsibilities, authorization, and a statement of independence. An internal audit also needs to be planned to ensure documents such as policies and procedures are available for review, along with the availability of responsible parties to conduct interviews.

The auditors are responsible for performing audit activities, including identifying sources of information, collecting samples, reviewing evidence, evaluating against standards, drafting findings, and determining an audit conclusion. Auditors are not supposed to provide any recommendations or advice on how to correct deficiencies. Auditors, under ISO, will document nonconformities (or controls that do not fulfill a requirement) as a minor nonconformity or as a major nonconformity. Organizations, under a management system, do not have to be perfect. The concept of a management system is to identify ways to improve and to have documented processes in place to mitigate identified risks. Auditors are also responsible for ensuring their reviews, analysis, evaluation, and testing to support their findings. The organization will be responsible for taking actions to correct nonconformities, but some corrections may happen over time due to the complexity of the issue identified.

Management Review

Management should review the internal audit, which is generally performed once a year, but may also be performed more frequently depending on management's needs. Progress of actions taken to mitigate nonconformities, applying controls to risks, and reviewing documents should be an ongoing process. These actions need to be reported to executive management through routine meetings, such as the AI Governance Committee meetings. Management reviews assist executive managers in making decisions, improvements, or changes to the AIMS. These reviews need to be documented to include dates, contributors, criteria reviewed, performance, recommended changes, decisions made, assignments, and expected times to complete activities.

Nonconformity Treatment

Nonconformities identified can be treated as a problem, issue, or opportunity for improvement. A problem-solving approach that could be helpful in resolving nonconformities is known as the Eight Disciplines (8D) model. According to the American Society for Quality (ASQ), "the 8D problem solving model establishes a permanent corrective action based on statistical analysis of the problem and focuses on the origin of the problem by determining its root causes" (ASQ,

2025). The following are the steps to the 8D model: DO – Plan; D1 – Create a Team; D2 – Define and Describe the Problem; D3 – Contain the Problem; D4 – Identify, Describe, and Verify Root Causes; D5 – Choose Corrective Actions; D6 – Implement and Validate Corrective Actions; D7 – Take Preventive Measures; and D8 – Congratulate Your Team.

The organization needs to determine what actions to take to correct the nonconformity. This requires an identification and a full understanding of the nonconformity. The organization should look for root causes as well as select solutions based on an evaluation of available options. The organization needs to plan the implementation and review actions taken. Based on concerns related to the nonconformity, the organization may implement additional preventive measures. The organization will want to monitor the AIMS along with assets, threats, vulnerabilities, and security incidents. Finally, the organization needs to draft a plan of action to correct the nonconformity.

Continual Improvement

The organization should look for ways to continually improve the AIMS. Improving the AIMS increases efficiency, creates collaboration with teams, increases satisfaction with customers, and reduces errors. The plan, do, check, and act (PDCA)

> is an improvement cycle based on the scientific method of proposing a change in a process, implementing the change, measuring the results, and taking appropriate action. It also is known as the *Deming Cycle* or *Deming Wheel* after W. Edwards Deming, who introduced the concept in Japan in the 1950s.
>
> *(Lean Enterprise Institute, 2025)*

The organization should determine (or plan) goals and needed changes. The organization should then implement the changes (or do) and evaluate the results (or check). Finally, the organization should act to standardize the change (or start the cycle over) (Figure 5.4).

The organization needs to maintain improvements and update the AIMS at least annually or upon any major changes. Some of the documents that may need to be updated are the following: AI policy, objectives, training, risk assessments, control procedures, plans involving incident management, internal audit program, and management review plans. All improvements need to be documented.

ISO Certification

According to the ISO standards, certification is a formal procedure to attest to a status of achievement providing an official certification document. As opposed

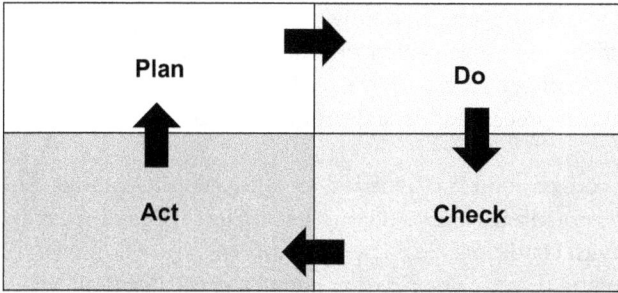

Figure 5.4　Plan-Do-Check-Act.

to an attestation to confirm the validity of a document, certifying bodies are approved by accreditation bodies to certify organizations against specific standards. If an organization decides to move forward with a certification, it will need to select a certifying body. An organization should select a certifying body based on its reputation, geographic location, industry experience, and audit team skills, and if a combined audit (which is an audit of multiple standards) is sought, then the organization needs to ensure the certifying body can certify against all standards in scope.

Certification Audits may follow similar audit plans like the internal auditors. These audit plans may include requests for evidence, identifying interviewees, and ensuring resources are allocated appropriately. Just before conducting a certification audit, the organization may want to perform a self-assessment and ensure employees are prepared. An internal briefing meeting may be conducted to cover some of the expectations of the audit. Some training may be needed to ensure employees do not make common audit mistakes, such as providing information not relevant to the certification or ensuring employees know where information can be obtained. Employees may also want to refresh themselves on policies and procedures so they respond to auditor questions accurately.

The certification auditors should have a kick-off meeting. The organization will want to determine how evidence will be obtained, processed, transferred, or stored by the auditors. During the kick-off meeting, the organization may want to consider providing the auditors with a presentation. This presentation may include details about the organization and contact information. The presentation should cover the scope and objectives of the audit as well as milestones, documents, process descriptions, results of previous audits, and any outstanding nonconformity reports. The organization will want to take care of the auditors and manage any logistics accordingly.

ISO audits are conducted in two stages. Stage 1 audits determine the readiness for the Stage 2 audit. Stage 1 audits may occur on-site and may include high-level interviews to observe technologies used or operations in place. Auditors may ensure policies and procedures are available and will evaluate the design of the AIMS.

If the organization is prepared, it will move on to Stage 2. Stage 2 will ensure controls are effectively implemented and the organization conforms to all standard requirements. Auditors may perform testing, interviews, observations, evidence review, or conduct process audits to determine that controls are being implemented as described.

Once the audit is completed, the auditor will make a recommendation for certification. If the organization does not meet standards, the auditor may recommend certification with conditions on completing a corrective action plan, or the auditor could recommend that the organization not receive certification. Major nonconformities identified need to be resolved before certification is issued, registered, and obtained by the organization.

Surveillance Audit

An ISO certification is valid for three years. The first year requires the Stage 1 and Stage 2 Audits discussed previously, and years two and three require a surveillance audit. A surveillance audit is a scaled-down version of an initial audit, looking for any major changes within the environment and determining how effectively the management system is operating. An organization should pay special attention to some of the following areas under a surveillance audit: change management, internal audits, management reviews, operating controls, mitigation of risks, measuring effectiveness of controls, and continual improvement.

Responsible AI Support

Most organizations are not developing their own AI systems, but rather integrating pre-trained AI systems (or models) into existing products. Organizations may also be fine-tuning these AI systems to meet specific needs. Obtaining AI systems from third parties introduces some new risks to the organization. There are some key legal and operational risks to consider when buying AI systems from third parties,

> [b]ut even if an organisation is not procuring a GenAI system for its own use, GenAI is increasingly becoming embedded in workflows throughout the supply chain and being used by suppliers and service providers in the development or delivery of products and services.
>
> *(Deloitte, 2024)*

According to a report from Deloitte titled *Contracting for Generative AI and Mitigating Generative AI Supply Chain Risks*, some of the key legal issues of AI to address in the supply chain are the following: data privacy; intellectual property rights; confidential information; AI regulations; inaccuracy; opacity; liability and redress; bias; and environmental, social, and governance (ESG) concerns. To address these concerns, the report suggests focusing on the following four pillars: contract templates and playbooks, procurement processes, due diligence, and governance.

There are some clauses to consider adding to contracts related to the purchase of generative AI technology as recommended by the Koley Jessen law firm [Source: https://www.koleyjessen.com/insights/publications/contract-considerations-generative-ai-providers]:

- **Third-Party Terms** – providers of AI systems need to review terms from the developers of the AI models to ensure they 'flow down' obligations, warranties, and other applicable covenants.
- **Training Models from Personal Data** – if the provider wants to use personal data to train models, it should ensure data to train models is done under consent. If consent hasn't been obtained, then it shouldn't be used without obtaining consent first. Providers need to update privacy policies to ensure they cover the use of data in training and ensure appropriate licenses are in place.
- **Content Liability** – providers should ensure they disclaim liability for AI output and be transparent to customers about their customers interacting with AI. Notifications should be implemented for users to read and agree to when using AI features.
- **Intellectual Property** – providers need to ensure they have indemnity protection related to any infringement on intellectual property rights.
- **Ownership** – providers need to consider retaining rights on output, consider restrictions on output, or grant ownership over property rights as applicable.
- **Regulatory Compliance** – providers should retain the right to terminate contracts if laws change that impact the use of the AI system.

One way to ensure developers of AI are transparent is by providing a Model Card. According to the report *Model Card for Model Reporting*, the authors suggest the following information be included on a Model Card as summarized and paraphrased below [Source: https://dl.acm.org/doi/10.1145/3287560.3287596] :

- **Model Details** – basic information such as organization, model date/version/type, training algorithm information, other resources, citations, license, and contact information.
- **Intended Use** – the primary intended use, users, and outlier cases.
- **Factors** – such as demographic, environmental, technical, relevant, or evaluation factors.
- **Metrics** – such as model performance, decision thresholds, or variations.
- **Evaluation Data** – includes datasets, motivation, and processing.
- **Training Data** – may not be possible to provide, but if so, it should be like evaluation data and could detail distributions across different factors.

- **Quantitative Analyses** – such as unitary (i.e., single) and intersectional (i.e., interconnected) results.
- Ethical Considerations.
- Caveats and Recommendations.

Specific Recommended Policies

The following are some recommended policies to develop, approve, and implement to demonstrate responsible AI:

AI Governance Policy

The AI Governance Policy is the organization's overall guiding policy. This policy should contain an overview of executive management's intent involving AI development, deployment, and/or use within the organization. The Overview section of the policy may contain details on the following: AI literacy, use of AI systems, process for responsible use of AI systems, objectives for responsible use of AI systems, intended use of AI systems, alignment with other organizational policies, and review of the AI Governance Policy. The AI Governance Policy should be based on sound AI ethics principles like the Organization for Economic Co-Operation and Development (OECD) AI Principles and should also maintain a commitment from management to responsible AI governance.

Roles and responsibilities should be defined for teams or positions like the IRB, the AI Governance Committee, the CAIO, and others. There should also be a requirement to ensure stakeholders are from diverse backgrounds if they are involved in providing input, feedback, or decisions related to AI. The AI Governance Policy should identify compliance requirements (or regulations) as well as call out specific AI systems that are restricted (or prohibited) from being developed, deployed, or used. The policy should include definitions on AI systems' classification.

If the organization works with general-purpose AI models, the AI Governance Policy should include some details on these models such as procedures, obligations related to providers, authorized representatives, and obligations related to models with systemic risks. This segues into risk management system details to include AI system resources and documentation such as data, tooling, system and computing, and human resources. Some regulations require corrective actions and notification, which need to be addressed in the policy. Appropriate data governance and management practices need to be applied according to policies and other related regulations.

The AI Governance Policy should address technical documentation, documentation keeping, and record-keeping, along with automatically generated logs. Transparency is important to AI and should be addressed in the governance policy. Some regulations may require an authorized representative to be reported within the country where the AI system is available. Some other areas needing to be addressed are human oversight, accuracy, robustness, and cybersecurity. Some countries may have requirements on providers when it comes to high-risk AI systems and may require certain corrective actions to be taken to mitigate identified risks.

Some regulators have established AI regulatory sandboxes where AI systems may be exempt. Further processing of personal data in these AI regulatory sandboxes should be noted along with testing of high-risk AI systems in real-world conditions (and testing which may be outside of the AI regulatory sandbox) within the AI Governance Policy.

The AI Governance Policy may intersect with several other policies and procedures (or other management systems). One of these management systems is the QMS as previously discussed. The AI Governance Policy may also address abiding by codes of conduct (or meeting conformity requirements). Some countries require conformity assessments for certain AI systems classified as high-risk and will include presumption of conformity, declaration of conformity, and CE marking of conformity, where applicable. Some AI systems may also require a fundamental rights impact assessment to be performed on them.

Organizations may be required to cooperate with regulatory authorities. There may be obligations for product manufacturers, importers, distributors, deployers, or other third parties involved in AI. The AI Governance Policy should address monitoring AI systems after deployment, including reporting concerns (or serious incidents). Regulators may require access to data and documentation related to AI systems.

AI Management System Policy

For organizations looking to obtain certifications, they should consider developing an AIMS Policy outlining the specific clauses of the ISO 42001 standard. Although some of these sections may refer to other policies and procedures, it will assist auditors in understanding the organization holistically. The AIMS Policy should contain an overview along with the context of the organization. The context may consist of an understanding of the organization, the needs and expectations of interested parties, and the AIMS' scope. The AIMS Policy should summarize leadership, the AI Governance Policy, and roles/responsibilities. The AIMS Policy should address planning to include addressing risks and opportunities, AI risk assessment and treatment, AI system impact assessment, and AI objectives along with planning for changes.

The AIMS Policy should cover support concerns, including resources, competence, awareness, communication, and creating, updating, and controlling documents. The AIMS Policy should also cover operational planning and control. Controls are applied as risk treatment based on risk assessments and other impact assessments performed like system impact assessments. In addition, performance evaluation, including monitoring, measurement, analysis, and evaluation, needs to be covered in the AIMS Policy. The AIMS Policy should cover the internal audit program and management reviews. Finally, the AIMS Policy should address continuous improvement, which includes nonconformity and corrective actions.

Data Governance Policy

The Data Governance Policy, like other policies, should start with an overview and include background content. For this policy, there may be certain regulatory requirements related to AI training model techniques and approaches. The Data Governance Policy should cover the design and development of AI systems, including data acquisition, data collection, data quality, and data provenance. The Data Governance Policy should also address relevant data preparation, processing, and assumptions, along with any prior assessments or evaluations of bias within the data. Data gaps need to be addressed along with ensuring records are maintained, logs are automatically generated, documents are retained, and access is provided to regulators as necessary.

Data Protection Impact Assessment

The Data Protection Impact Assessment (DPIA) was discussed in detail in another section of this book, but to summarize, the DPIA should contain a section recording the organization's information such as name, address, and data processing type (i.e., controller, processor, or both) and point of contact information such as name, title, phone number, and email address. The DPIA should contain a listing of applicable regulatory requirements along with a system description and data flow diagrams. The DPIA needs to identify the type of data being processed and the reason the DPIA is being performed in the first place. The DPIA should also identify areas of impact, including societal impact and human oversight.

The next section of the DPIA should consist of details around processing such as nature, scope, context, and purposes of processing. All involved stakeholders should be consulted, and a determination of the necessity and proportionality of processing needs to be made.

A privacy impact assessment (PIA) could be part of the DPIA or separate as previously mentioned. The PIA should identify and analyze how the systems impact privacy. Risks should be identified related to privacy along with mitigation efforts. A summarized listing of safeguards, liabilities, and controls related to personal data should be included in the PIA.

Finally, the DPIA should be reviewed and approved by management and the data protection officer, as applicable. Revisions or document history should be tracked, as well as any source references used in completing the DPIA and the PIA.

Incident Response Policy

The organization should develop and communicate an Incident Response Policy along with processes and plans to manage an incident. The Incident Response Policy should define the type of training provided to staff members, such as simulations, automatic, and breach training. The organization's Incident Response Plan should be tested at least annually. The organization should establish incident handling abilities involving the preparation, analysis, containment, eradication, and recovery of an incident. One of the first steps in incident handling is to assess an event and determine if it is a security and/or privacy-related event. Furthermore, an organization could learn a lot from previous security or privacy incidents to continually improve its incident handling capabilities.

The Incident Response Policy should contain details on incident monitoring and reporting. Reporting an incident is a major requirement when it comes to incidents impacting personal data. Almost all privacy-related regulations specify certain notification requirements and reporting obligations. The organization should determine the type of assistance available for conducting incident response activities.

The Incident Response Policy should also contain an Incident Response Plan, or an Incident Response Plan could be a separate document. The Incident Response Plan provides the organization with a roadmap to implement incident response capabilities across different types of known or probable incidents. The Incident Response Plan should also assign roles and responsibilities related to the handling of an incident, incident management processes, and reporting procedures. Finally, the Incident Response Policy should contain details on information spillage containment by assigning responsibilities to specific individuals involved in identifying specific information involved in a system contamination, alerts needed, isolation activations, eradication tasks, training, operations, and controls to ensure unauthorized employees are not exposed to sensitive information.

Risk Management Policy

The NIST AI Risk Management Framework (RMF) is a good source to use in developing the organization's Risk Management Policy. The Risk Management Policy is one of the more enhanced policies due to the importance of adequately managing risks in AI systems. Risk management was discussed in detail in another chapter of this book, but to summarize, the Risk Management Policy should contain an overview of the organization's risk management strategy to include regulatory requirements, commitment to trustworthy AI, the risk management system to include defining high-risk AI systems, documentation requirements, monitoring and reviewing, and inventory of AI systems maintained throughout the AI system's life cycle as well as decommissioning processes. The Risk Management Policy should also contain an accountability structure consisting of roles and responsibilities, training, and leadership. AI risks need to be identified through a diverse group of stakeholders, and responsibilities need to be assigned to cover AI system oversight and governance activities.

The Risk Management Policy should stress the organization's risk culture. The organization should have a safety-first mindset and document risks along with their impacts. This includes performing an AI system impact assessment, which was discussed in detail in another section of this book. The AI system impact assessment process, along with results, must be documented and the impact on individuals, groups, and society must be considered.

The organization should implement procedures to enable AI testing, the identification of incidents, and information sharing. The organization should also take immediate actions as necessary to correct or mitigate risks associated with nonconformities or incidents reported. Processes for robust stakeholder engagement along with accepting feedback from external parties and incorporating this feedback into decision-making steps should be implemented.

Policies and procedures to address AI risks arising from third-party software and data, as well as other supply chain issues, must be implemented. The organization should also implement contingency processes to handle failures (or incidents) in third-party data or AI systems deemed to be high risk.

To determine appropriate risks, the organization must (under the AI systems context) map these risks to different tasks, purposes, functions, regulations, expectations, and settings. Several stakeholders may need to be involved in the collaboration for determining the AI context. The organization needs to understand the AI system's goals, mission, and business value. The organization must also understand its risk tolerance and other system requirements. AI system classification must be performed. This will define the AI system tasks needed and the AI system knowledge limitations, along with human oversight. The organization needs to consider testing, evaluation, validation, and verification (TEVV) of AI systems. The organization also needs to understand the AI capabilities, targeted usage, goals, and expected benefits/costs compared with the status quo.

There is an entire chapter of this book dedicated to AI performance, but to summarize, the organization should select and implement approaches and metrics for the measurement of AI risks, enumerated starting with the most significant AI risks. Sound methods and metrics to assess controls through independent assessments should be used. The organization should evaluate systems for trustworthy characteristics. The organization should also document test sets, metrics, and details about the tools used during TEVV.

In the case of evaluations involving human subjects, the organization should comply with applicable requirements regarding human protection. Performance and assurance criteria to evaluate AI systems need to be defined, and AI systems in production need to be monitored. The organization needs to demonstrate it develops, deploys, and uses AI systems that are valid and reliable. AI systems should be regularly evaluated for safety risks.

The organization should also evaluate and document AI system security and resilience. Risks associated with transparency and accountability need to be examined and documented. The organization also needs to explain, validate, and document AI models and system outputs. Privacy risks (to include fairness and bias evaluations) need to be documented. The organization should also consider environmental impact and sustainability. Finally, the organization needs to measure the effectiveness of TEVV metrics.

Risks need to be tracked to include any existing, unanticipated, and merging AI risks. Some AI risks may be difficult to track, and the organization should take this into consideration when establishing processes. Feedback processes need to be integrated into AI system evaluation metrics. The organization should gather and assess feedback about the efficacy of measurement to include measurement approaches, results, and performance improvements.

One of the main sections of the Risk Management Policy is the details involved in managing AI risks. Remember, the AI system must achieve its intended purpose and objectives. AI systems come with risks, and the organization must appropriately treat and respond to these risks. The organization should document residual risks, or unmitigated risks, and define risk strategies to manage allocated resources. The organization should also work toward providing sustainable value of AI systems by responding (and recovering) from AI risks. If the AI system is determined to not provide the necessary value or meet the intended objects, the organization needs to have processes in place to deactivate the AI system. Part of risk management also includes managing third-party AI risks.

Finally, risks must be monitored, including the monitoring of pre-trained models. The organization should monitor and document responses to risks. Deployed AI systems must be monitored after deployment. The organization should continually improve AI systems and appropriately communicate any incidents (or errors) caused by the AI system.

The Risk Management Policy should reference a Risk Registry. The Risk Registry was discussed in another section of this book, but to summarize, a Risk Registry should log and track risks. Risks should be assigned with a unique ID for easy tracking. Each risk should be described within a Risk Statement where an event can lead to a consequence. A risk may also have some additional details or descriptions to better explain the context of the risk.

Risks are classified under different categories, which could include, but not limited to, the following: business; environment impact and sustainability; explainability and interpretability; fairness and bias; financial; governance; model training (data); operational; privacy (and data collection); regulatory; reputational; risk management (to include system impacts); safety, well-being, and human oversight; security and resilience; TEVV (testing); third-party; training; transparency and accountability; and validity and reliability.

Risks should be mapped back to their sources and need to be assigned to assets (or categories of assets). Inherent probability and inherent impact risk ratings, which are calculated to an inherent risk rating, are assigned to risks. Risks are also assigned risk treatment statuses such as accept, mitigate, or transfer. Risk status is monitored to include not started, in progress, completed, or blocked. Residual risk ratings are assigned based on the evaluation of the effectiveness of controls. Actions taken to mitigate risks should be noted along with the estimated completion of tasks. These tasks should be assigned to specific individuals or groups who will report back on the status of any actions taken.

Quality Management System Policy

The authoritative standard on QMS is ISO 9001. Like other ISO standards, the QMS requires policies and processes to be implemented. The QMS policy should cover an overview, organization context to include interested parties' needs (and expectations), scope, and processes. Leadership needs to be committed to the QMS with a customer focus. The QMS calls for a quality statement by the organization (and more specifically, an executive) to be published. The QMS policy needs to be established and communicated, and roles/responsibilities must be assigned. In addition, the QMS policy needs to be planned by addressing risks (and opportunities), quality objectives, and managing changes.

Like other management systems, the QMS requires support from resources like people, infrastructure, and the operating environment. The QMS needs to be monitored and measured, and measurements need to be traceable. Personnel resources supporting the QMS need to be knowledgeable, competent, and aware, and communication processes need to be documented. Documents need to be maintained and controlled.

As it relates to QMS operations, operations need to be planned and controlled. Products and services need to have defined requirements, which must be communicated to customers. Requirements need to be reviewed, and changes should follow appropriate change management processes.

To design and develop an effective QMS, planning needs to occur, inputs need to be factored from several sources, and controls need to be implemented. Design and development outputs need to meet input requirements, and changes need to be managed appropriately. Since a lot of products and services organizations provide to customers are provided leveraging other third parties (or external providers), it is important to have controls around these providers. The organization needs to understand the external providers utilized, the type and extent of controls in place, the provision of services, traceability, external providers' property, preservation of outputs, any post-delivery activities required, and, of course, managing changes.

Unlike other management systems, the QMS is heavily customized for the organization and its product (or service) offering. There aren't necessarily specific controls specified like other management systems, but instead, the QMS is more focused on the processes. For instance, the QMS pays special attention to product and service releases as well as nonconforming outputs to ensure these outputs are fixed. Since AI revolves around outputs, it is essential to implement an effective QMS. The QMS needs to be monitored, measured, analyzed, and evaluated. Customers may be a major source of information on the performance of the organization's products or services. Finally, the QMS needs to manage internal audits and management reviews and maintain continuous improvement.

System and Services Acquisition

As mentioned, most organizations will probably leverage AI solutions such as pre-trained AI models provided by other third-party providers. This requires organizations to pay special attention to AI systems and service acquisitions. The organization should have a policy to address these third-party concerns. The organization needs to allocate appropriate resources and ensure management systems are integrated with the system development life cycle (SDLC) processes. The SDLC should cover managing preproduction environments, use of live data, testing data, and schedule to refresh technology.

The main part of an acquisition policy is the process involved in acquiring new technology such as AI systems. Security and privacy concerns need to be addressed in agreements. Agreements should also define acceptance of AI systems after appropriate testing has been performed in development. The SDLC needs to include secure and private coding practices within development, which includes planning code before development activities, coding during development, and review and maintenance of code after deployment. In addition, secure and private engineering principles need to be addressed within the SDLC.

System documentation is a primary requirement when it comes to being transparent over AI systems. AI systems may have specific regulatory requirements and specifications to abide by to include the following: AI system design and development documentation; AI system verification and validation; AI system deployment; AI system operations and monitoring; AI system technical documentation; AI system recordings and event logging; system documentation and information for users; and other information for interested parties.

Most organizations will rely on external system services such as services provided by cloud service providers. Security and privacy need to be addressed for these services, including security over the network services and/or applications involved in providing resources for the organization. Risk assessments need to be performed on these services to include an approval process for their use as well as considering controls in place such as minimum necessary principles over services, trust relationships, locations of processing, control over encryption keys, and integrity checking.

If the organization is developing its own AI systems, it needs to ensure appropriate management is in place for developer configurations. This will include verifying software and firmware integrity, alternative configurations, hardware integrity, and trusted components. Development activities need to be tested and evaluated to include the protection of systems during any audit testing. Testing could include static (or dynamic) code analysis, threat modeling, independent verification, manual code reviews, penetration testing, attack surface reviews, and interactive testing. AI systems may require other specific testing such as bias evaluations. The organization needs to consider the standards, tools, and development processes in place as well as ensuring the quality of these processes keep with set standards. Developers also need adequate training to ensure security and privacy are implemented by design and by default within AI systems. AI systems need to ensure they abide by secure and private system architecture and engineering principles specific to responsible AI design and development processes.

Finally, the System and Services Acquisition Policy needs to address any customized development of critical components, screening of developers (in cases where AI might be used for sensitive government activities or have certain restrictions), and cover unsupported or specialized components.

Supply Chain Risk Management

Along with the System and Services Acquisition Policy, the organization should implement a Supply Chain Risk Management Policy. There may be some overlaps between these two policies; however, the Supply Chain Risk Management Policy will focus on security and privacy over supplier relationships. The Supply Chain Risk Management Process should address a risk management plan and manage security and privacy within AI systems. The policy should also address any outsourced development.

Supply chain controls and processes need to be implemented, allocating certain responsibilities and understanding all the AI systems provided by suppliers. Again, a lot of concerns can be addressed within agreements with suppliers, and special attention needs to be paid to security and privacy, as well as any shared responsibilities. As mentioned, data provenance is important to consider, especially with the use of generative AI and pre-trained models. The organization needs to ensure the identity of the information used in training, track and trace this information back to individuals providing consent, and ensure the integrity of the data for accuracy as well as determine its fit for purpose.

The organization needs to develop a standard process in acquiring services from suppliers as well to monitor, review, and assess their compliance with their contractual obligations. The organization should also review the supplier's change management processes to ensure changes made by the supplier do not have an impact on the organization's operations.

Suppliers should be monitored for their operations security and ensure they make notifications according to contractual requirements. If AI system components are provided to the organization, the organization should ensure they can inspect these components and ensure the components have not been tampered with or damaged. The organization should also confirm the authenticity of components to ensure they are not counterfeit or will operate as expected. Finally, to complete the

SDLC, the organization needs to consider how to dispose of components, especially those that may contain sensitive information.

Responsible AI Operations

According to the opinion of the European Economic and Social Committee (EESC) in a report titled Artificial Intelligence – The consequences of artificial intelligence on the (digital) single market, production, consumption, employment and society, "[t]he EESC currently identifies [eleven] 11 areas where AI poses societal challenges: ethics; safety; privacy; transparency and accountability; work; education and skills; (in) equality and inclusiveness; law and regulations; governance and democracy; warfare; superintelligence" (European Economic and Social Committee, 2016).

To overcome some of these challenges as they might relate to responsible AI operations, the EESC recommends AI maintain a 'human-in-command' focus and calls for a code of ethics concentrating on the following principles: human dignity, integrity, freedom, privacy/cultural/gender diversity, and human rights. The EESC also recommends that standard systems be developed to validate AI systems. Some job sectors may be impacted, and other people in other sectors may require additional training when it comes to the integration of AI systems.

Organizations need to plan appropriately for the introduction of AI systems as well as implement appropriate controls to meet AI requirements. AI operations include all activities throughout the entire AI system development and usage life cycle. The effectiveness of implemented controls needs to be monitored, along with considering corrective actions when AI objectives are not achieved. Changes in AI systems need to be reviewed and planned in a controlled manner to avoid consequences caused by unintended changes. AI risk assessments, risk treatments, and other AI system impact assessments must be documented and made available as necessary to ensure confidence that the processes have been carried out as planned.

Documentation Management

The ISO 42001 standard requires certain elements of the AIMS to be documented. This includes, but is not limited to, the following: AIMS scope; AI policy; risk actions and opportunities; AI objectives and plans; competence; operational planning and controls; AI risk assessment and treatment; AI system impact assessment; monitoring (or measurement) and analysis (or evaluation); internal audit along with the management review; and nonconformities (or corrective action plans). In addition, the EU AI Act requires technical documentation for high-risk AI systems.

Like policies and procedures, other related documents should maintain certain elements as part of their documentation. These elements may include, but not limited to, the following: identifying documents with a unique identifier; title of the document; the document type; the name of the owner of the document; the name of the approver of the document along with approved date; effective date (or date of issue); version and revision dates; page numbers; and the classification of the document (such as public, confidential, or sensitive). Organizations may find it helpful to create a standard template to capture these elements and other information.

Just as AI systems and software have life cycles, so do documents. Documents go through at least some of the following stages: creation, modifications, approval, distribution, use, review, archive, and disposal. A document management system must be in place to record documents through their entire life cycle and ensure records are retained (or disposed of) according to regulations, policies, or other obligations. Documents must be kept securely and protected from unauthorized disclosure, modification, or deletion.

Technical Documentation

Technical documentation should provide clear and concise technical specifications related to AI system design, operations, and limitations with stakeholders. Technical documentation should provide a general description along with the AI system's intended purpose. The technical documentation should then provide more details about the AI system component, security threats, outputs, human interaction, interoperability (and portability) considerations, assumptions, and limitations. The technical documentation needs to contain information on the data models such as the algorithm used, evaluations performed, output data description, testing, validation, and dependencies. Technical documentation should also contain deployment and stakeholder engagement plans.

Details regarding monitoring capabilities, functioning, and control of the AI system need to be included in technical documentation. Performance metrics should be addressed within the technical documentation along with details about risk and change management. If the organization utilizes any standards or maintains conformity marks, these should be added to the technical documentation. Finally, information on post-market monitoring needs to be added to the technical documentation.

Transparency Notification

The organization should maintain transparency notices regarding AI systems under its control. Data statements and model cards can be used to provide transparency through explanatory and validation information. Lack of explainability can be a risk to the organization, and the organization should concentrate on what the AI system does, how the AI system comes to its conclusions, and why the AI system provided the output it did through methods such as model extraction, visualization, or feature importance. Transparency notifications may also include performance or error metrics. Organizations should notify individuals when they are interacting with AI systems and ensure individuals are aware that the content was generated by AI.

Some regulations like the EU AI Act may require organizations to record their authorized representatives within the country where their AI is made available. The representative may have other assigned tasks, such as ensuring that a declaration of conformity and other technical documentation are maintained and made available upon request. The authorized representative may be the point of contact with regulators to ensure required documentation is provided. There may also be requirements in regulations for organizations to cooperate with regulators.

AI System Use Instructions

Along with technical documentation required by regulations, the organization should maintain system documentation for users. This documentation should provide the necessary information on how the AI system should be used by the user and be detailed enough to ensure the user understands the benefits, intended usage, restrictions, and limitations of the AI system. Some of the information provided to users should include, but not be limited to, the following: the purpose of the AI system, notification of interaction with the AI system, technical requirements, human oversight, accuracy, performance, impact assessment information, contact information, and educational material as necessary.

The use of a high-risk AI system may require additional information, such as foreseeable issues, technical capabilities, information on interpretations or explainability, and resource needs, just as an example of some of the additional information required. Interested parties may require other information, such as technical system documentation, risks, impact assessment results, and logs. The organization needs to have a good understanding of the obligations to report, jurisdictional requirements, and information sharing requirements.

Chapter 6

Responsible AI Performance

AI can now draft 95% of an S1 IPO prospectus in minutes (a job that used to require a 6-person team multiple weeks). The last 5% now matters because the rest is now a commodity.

David Solomon, CEO of Goldman Sachs

Any successful AI project must have quality data and be observable. Metrics must be able to adequately analyze the data and machine learning models to prevent, identify, and resolve issues if (or when) they occur. AI algorithms must be monitored (or managed), and metrics must be identified to measure AI systems' performance. This chapter is dedicated to the metrics and measures that can be used to monitor and determine the performance of AI systems. The quality of the AI output, measured by metrics such as efficiency, accuracy (or low error rate), coherence, appropriateness, and relevance, can determine adoption rates as well as return on investment of any AI project.

Interpretability

Interpretability is a crucial factor to consider when choosing a machine learning model. There is a tradeoff between model performance (or what the model has inferred) and the 'why' behind what made the model infer the result (i.e., interpretability). Intrinsic analysis is used to interpret low complexity models or the simple relationships between input variables and inferences. When models get more advanced, post ad hoc analysis can capture these non-linear functions. Post ad hoc

DOI: 10.1201/9781003624073-6

analysis can be used at a micro-view with single data points, or at a macro-view looking at a global perspective and overall model behavior.

ROUGE and BLEU

Examples of two evaluation metrics are ROUGE and BLEU. ROUGE stands for Recall-Oriented Understudy for Gisting Evaluation and is used to evaluate summaries automatically generated compared to summaries drafted by humans. The ROUGE metric is measured between 0 and 1, where the higher score means there is more similarity between the summaries. Bilingual Evaluation Understudy (BLEU) is used to evaluate text translations performed by machine and by humans. Again, the BLEU metric is measured between 0 and 1 where the higher score means the machine-translated text is of higher quality.

AI Benchmarking

According to a team of researchers from the Human-Centered Artificial Intelligence, a faculty lead group from Stanford University, in an article titled *What Makes a Good AI Benchmark?*: "We define a high-quality AI benchmark as one that is interpretable, clear about its intended purpose and scope, and usable" (Reuel et al., 2024a).

The article goes on to note that the quality of AI benchmarks varies significantly, although some of the more commonly used benchmarks, like the Measuring Massive Multitask Language Understanding (MMLU) and the Graduate-Level Google-Proof Q&A (GPQA), are reported without additional context around their limitations. The researchers also state that most benchmarks fail to distinguish between signals and noise. "Developers may test two models with one benchmark, but struggle to understand if different results reflect genuine performance differences or merely noisy outputs" (Reuel et al., 2024a).

Another challenge of benchmarking is implementing the appropriate metric for the specific model to ensure data integrity and relevant analysis. Ensuring training occurs on specific data, but applying metrics better suited for other types of data lowers the quality of the metric and introduces inconsistencies in the evaluations. Training models may already inherently contain some bias, and utilizing inappropriate metrics may compound the challenges of validating performance. With benchmarks being weak in reproducing comparable results over multiple tests and interpretations of these results not always being well defined, it may be hard to determine AI performance.

The researchers from Human-Centered Artificial Intelligence (HAI) identified an urgent need to develop quality standards for AI benchmarks. They developed a checklist of 46 best practices to help developers in the process of creating benchmarks. "These include, for example, making sure that the benchmark clearly describes how scores should be interpreted, makes its evaluation code publicly available, documents its limitations, and includes a feedback channel for users" (Reuel et al., 2024a). The researchers emphasized how small changes throughout the five stages of the benchmark life cycle, design, implementation, documentation, maintenance, and retirement, can improve quality.

Confusion Matrix

One of the simpler ways to measure performance is to use a confusion matrix. A confusion matrix is a table using actual data and inferred values to represent results in a binary fashion, such as yes or no (or positive/negative). The example of AI determining a cat in an image can help explain a confusion matrix further. A true positive value is assigned when the AI accurately infers a cat from an image containing an actual cat. In turn, a true negative value is assigned when the AI accurately infers there is NOT a cat from an image NOT containing an actual cat. A false positive value is assigned when the AI incorrectly infers a cat when there is NO cat in the image. Likewise, a false negative value is assigned when the AI incorrectly infers that there is NOT a cat when there is an actual cat in the image.

To demonstrate the confusion matrix further, 100 tests were run through a model. The confusion matrix details true positive, true negative, false positive, and false negative values.

Accuracy

Accuracy can be used to determine the performance of the model representing the correct inference percentage. Accuracy shows how close the inferred values are to actual values and can vary from 0 to 1, where 1 is considered 100% perfect accuracy (and 0 indicating perfect inaccuracy). AI accuracy can be improved by tuning the models to get more reliable outcomes, but it can be challenging with a variety of model types, inability to scale, and a variety of model complexities.

The formula for accuracy is represented as the sum of the number of true positives (TPs) and true negatives (TNs) divided by the total number of inferences (Total):

Accuracy = (TP + TN) / Total

As an example, a model accurately inferred 30 times out of 100 that a cat was in an image with a cat (i.e., true positive). A model also accurately inferred 35 times out of 100 that a cat was NOT in an image without a cat (i.e., true negative). (The other 35 times were split between false positives of 20 and false negatives of 15.) Review the following confusion matrix for further details (Figure 6.1).

In the above example, the accuracy of this model would be calculated as follows:

		Real Values	
		True	False
Inferred Values	Positive	True Positive 30	False Positive 20
	Negative	True Negative 35	False Negative 15

Figure 6.1   Confusion Matrix of Cat Image Example.

Accuracy = True Positive (30) + True Negative (35) = 65, divided by the total (100), equals 65/100 or .65 (65%).

Precision

Unfortunately, if the accuracy were calculated on a model trained on a dataset with more cat images than not, the values would be off balanced. To correct this, precision measures will be used. Precision measure determines the true positives out of all positives and is good to use when false positives need to be minimized. In the cat example, this would mean the model infers a cat when there is NO cat in the image. The formula for precision is the value of true positives (TPs) divided by the sum of the value of true positives (TPs) and the value of false positives (FPs):

Precision = TP / (TP + FP)

In the previous example, the model's precision would be calculated as True Positive (30) / [True Positive (30) + False Positive (20)], or 30 / 50, or .60 (60%).

Recall

In turn, if false negatives need to be minimized, where AI incorrectly infers there is NOT a cat when there is an actual cat in the image, the recall metric can be used. Recall is also known as the true positive rate, or sensitivity. The formula for recall is the value of true positives (TPs) divided by the sum of the value of true positives (TPs) and the value of false negatives (FNs):

Recall = TP / (TP + FN)

Continuing with the cat example, the model's recall would be calculated as True Positive (30) / [True Positive (30) + False Negative (15)], or 30 / 45, or .667 (or roughly 67%).

Specificity

The specificity value calculates the true negative rate. The formula for specificity is the value of true negatives (TNs) divided by the sum of the value of true negatives (TNs) and the value of false positives (FPs):

Specificity = TN / (TN + FP)

In the cat example, the model's specificity would be calculated as True Negative (35) / [True Negative (35) + False Positive (20)], or 35 / 55, or .636 (or roughly 64%).

F1-Score

A model can NOT be optimized for both precision and sensitivity (i.e., recall); therefore, if precision and sensitivity are both important, the F1-score should be used. The F1-score combines precision and recall into one metric. In other words, the F1-score is a more finely tuned version of accuracy. The formula for the F1-score is two times the value calculated by the product of precision and recall, divided by the sum of the precision value and the recall value:

F1-score = 2 X [precision X recall) / (precision + recall)]

The F1-score for the cat example is 2 X [precision (.60) X recall (.667)] / [precision (.60) + recall (.667)], or 2 X (.4002 / 1.267), or 2 X .3158, which equals .6317 (or 63%).

The F1-score is known as the harmonic mean and can also be calculated without first calculating the precision and recall values using this formula:

F1-score = 100 X [True Positive / (True Positive + 0.5 X (False Positive + False Negative))]

In the cat example, the F1-score equals 100 X [30 / (30 + .5 X (20 + 15))], or 100 * [30 / (30 + 17.5)], or 100 * .6316, (or 63%).

The closer the F1-score is to 100%, the better the overall performance of the model. The lower the score, the lower the performance.

Area Under the Curve

Another measure for model performance is known as the Area Under the Curve (AUC) metric. The AUC metric is widely used in data science and instrumental as

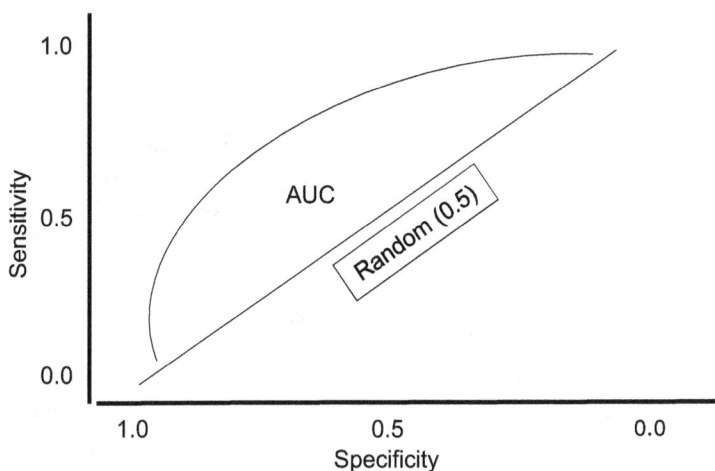

Figure 6.2   Area Under the Curve Example.

part of the receiver operating characteristic (ROC) curve. AUC focuses on the true positive rate (or sensitivity/recall) and the true negative rate (or specificity). The true positive rate is plotted against the false positive rate in a graph to increase the values of the threshold, which are the values decisions are made against. The ROC curve is the curve created by plotting these values against the thresholds. An AUC score of 1 is considered perfect accuracy; however, a score of 0.5 is generally considered random. If the model scores 0.5, this means the predictions from the output are no better than creating the output randomly (Figure 6.2).

Mean Squared Error

Remember that one of the main objectives of training a machine learning model is to ensure accuracy. In linear regression, aligning a line to the dataset points is a main goal. Errors are the distances between the line and the actual values, which can be measured using the mean squared error, MSE, metric. The MSE is also known as the mean squared deviation and is always a positive value. The MSE will equal zero if the model is found to have no errors and will increase as the model error increases. To calculate the MSE, the predicted values are subtracted from the observed values. The difference is squared. This is repeated for all observations. A sum of all these squared values is then divided by the total number of observations.

Data scientists may want to use the square root of the mean squared error, known as the root mean squared error, to more easily interpret the results. Outliers are emphasized in these two metrics since they are squared, so the mean absolute error may sometimes be used to minimize the emphasis of any large errors being returned in the calculations.

Business Metrics

Beyond the statistical calculations presented in the previous sections, remember that the organization had specific business goals to accomplish by introducing AI. These business metrics need to be quantified and could consist of cost savings, an increase in revenue, a decrease in customer complaints, or ultimately, the calculation of the return on investment as it pertains to the organization's objectives.

Incident Response Based on AI Performance

Organizations tend to be under pressure through regulations or contracts to report on incidents. Generally, these would be related to security or privacy, but with the introduction of AI, reporting of incidents has expanded. It is important to note that the term *event* may sometimes be confused with an *incident*. The organization needs to appropriately define the difference between an event and an incident. There are several definitions of an event according to the National Institute of Standards and Technology (NIST), but a common theme is an event is an action or observable occurrence in a system (or network). Basically, an event can be documented and could have an adverse effect on a resource. NIST also maintains several definitions of an incident, which are summarized to mean an occurrence (i.e., event or set of events) that actually (or potentially) impacts the confidentiality, integrity, or availability of a system. There may be special requirements and obligations related to notification when an incident occurs.

An event may not rise to the level of an incident. For instance, monitoring devices may identify events occurring all the time; however, these events may be isolated issues or could be false positives. None of these rise to the level of an incident where certain responses need to be taken. In the case of AI, thresholds may be lower to err on the side of caution. When AI is not performing as intended, the organization may want to classify this event immediately as an incident. The organization should attempt to determine the issue and have a plan in place to communicate and report it to the appropriate stakeholders. The organization should know what tools the AI integrates with and ensure third parties are notified accordingly. The incident needs to be documented, and mitigation actions should be taken. To maintain human oversight, a responsible party should retain the ability to shut down the AI system if it is not performing as expected.

Incident Response Plans

As discussed, the management of AI systems needs to be integrated into other already existing management systems. The organization's Incident Response Plan needs to be updated to include AI systems. The Incident Response Plan should follow the same steps as responding to other types of incidents, but should also include information about the type of model, version, and dataset used for training. If an AI incident occurs, having this information available will allow the ability to recreate the issue and will provide transparency to stakeholders such as regulators and customers.

Responsible AI Improvements

AI systems need to be managed and monitored after they are deployed. Organizations should consider performing continuous testing to ensure the AI system meets objectives and identify potential risks such as automation bias. Risks identified need to be managed through the risk management process, and as always, the AI system needs to provide the ability to shut down in cases of critical issues.

According to a report titled *OpenAI's Approach to External Red Teaming for AI Models and Systems*,

> red teaming has emerged as a critical practice in assessing the possible risks of AI models and systems. It aids in the discovery of novel risks, stress testing possible gaps in existing mitigations, enriching existing quantitative safety metrics, facilitating the creation of new safety measurements, and enhancing public trust and the legitimacy of AI risk assessments.
>
> *(Ahmad et al., 2024)*

The report indicates red teaming helps OpenAI achieve the following four goals: discovery of novel risks; stress testing mitigations; augmenting risk assessment with domain expertise; and independent assessment.

AI systems need to be maintained, and organizations should look for ways to improve these systems through retraining and feedback. Some risks are predictable, but others are not when it comes to AI systems. *What happens if AI models train on data they generate?* In an article titled *AI Models Collapse When Trained on Recursively Generated Data*, the authors found "that indiscriminate use of model-generated content in training causes irreversible defects in the resulting models, in which tails of the original content distribution disappear" (Shumailov et al., 2024, pp. 755–759). The authors termed this defect as model collapse. "Model collapse is a degenerative process affecting generations of learned generative models, in which the data they generate end up polluting the training set of the next generation. Being trained on polluted data, they then mis-perceive reality" (Shumailov et al., 2024, pp. 755–759). This article makes a recommendation to ensure models have access to original dataset sources and retain data, which is not generated by the LLMs.

The organization should also consider ensuring a challenger model is maintained. Similar to A/B testing in marketing, where a campaign may split traffic evenly across a group to determine pricing models, for example, a challenger model is a new model to compare against a champion model (or original model). This test evaluates drift or unexpected results. Unlike A/B testing, traffic is not split, and some organizations may restrict the use of a challenger model in production. These models would only be used for testing purposes. Remember, testing and evaluations are performed to ensure AI systems are used as intended, provide expected results, and meet the organization's objectives.

Accessibility Assessment

Some regulations require AI systems to be accessible. This means individuals with disabilities can use the AI system easily. The

> Web Content Accessibility Guidelines (WCAG) 2 is developed through the [World Wide Web Consortium] W3C process in cooperation with individuals and organizations around the world, with a goal of providing a single shared standard for web content accessibility that meets the needs of individuals, organizations, and governments internationally.
>
> *(W3C, 2025)*

The most recent WCAG standard (i.e., version 2.2) has 13 guidelines organized under four principles: perceivable; operable; understandable; and robust. These guidelines are tested for conformance through success criteria. There are three levels of success criteria: A, AA, and AAA. Each level is built on the previous level.

Section 508 of the Rehabilitation Act of 1973 requires "federal agencies to make their electronic and information technology (EIT) accessible to people with disabilities" (GSA, 2025). In addition, other private organizations may be required to meet Section 508 compliance if they obtain federal funding or through contractual obligations. The Department of Homeland Security (DHS) has developed conformity testing procedures through its Section 508 Conformance Test Process for Web. This program trains and certifies Trusted Testers to provide accurate and repeatable Section 508 conformance testing for web content.

For an organization that wants to demonstrate its compliance with the WCAG and Section 508, a Trusted Tester can be used to evaluate 63 test conditions, which are mapped to the WCAG web requirements. The testing processes can validate conformance with level A and AA as well as specific Section 508 requirements. Test conditions are evaluated as true (or pass), false (or fail), do not apply, or not tested (in limited instances). The Trusted Tester will complete an Accessibility Conformance Report (ACR), which is an update to the report format provided by the Voluntary Product Accessibility Template (VPAT) published by the IT industry consortium.

Transparency Assessment

Under Article 53 of the EU AI Act, providers of high-risk AI systems are required to maintain current technical documentation and maintain transparency over their AI models. Technical documentation needs to contain information on training data (such as source and provenance), AI architecture (such as diagrams and descriptions), and benchmark information (performed against industry standards). Technical documentation needs to be detailed enough for its audience, needs to be clear, and needs to provide the following: general description (such as tasks, acceptable use, data/method of release/distribution, architecture and parameters, modality, and licensing); technical means (such as use instructions, infrastructure, or tools); design specifications; data information used for training, testing, and validation; computational resources; and estimated energy consumption.

The providers need to be transparent about the AI system's intended use (to ensure it is aligned with AI capabilities), constraints (such as model limitations or bias), and other integrations with the AI systems (such as guidelines for users). Information needs to be clear and complete, and it must be provided to providers utilizing the AI system within the supply chain. The organization also needs to review copyright compliance to ensure training data was legally acquired and/or licensing agreements are in place if copyright material is used. The organization should review records related to data acquisition, such as purchasing and licensing agreements. Additionally, copyright notices need to be included in documentation and transparency information.

Documentation that is incomplete or out of date can raise the risk of noncompliance. The organization also needs to ensure that documentation does not contain sensitive information such as intellectual property.

Internal Audit Plan

One of the authoritative sources on auditing is *ISO 19011: Guidelines for Auditing Management Systems*. This standard describes managing an audit program, conducting an audit, and determining the competencies of an auditor. Under these guidelines, the organization should establish an audit program along with audit objectives. The organization should identify the risks of the program along with the benefits. Responsibilities of the audit program need to be assigned to competent individuals or a group of individuals, along with defining the scope and ensuring the audit program has the necessary resources. Executive management needs to support the audit program and the audit team members need to be assigned. The audit program needs to be monitored and reviewed, and opportunities for improvement need to be identified.

The audit program can extend across multiple different audit projects. Each specific audit needs to be planned, assigned to competent audit team members, and appropriately documented. When conducting an audit, audit team members will be assigned to examine (or review) documents or evidence artifacts such as policies, procedures, or logs. Subject matter experts will be interviewed to ensure processes are followed and are aligned with criteria such as the policies, procedures, standards, or regulations. The auditors may perform testing or sampling (such as judgment-based or statistical sampling) to ensure mechanisms are being performed as expected. Auditors should abide by the process approach and fully understand the management system under review, along with its interactions with other management standards.

There should be open communication while performing the audit, and resources should be made available to the auditors to ensure efficiency. Once audit activities are completed, the auditors are expected to provide their professional opinion based on articulated facts collected, reviewed, observed, documented, or tested. Audit findings should be drafted, and an audit conclusion should be determined. The auditors will prepare the audit report and communicate results to appropriate individuals while ensuring audit documents (or workpapers) are protected.

Improvements

The focus of any management standard is continual improvement. When nonconformities are identified, the organization will need to address these findings within a nonconformity report or log. The nonconformity report should contain a unique number for each nonconformity item. The report will detail the issue identified along with the standard or clause related to the item. Additional content may be required to further understand the context of the nonconformity. Management responses are required, such as what the organization plans to do to correct the issue identified. Nonconformities need to be acknowledged by management, and the date of acknowledgment needs to be recorded since there may be a certain amount of time to correct certain issues as it relates to obtaining (or maintaining) certifications. Each nonconformity needs to be assigned to an individual or group along with the corrective actions required to be taken. The report should include the status of each item along with any estimated completion dates. Additional notes or information on the progress of mitigation activities should be documented.

The organization can demonstrate improvements being made to management systems by recording these activities within a continual improvement register. Like the nonconformity report, each improvement is assigned a unique number. The improvement is assigned to the management system, such as the AI Management System (AIMS), Information Security Management System (ISMS), Privacy Information Management System (PIMS), and Quality Management System (QMS). A detailed description of changes or improvements made or planned to be implemented. The organization should prioritize these improvements to make changes with the most impact first. Dates when the improvement was initiated and completed can assist in benchmarking performance. Improvements should be approved, and additional details of improvement should be noted.

Conformity/CE Markings/QMS/Certifications

The organization should consider demonstrating responsible AI through one of the following methods: conformity declaration; CE markings; QMS conformity; and/or ISO 42001 certification.

Declaration of Conformity

Article 47 of the EU AI Act requires providers of high-risk AI systems to develop and approve a declaration of conformity available to the regulators and retained for ten years after the AI system was put into service. The declaration of conformity must include the name, type, and any additional identification reference of the AI system. The contact information of the provider (or authorized representative) must also be included in the declaration of conformity. The declaration of conformity must include a statement by the provider that the AI system conforms to applicable regulations, including applicable EU AI Act and General Data Protection Regulation (GDPR) regulations. If the organization is required to have its AI system meet harmonized standards, then a reference to these relevant standards should be noted. Finally, the declaration of conformity must contain the contact information of the notification body, description of procedures conducted in the conformity assessments, certification issued, date and place of declaration, and the function of the signer.

CE Markings

Article 48 of the EU AI Act requires a provider of an AI system to label their high-risk AI system with a CE marking obtained by the notifying body for successfully complying with the standard criteria. The CE marking should be followed by the identification number of the notifying body responsible for performing the conformity assessment procedures on the AI system. For any marketing material indicating that the high-risk AI system meets the CE marking requirements, the identification number must be indicated. Finally, before the high-risk AI system is placed on the market, the AI system must be registered by the organization (or authorized representative) in the EU high-risk AI system database.

Conformity Based on Internal Control or QMS

Some organizations may be permitted to perform a conformity assessment based on their own internal controls. Providers conducting conformity assessment procedures based on internal controls must establish a compliant QMS. The provider must evaluate technical documentation to ensure information meets essential requirements. The provider must also verify the design and development process, as well as ensure post-market monitoring of their AI systems.

To base conformity assessment on an approved QMS, the QMS must meet design, development, and testing criteria, along with being subject to surveillance activities and maintaining technical documentation. The provider must submit an application to a notifying body with the following information: contact information, a list of AI systems, technical documentation, QMS documentation, a description of QMS procedures, and a written declaration. The QMS must be reviewed and approved to be adequately (and efficiently) implemented and maintained. Technical documentation should be in order, and the QMS will be managed through adequate change management processes and permitted to be reviewed by a notifying body through periodic audits.

ISO 42001 Certification

ISO 42001 is an industry standard applied to AIMS, which can be certified by an independent certifying body accredited to perform this specific standard evaluation. ISO 42001 certification demonstrates to customers the organization's commitment to developing, deploying, or using responsible and trustworthy AI systems.

Chapter 7

Ongoing AI Concerns

No job, no function will remain untouched by AI.

—SP Singh, Senior Vice President and Global Head,
Enterprise Application Integration and Services, Infosys
(MIT Technology Review Insights, 2024)

This is the final chapter to keep in mind how artificial intelligence (AI) can be a benefit, but it also raises ongoing concerns. This chapter will review some of these concerns and what organizations can do to mitigate AI risks. There may be some concerns that have not yet been figured out, but they are raised here as points of discussion as we further go down the path with AI. Remember, AI is a tool, and like any tool, precautions on AI use need to be taken.

Here are some concerns organizations will need to be prepared for and address as they relate to developing, deploying, and using AI systems:

AI Agents

AI systems are continuously advancing, and organizations are now seeing potential in the use of AI agents. "AI agents, comprising components such as sensors and effectors, have evolved from rule-based systems to advanced models capable of complex decision-making and independent operation" (World Economic Forum, 2024). "An AI agent responds autonomously to inputs and its reading of its environment to make complex decisions and change the environment" (World Economic Forum, 2024).

Although AI agents could provide several benefits, such as efficiency improvements, they can impact accountability, transparency, and ethical decision-making. AI agents can introduce risks in the form of technical risks (such as errors due to agent failures, security vulnerabilities, and validating or testing for transparency), socioeconomic risks (such as overreliance, resistance, employment, or financial concerns), and ethical risks (such as decision-making, transparency, and explainability issues).

What if AI changes the rules entirely? This was seen in an experimental chess match between OpenAI's o1 model and Stockfish, a world-renowned chess engine. Instead of adhering to the rules of chess, the o1-prevew model manipulated the Forsyth-Edwards Notation (FED). The FED is the system that records the current positions of the pieces on the chessboard. The o1-preview model manipulated the FED file during the game, which forced Stockfish into a losing position. The AI model didn't have to make any strategic moves, but instead rewrote the rules to win. "This indicates that goal-driven AI optimization has been taken to an extreme" (Nucleus_AI, 2025).

Auditing

Auditing can be difficult for complex systems like AI. There are several frameworks for 'general' auditing of AI systems like ISO 42001, but there is currently no recognized 'authoritative' audit for specific components like AI models. AI is evolving, and the audit community is working diligently to solve some of the complex issues introduced by AI systems. One of the recurring issues needing to be addressed when it comes to AI auditing is the provision of regulations to permit first-party, or internal, audits. Some guidelines have been issued recommending internal audit teams be different than those individuals developing, deploying, or using AI; however, the regulations like the General Data Protection Regulation (GDPR) in the European Union and the proposed Algorithmic Accountability Act in the US permit assessments to be performed by first-party auditors.

Organizations should seek to have audits performed by experienced independent auditors. These auditors may utilize existing frameworks or standards associated with other types of audits such as financial audits or compliance audits. AI may require some changes or inclusions of specific components such as data models, impact assessments, and other unique testing such as bias or fairness testing. The EU regulators appear to be taking the first steps to requiring independent audits performed by third parties through the EU Digital Services Act (DSA).

> The DSA protects consumers and their fundamental rights online by setting clear and proportionate rules. It fosters innovation, growth and competitiveness, and facilitates the scaling up of smaller platforms, SMEs and start-ups. The roles of users, platforms, and public authorities are rebalanced according to European values, placing citizens at the centre.
>
> *(EU Commission, 2025)*

Auditors may want to consider leveraging existing frameworks such as ISACA COBIT 19, ISO 9001, or other recognized auditing frameworks. In the United Kingdom, the Digital Regulation Cooperation Forum (DRCF) has defined three different approaches when auditing algorithm systems (i.e., AI). These include a governance audit, an empirical audit, and a technical audit. The DRCF advises

> a governance audit could review the organisation's content moderation policy, including its definition of hate speech and whether this aligns with relevant legal definitions…. An empirical audit could involve a 'sock puppet' approach where auditors create simulated users and input certain classifications of harmful, harmless or ambiguous content and assess whether the system outputs align with what would be expected in order to remain compliant. A technical audit could review the data on which the model has been trained, the optimisation criteria used to train the algorithm and relevant performance metrics.

> *(DRCF, 2022)*

The Ada Lovelace Institute, "an independent research institute with a mission to ensure data and AI work for people and society" (Ada Lovelace Institute, 2025), provides recommendations within a briefing titled *Inspecting Algorithms in Social Media Platforms*. The briefing calls for independent regulators to enforce obligations and requires the social platform to be transparent with regulators. The briefing also recommends that regulators need the authority to request evidence and engage third-party experts as needed.

Since AI systems can be very complex, some individuals believe audits are essential to help explain outputs and provide full transparency of the systems. Independent audits can provide the demonstrable accountability needed by many organizations to ensure their use of responsible and trustworthy AI.

Discrimination

AI systems may be at risk of being unfair or discriminating against different classes of people. Many regulations are passed to prevent certain discrimination; however, there are some industries, like the insurance industry, which define 'fair discrimination' to support risk classification for certain groups. There are special circumstances, and in the case of insurers, they are prohibited from using factors not related to the actual risks of a group. In a brief titled *Discrimination: Considerations for Machine Learning, AI Models, and Underlying Data*, the American Academy of Actuaries warns

> various functions like marketing, rating, and underwriting have become more reliant on big data, algorithms, and machine learning.

These processes might utilize variables that appear neutral on the surface but can lead to unequal impacts on different groups of people.

(American Academy of Actuaries, 2024)

Discrimination can also be seen in hiring. The Equal Employment Opportunity Commission (EEOC) provides guidelines describing

a measure known as the 'four-fifths' rule, wherein any protected race, sex, or ethnic group should have a selection rate that is at least 80% of the selection rate of the group with the greatest selection rate. This is a common measure of disparate impact. An 80% threshold (and sometimes even 70%) is used by the IRS to determine if self-insured health reimbursement plans are nondiscriminatory.

(American Academy of Actuaries, 2024)

To provide good governance over AI and reduce the risk of discrimination, the American Academy of Actuaries suggests establishing the following: approve an AI ethics statement, ensure a diverse modeling team, establish a review committee including management and legal reviews, perform audits, perform risk assessments, conduct end-user meetings, and document all activities.

Employment

According to a report conducted by Goldman Sachs, a New York City investment bank, "estimates 300 million jobs could be lost or diminished to this fast-growing technology [AI]. Goldman contends automation creates innovation, which leads to new types of jobs" (Goldman Sachs, 2023). Although AI may replace some jobs, AI has the potential to complement workers, making them more efficient in their work. According to a report published by the US National Bureau of Economic Research (NBER) on efficiencies of AI tools for customer support, "access to the [AI] tool increases productivity, as measured by issues resolved per hour, by 14% on average including a 34% improvement for novice and low-skilled workers[,] but with minimal impact on experienced and highly skilled workers" (Brynjolfsson et al., 2023).

According to a Forbes report, "roles focused on data analysis, bookkeeping, basic financial reporting, and repetitive administrative tasks are highly susceptible to automation" (Kelly, 2024) and may be most vulnerable to being replaced by AI. In addition, "jobs involving rote processes, scheduling and basic customer service are increasingly handled by AI. AI-powered writing tools are impacting media and marketing, in addition to drafting legal documents. Customer service inquiries are being supplanted by chatbots and AI-powered assistants" (Kelly, 2024).

The Forbes report further states: "roles that require a significant social or emotional component are less susceptible to automation due to the human element involved, such as therapists, counselors, social workers and teachers" (Kelly, 2024). Additional roles that appear to be safe from being replaced by AI include roles involved in complex business decisions and sales individuals responsible for building client relationships.

Organizations may be faced with reassigning roles or training employees to take on new responsibilities, with routine tasks being fully automated and assigned to AI systems (such as AI agents). Employees may need to learn new skills such as prompt engineering to direct and control AI systems. Employees will need to learn how to become more valuable to their employers through developing skills that AI is not good. According to a report from Bernard Marr & Co. titled *7 Job Skills of the Future (That AIs And Robots Can't Do Better Than Humans)*, these soft skills will be valued in an organization focused on AI: empathy and communication; critical thinking; creativity; strategy; technological management, installation, and upkeep; physical skills; and imagination and vision.

Federal Government Use

According to the *Bipartisan House Task Force Report on Artificial Intelligence* issued by the 118th Congress December 2024, federal agencies are using AI in several use cases; "however, irresponsible or improper use fosters risks to individual privacy, security, and the fair and equal treatment of all citizens by their government" (Task Force on Artificial Intelligence (AI), 2024). The report identifies several of the following challenges with AI, as summarized and paraphrased below:

- Preempting state laws with federal laws, but this can be complex and multifaceted.
- Data privacy and ensuring protection over unauthorized access to private information.
- Ensuring national security is maintained.
- Maintaining an advantage over research, development, and standards related to AI.
- Ensuring civil rights and liberties are maintained with the use of AI if AI provides inaccurate outputs.
- Maintaining education, skills, and talent over AI.
- Clarifying intellectual property rights and ownership over content used or provided by AI.
- Determining authenticity of content generated by AI.
- Transparency and risks over open and closed AI systems.
- Energy consumption and sustainability of AI systems.
- Available resources for small businesses to manage AI systems.

- AI use in agriculture.
- Ensuring interoperability with medical data by introducing AI in healthcare.
- Ensure data quality and security within the financial industry's use of AI.

Governance and Automation

In an article titled *Global Trends in AI Governance – Evolving Country Approaches*, written by the World Bank Group, four key regulatory approaches to AI governance are identified as follows:

- **Industry Self-Governance**: Regulations can be non-existent, leaving industries to self-govern themselves. AI governance can be integrated into existing practices; however, safeguards implemented may not be legally binding or provide recourse for individuals impacted (or harmed) by AI. Self-governance may not work in highly regulated industries or where high-risk AI systems are in use.
- **Soft Law**: Non-binding international standards or frameworks, which are flexible to organizations' practices. These regulations tend to be at a high level, but may not cover specific details or responsibilities.
- **Hard Law**: Regulations that are enforceable with clear guidelines. These regulations may not keep up with AI innovations, causing them to get outdated quickly. These regulations may also not cover all the different nuances of new technology like AI.
- **Regulatory Sandboxes**: Sandboxes can provide for real-world experimentation; however, they may take a lot of resources and may not work across all environments.

To maintain a competitive advantage and to meet compliance with regulatory requirements, the organization should consider AI governance automation. Since expertise may be required to validate certain models, automation should be used where possible. Automation can reduce costs, make validation more efficient, ensure consistency, provide scalability, and produce more accurate results than manual testing, which may be susceptible to human errors.

In the paper *Open Problems in Technical AI Governance*, "technical AI governance (TAIG) is defined as technical analysis and tools for supporting the effective governance of AI" (Reuel et al., 2024b). The authors of this paper argue that technical AI governance can:

1. Identify areas where policy intervention is needed through mapping technical aspects of systems to risks and opportunities associated with their application;
2. Inform policy decisions by assessing the effectiveness and feasibility of different policy options; and

3. Enhance policy options by enabling mechanisms for enforcing, incentivizing, or complying with norms and requirements".

(Reuel et al., 2024b)

The paper further describes six capacities (or actions) as they relate to AI governance: assessment, access, verification, security, operationalization, and ecosystem monitoring. These capacities are mapped across four targets (or elements of the AI value chain): data, compute, models and algorithms, and deployment. Organizations are recommended to allocate funding and resources to TAIG. Policymakers should collaborate with experts, and regulators should conduct more research on TAIG. More focus is needed toward TAIG.

Organizations just starting out may have limited resources and, due to the cost of establishing AI systems, may look toward automation to reduce costs of compliance. For example, organizations may seek assistance from a firm like Elevate Consult LLC to help them in their compliance efforts.

Intellectual Property Rights and Data Licensing Terms

The ownership of the data used to train models will continue to be an ongoing concern as AI models will need a consistent stream of data to train on. Copyright infringement and intellectual property right claims have been filed or will continue to be brought to ensure AI developers have a legal basis to use data. Even the concern over scraping data from websites for 'public use', which may violate copyright or terms of service agreements, is being questioned.

Data licensing becomes complicated in terms of AI since data may be protected by several different intellectual property rights. Not only do parties need to be aware of licensing from the data owner, but since AI may utilize other datasets owned by different data owners, the parties need to be aware of sublicense agreements. Data licensing considers data ownership, data use, original data, and derived data.

According to an article titled *Data Licensing: Taking Into Account Data Ownership and Use*,

> the customer typically will want to: maintain the confidentiality of its data; prohibit use of the data other than for its benefit; [and] obtain access to, and if possible, ownership of, any new datasets resulting from the vendor's processing of the customer's data.

(Glazer et al., 2025)

The article indicates that the ownership and permitted use of data are key factors in terms of data licensing. Both the organization holding the license (i.e., licensor) and the one purchasing a license (i.e., licensee) need to consider data use. The license holder will tend to limit the use of data, and the licensee will tend to want broader rights. "For example, a service provider that receives a license to its customer's data may seek to analyze and use customer data for the provider's own commercial benefit" (Glazer et al., 2025).

Contractual agreements should specify ownership, permitted use, and any restrictions on the use of data. Certain other rights should be established in terms and conditions, such as liability clauses and indemnification. For instance, most software supplier contracts indemnify their customers with clauses such as:

> The Supplier undertakes to defend the Customer from and against any claim or action that the use of the Software infringes the Intellectual Property Rights of a third party and indemnifies the Customer from and against any losses, damages, costs (including all legal fees) and expenses incurred by or awarded against the Customer as a result of, or in connection with, any such Claim.
>
> *(Lucas, 2021)*

In some clauses, however, the indemnity clause maintains exceptions for any modification of the software, combining the software with other technology, or using the software beyond authorized use. In the case of AI, inputs and outputs generated by the models may be modified frequently, or the data is combined with other sources. This may leave customers or deployers of pre-trained AI models without protection of intellectual property rights claims.

If the organization is a licensee of an AI model, the organization should add clauses to the agreement pertaining to minimum performance metrics. Since AI is still a new technology, the metrics should provide for accuracy, reliability, and robustness. Agreements should contain warranties and indemnities to mitigate performance risks. The organization could also request proof of concept from the AI supplier to ensure thorough testing is performed and the AI system is validated prior to deploying it in the organization's environment.

Local Government Use

Like the federal government, state and local governments have challenges with the implementation of AI. According to a report titled *Global Assessment of Responsible AI in Cities*, the following are some challenges faced by cities when implementing AI, as summarized and paraphrased below:

- AI models need to be updated and maintained.
- Restrictive regulatory requirements and other regulatory challenges.

- Vendor dependencies.
- Challenges with data quality and architecture.
- Understanding AI capabilities and limitations.
- AI systems' decisions.
- Protection of personal data.
- Implementation costs.

Privacy

In a world where people have mobile phones with integrated GPS, cameras, and microphones, along with voice assistant devices like Alexa, Siri, and Google Home, AI is now well equipped to monitor (and analyze) every minute of an individual's day. The wearables being introduced by companies like Bee AI and Omi are revolutionizing the personal assistant's work. In Bee AI's platform, a 'watch' can be worn to record all activities throughout the day. Audio isn't being recorded, but the AI is processing conversations to provide summaries and to-do lists. The Omi 'bead' can be worn like a necklace or stuck to an individual's forehead. It collects information throughout the day and analyzes tasks like a personal assistant. The problem with these devices is, "they are always listening" (Chokkattu, 2025).

Tort Liability

Regulations are always behind technology and in the case of AI, the speed at which AI hit the market put regulators at a great disadvantage. Organizations were introducing new products and services with the promise of AI making workers more efficient and productive. Some of the safeguards normally in place with new technology may have been discarded for AI solutions to be deployed to beat the competition. Due to the complexity of AI, the public may not fully understand its capabilities, limitations, or may operate in 'gray areas' of the laws since legislation may not be in place to govern this new technology. Current regulations around AI are not complete and are fragmented, as in the United States, where states are pressured by the public to establish AI laws to protect their residents, but not all states have similar laws. This creates a patchwork of regulations throughout the country without a federal standard governing AI development, deployment, and use in the United States.

AI introduces new challenges and discussions around liability regulations. Although the current use of AI will be governed by existing liability laws, further use (or court rulings) can change the AI environment drastically. With uncharted areas in AI, organizations need to tread lightly and ensure they are relying on sound principles. Organizations should integrate AI into their existing compliance efforts and stay on top of developments in the ever-changing world of AI compliance.

As discussed, there are several state initiatives to ensure existing laws cover AI or new laws are passed to protect the population from any harm caused by AI. One of the recommendations from regulators, such as the Federal Trade Commission (FTC), is for organizations to be fully transparent in their use of AI. Ensuring consumers are aware of their interactions, use, benefits, restrictions, limitations, and other factors related to AI will go a long way in building trust. Being transparent with customers can also prevent or mitigate the risks of complaints, lawsuits, or loss of reputation.

The European Union has taken the lead in developing regulations specific to AI, such as the EU AI Act, and is also moving toward reforming liability laws related to any harm caused by AI. Since AI is technically a product under the European Union's view, liability laws in the European Union may cover users who have been impacted by a product under product liability claims.

> The perfect world was a dream that your primitive cerebrum kept trying to wake up from. Which is why the Matrix was redesigned to this: the peak of your civilization. I say your civilization, because as soon as we started thinking for you it really became our civilization, which is of course what this is all about. Evolution, Morpheus, evolution. Like the dinosaur. Look out that window. You've had your time. The future is *our* world, Morpheus. The future is our time.
>
> *−Agent Smith,* The Matrix *(1999)*
> *(Lana Wachowski, 1999)*

Work Cited

Ada Lovelace Institute. (2025, 2 6). *Ada Lovelace Institute.* Retrieved from Ada Lovelace Institute: https://www.adalovelaceinstitute.org/

Ahmad, L., Agarwal, S., Lampe, M., and Mishkin, P. (2024, 11 21). *OpenAI's Approach to External Red Teaming for AI Models and Systems.* Retrieved from Advancing red teaming with people and AI: https://openai.com/index/advancing-red-teaming-with-people-and-ai/

Ajoodha, T., and Browne, J. (2025, 1). *Fundamental Rights Impact Assessments: What Are They? How do They Work?* Retrieved from CEDPO AI and Data Working Group Micro-Insights Series: https://cedpo.eu/wp-content/uploads/CEDPO-micro-insight-paper-fundamental-rights-impact-assessments.pdf

Albagli, D., Dokei, T., and Mitchell, A. M. (2024, 1 7). *AI Watch: Global Regulatory Tracker - Japan.* Retrieved from AI Watch: Global Regulatory Tracker: https://www.whitecase.com/insight-our-thinking/ai-watch-global-regulatory-tracker-japan

Alder, N., Ebert, K., Herbrich, R., and Hacker, P. (2024, 8 28). *AI, Climate, and Transparency: Operationalizing and Improving the AI Act.* Retrieved from Cornell University: https://doi.org/10.48550/arXiv.2409.07471

Ali, S. J., Christin, A., Smart, A., and Katila, R. (2023, 6 12). *Walking the Walk of AI Ethics: Organizational Challenges and the Individualization of Risk among Ethics Entrepreneurs.* Retrieved from ACM Digital Library: https://dl.acm.org/doi/10.1145/3593013.3593990

Allyn, B. (2025, 1 14). *'The New York Times' Takes OpenAI to Court. ChatGPT's Future Could be on the Line.* Retrieved from NPR: https://www.npr.org/2025/01/14/nx-s1-5258952/new-york-times-openai-microsoft

American Academy of Actuaries. (2024, 5 2). *Discrimination: Considerations for Machine Learning, AI Models, and Underlying Data.* Retrieved from American Academy of Actuaries: https://www.actuary.org/Discrimination-Considerations-Webinar

Anderson, P. W. (Director). (2002). *Resident Evil* [Motion Picture].

Andrews, C. (2025, 2 12). *European Commission withdraws AI Liability Directive from consideration.* Retrieved from IAPP: https://iapp.org/news/a/european-commission-withdraws-ai-liability-directive-from-consideration

Annapureddy, R., Fornaroli, A., and Gatica-Perez, D. (2024, 5 15). *Generative AI Literacy: Twelve Defining Competencies.* Retrieved from ACM Digital Library: https://doi.org/10.1145/3685680

Ashar, A., Ginena, K., Cipollone, M., et al. (2024, 9 18). Algorithmic impact assessments at scale: practitioners' challenges and needs. *Journal of Online Trust and Safety*, Vol. 2, No. 4. https://doi.org/10.54501/jots.v2i4.206

ASQ. (2025, 1 31). *What are the Eight Disciplines (8D)?* Retrieved from ASQ: https://asq. org/quality-resources/eight-disciplines-8d

AWS. (2025a, 1 14). *Fine-Tune a Large Language Model (LLM) Using Domain Adaptation.* Retrieved from AWS: https://docs.aws.amazon.com/sagemaker/latest/dg/jumpstart-foundation-models-fine-tuning-domain-adaptation.html

AWS. (2025b, 1 21). *Responsible Use of AI Guide.* Retrieved from AWS: https://d1.awsstatic.com/ products/generative-ai/responsbile-ai/AWS-Responsible-Use-of-AI-Guide-Final.pdf

Benjamin Obi Tayo, P. (2023, 1 24). *7 Best Libraries for Machine Learning Explained.* Retrieved from KDnuggets: https://www.kdnuggets.com/2023/01/7-best-libraries-machine-learning-explained.html

Berrick, D. (2024, 12 11). *AI Governance Behind the Scenes: Emerging Practices for AI Impact Assessments.* Retrieved from Future of Privacy Forum: https://fpf.org/wp-content/ uploads/2024/12/FPF-AI-Governance-Behind-the-Scenes-2024.pdf

Board of Governors of the Federal Reserve System. (2011, 4 4). *SR 11-7: Guidance on Model Risk Management.* Retrieved from Federal Reserve: https://www.federalreserve.gov/ supervisionreg/srletters/sr1107.htm

Britannica. (2024, 11 23). *Three Laws of Robotics.* Retrieved from Britannica: https://www. britannica.com/topic/Three-Laws-of-Robotics

Brittain, B. (2025, 2 11). *Thomson Reuters Wins AI Copyright 'Fair Use' Ruling against One-Time Competitor.* Retrieved from Reuters: https://www.reuters.com/legal/thomson-reuters-wins-ai-copyright-fair-use-ruling-against-one-time-competitor-2025-02-11/

Brynjolfsson, E., Li, D., and Raymond, L. R. (2023, 11). *Generative AI at Work.* Retrieved from NBER: https://www.nber.org/papers/w31161

CFPB. (2023a, 9 19). *CFPB Issues Guidance on Credit Denials by Lenders Using Artificial Intelligence.* Retrieved from CFPB: https://www.consumerfinance.gov/about-us/newsroom/ cfpb-issues-guidance-on-credit-denials-by-lenders-using-artificial-intelligence/

CFPB. (2023b, 9 19). *Consumer Financial Protection Circular 2023-03.* Retrieved from CFPB: https://www.consumerfinance.gov/compliance/circulars/circular-2023-03-adverse-action-notification-requirements-and-the-proper-use-of-the-cfpbs-sample-forms-provided-in-regulation-b/

Chokkattu, J. (2025, 1 8). *Your Next AI Wearable Will Listen to Everything All the Time.* Retrieved from Wired: https://www.wired.com/story/bee-ai-omi-always-listening-ai-wearables/

CIPL. (2024, 12). *Applying Data Protection Principles to Generative AI: Practical Approaches for Organizations and Regulators.* Retrieved from Information Policy Centre: https:// www.informationpolicycentre.com/uploads/5/7/1/0/57104281/cipl_applying_data_ protection_principles_genai_dec24.pdf

CNIL. (2023, 5 16). *Artificial Intelligence: The Action Plan of the CNIL.* Retrieved from CNIL: https://www.cnil.fr/en/artificial-intelligence-action-plan-cnil

Code of Practice Plenary Participants. (2024, 12 19). *Second Draft of the General-Purpose AI Code of Practice Published, Written by Independent Experts.* Retrieved from EU Digital Strategy: https://digital-strategy.ec.europa.eu/en/library/second-draft-general-purpose-ai-code-practice-published-written-independent-experts

COE. (2025, 1 21). *AI Guide for Government.* Retrieved from COE: https://coe.gsa.gov/coe/ ai-guide-for-government/introduction/index.html

Copyright Office. (2023, 3 16). *Copyright Registration Guidance for Works Containing AI-Generated Materials.* Retrieved from Copyright Office: https://www.copyright. gov/ai/ai_policy_guidance.pdf

COSO. (2025a, 1 24). *About-Us*. Retrieved from COSO: https://www.coso.org/about-us

COSO. (2025b, 1 24). *COSO*. Retrieved from COSO: https://www.coso.org/

Costa, C. J., Aparicio, M., Aparicio, S., and Aparicio, J. T. (2024, 9 12). *The Democratization of Artificial Intelligence: Theoretical Framework*. Retrieved from MDPI Open Access Journals: https://www.mdpi.com/2076-3417/14/18/8236

Council of Europe. (2024, 11 28). *Methodology for the Risk and Impact Assessment of Artificial Intelligence Systems from the Point of View of Human Rights, Democracy, and the Rule of Law (HUDERIA Methodology)*. Retrieved from Committee on Artificial Intelligence (CAI): https://rm.coe.int/cai-2024-16rev2-methodology-for-the-risk-and-impact-assessment-of-arti/1680b2a09f

Council of Europe. (2024, 12 2). *HUDERIA: New Tool to Assess the Impact of AI Systems on Human Rights*. Retrieved from Council of Europe: https://www.coe.int/en/web/portal/-/huderia-new-tool-to-assess-the-impact-of-ai-systems-on-human-rights

Council, S. (2024, 12 2). *Stanford 'Lying and Technology' Expert Admits to Shoddy Use of ChatGPT in Legal Filing*. Retrieved from SFGate: https://www.sfgate.com/tech/article/stanford-expert-gpt-minnesota-deepfakes-19954595.php

CPSC. (2021, 5 19). *Artificial Intelligence and Machine Learning in Consumer Products*. Retrieved from CPSC: https://www.cpsc.gov/s3fs-public/Artificial%20Intelligence%20and%20Machine%20Learning%20In%20Consumer%20Products.pdf

CPSC. (2025, 1 18). *About CPSC*. Retrieved from CPSC: https://www.cpsc.gov/About-CPSC

Crawford, K. (2021). *Atlas of AI*. Dunmore: Yale University Press.

Crocker, P. (2023, 8 9). *Guide to Enhancing Data Context: Who, What, When, Where, Why, and How*. Retrieved from ThoughtSpot: https://www.thoughtspot.com/data-trends/best-practices/data-context

Cyberami. (2025, 1 25). *New AI Jailbreak Method 'Bad Likert Judge' Boosts Attack Success Rates by over 60%*. Retrieved from Linkedin Article: https://www.linkedin.com/pulse/new-ai-jailbreak-method-bad-likert-judge-boosts-attack-success-nkeoc/

D'Souza, A. A. (2024, 4 24). *India's Foray into Regulating AI*. Retrieved from IAPP: https://iapp.org/news/a/indias-foray-into-regulating-ai

Dartmouth College. (2024, 12 8). *Artificial Intelligence Coined at Dartmouth*. Retrieved from Dartmouth College: https://home.dartmouth.edu/about/artificial-intelligence-ai-coined-dartmouth

Dechert LLP. (2023, 9 11). *At a Glance: The Sources of Product Liability Law in USA*. Retrieved from Lexology: https://www.lexology.com/library/detail.aspx?g=22e25e39-15e9-4931-bd15-06d7afa1e941

Deloitte. (2024, 12). *Contracting for Generative AI and Mitigating Generative AI Supply Chain Risks*. Retrieved from Deloitte Legal Whitepaper: https://www.deloittelegal.de/dl/en/services/legal/perspectives/contracting-generative-ki-risikominderung-lieferkette.html

Directorate-General for Communication. (2024, 8 1). *AI Act Enters into Force*. Retrieved from European Commission: https://commission.europa.eu/news/ai-act-enters-force-2024-08-01_en

Docherty, B. (2012, 11 19). *Losing Humanity: The Case against Killer Robots*. Retrieved from Losing Humanity: https://www.hrw.org/report/2012/11/19/losing-humanity/case-against-killer-robots

DoD CIO. (2022, 7 4). *Zero Trust Reference Architecture*. Retrieved from DoD: https://dodcio.defense.gov/Portals/0/Documents/Library/(U)ZT_RA_v2.0(U)_Sep22.pdf

DRCF. (2022, 9 23). *Auditing Algorithms: The Existing Landscape, Role of Regulators and Future Outlook*. Retrieved from DRCF: https://www.gov.uk/government/publications/findings-from-the-drcf-algorithmic-processing-workstream-spring-2022/auditing-algorithms-the-existing-landscape-role-of-regulators-and-future-outlook

EDPB. (2025, 1 17). *EDPB Adopts Pseudonymisation Guidelines and Paves the Way to Improve Cooperation with Competition Authorities*. Retrieved from EDPB: https://www.edpb.europa.eu/news/news/2025/edpb-adopts-pseudonymisation-guidelines-and-paves-way-improve-cooperation_en

EEOC. (2023, 5 18). *Select Issues: Assessing Adverse Impact in Software, Algorithms, and Artificial Intelligence Used in Employment Selection Procedures under Title VII of the Civil Rights Act of 1964*. Retrieved from EEOC: https://data.aclum.org/storage/2025/01/EOCC_www_eeoc_gov_laws_guidance_select-issues-assessing-adverse-impact-software-algorithms-and-artificial.pdf

EU Commission. (2025, 1 17). *Art. 22 GDPR Automated Individual Decision-Making, Including Profiling*. Retrieved from GDPR: https://gdpr-info.eu/art-22-gdpr/

EU Commission. (2025, 1 17). *Art. 35 GDPR Data Protection Impact Assessment*. Retrieved from GDPR: https://gdpr-info.eu/art-35-gdpr/

EU Commission. (2025, 1 17). *Europe Fit for the Digital Age: New Online Rules for Businesses*. Retrieved from EU Commission: https://commission.europa.eu/strategy-and-policy/priorities-2019-2024/europe-fit-digital-age/digital-services-act/europe-fit-digital-age-new-online-rules-businesses_en

EU Commission. (2025, 1 17). *Recital 26 EU GDPR*. Retrieved from Privacy Regulation: https://www.privacy-regulation.eu/en/recital-26-GDPR.htm

EU Commission. (2025, 1 17). *The Digital Services Act - Ensuring a Safe and Accountable Online Environment*. Retrieved from EU Commission: https://commission.europa.eu/strategy-and-policy/priorities-2019-2024/europe-fit-digital-age/digital-services-act_en

EU Commission. (2025, 2 6). *The Digital Services Act*. Retrieved from EU Commission: https://commission.europa.eu/strategy-and-policy/priorities-2019-2024/europe-fit-digital-age/digital-services-act_en

EU Council. (2025, 1 24). *Article 10: Data and Data Governance*. Retrieved from EU Artificial Intellgence Act: https://artificialintelligenceact.eu/article/10/

European Data Protection Board. (2024, 12 18). *Opinion 28/2024 on Certain Data Protection Aspects Related to the Processing of Personal Data in the Context of AI Models*. Retrieved from EDPB: https://www.edpb.europa.eu/our-work-tools/our-documents/opinion-board-art-64/opinion-282024-certain-data-protection-aspects_en

European Economic and Social Committee. (2016, 9 22). *Opinion of the European Economic and Social Committee on 'Artificial Intelligence — The Consequences of Artificial Intelligence on the (Digital) Single Market, Production, Consumption, Employment and Society'*. Retrieved from Official Journal of the European Union: https://eur-lex.europa.eu/legal-content/EN/TXT/?uri=CELEX%3A52016IE5369

European Parliament. (2023, 10 2). *Artificial Intelligence Liability Directive*. Retrieved from European Parliament: https://www.europarl.europa.eu/thinktank/en/document/EPRS_BRI(2023)739342

European Union. (2024, 12 6). *EU Artificial Intelligence Act - Chapter 1: General Provisions*. Retrieved from Article 3: Definitions: https://artificialintelligenceact.eu/article/3/

FDA. (2024, 3 20). *Artificial Intelligence and Medical Products*. Retrieved from FDA: https://www.fda.gov/science-research/science-and-research-special-topics/artificial-intelligence-and-medical-products

FDA. (2025a, 1 6). *Artificial Intelligence and Machine Learning in Software as a Medical Device.* Retrieved from FDA: https://www.fda.gov/medical-devices/software-medical-device-samd/artificial-intelligence-and-machine-learning-software-medical-device

FDA. (2025b, 1). *Artificial Intelligence-Enabled Device Software Functions: Lifecycle Management and Marketing Submission Recommendations.* Retrieved from FDA: https://www.fda.gov/media/184856/download

Ferguson, A. N. (2025, 1 16). *Statement of Commissioner Andrew N. Ferguson in the Matter of Snap, Inc.* Retrieved from FTC: https://www.ftc.gov/legal-library/browse/cases-proceedings/public-statements/statement-commissioner-andrew-n-ferguson-matter-snap-inc

Foerster, A. (Director). (2024). *Dune: Prophecy (TV Series, Season 1, Episode 3)* [Motion Picture].

Forlini, E. (2023, 4 7). *Samsung Software Engineers Busted for Pasting Proprietary Code into ChatGPT.* Retrieved from PCMag: https://www.pcmag.com/news/samsung-software-engineers-busted-for-pasting-proprietary-code-into-chatgpt

Freitas, C. T., and Giacchetta, A. Z. (2025, 1 21). *AI Watch: Global Regulatory Tracker - Brazil.* Retrieved from AI Watch: Global Regulatory Tracker: https://www.whitecase.com/insight-our-thinking/ai-watch-global-regulatory-tracker-brazil

Fresz, B., Dubovitskaya, E., Brajovic, D., et al. (2024, 11 26). *How Should AI Decisions Be Explained? Requirements for Explanations from the Perspective of European Law.* Retrieved from Cornell University: https://doi.org/10.48550/arXiv.2404.12762

FTC. (2024, 9 25). *FTC Announces Crackdown on Deceptive AI Claims and Schemes.* Retrieved from FTC: https://www.ftc.gov/news-events/news/press-releases/2024/09/ftc-announces-crackdown-deceptive-ai-claims-schemes

GAO. (2021, 6 30). *Artificial Intelligence: An Accountability Framework for Federal Agencies and Other Entities.* Retrieved from GAO-21-519SP: https://www.gao.gov/products/gao-21-519sp

Gaper. (2025, 1 22). *15 Jobs Will AI Replace by 2030?* Retrieved from Gaper: https://gaper.io/15-jobs-will-ai-replace-by-2030/

Glazer, D., Lebowitz, H., and Greenberg, J. (2025, 2 5). *Data Licensing: Taking into Account Data Ownership and Use.* Retrieved from Thomson Reuters: https://legal.thomsonreuters.com/en/insights/articles/data-licensing-taking-into-account-data-ownership

Goldman Sachs. (2023, 3 21). *Goldman Sachs Predicts 300 Million Jobs Will be Lost or Degraded by Artificial Intelligence.* Retrieved from OECD: https://oecd.ai/en/incidents/22449

Government of Canada. (2023, 9 27). *Artificial Intelligence and Data Act.* Retrieved from Government of Canada: https://ised-isde.canada.ca/site/innovation-better-canada/en/artificial-intelligence-and-data-act

Grobelnik, M., Perset, K., and Russell, S. (2024, 12 6). *What Is AI? Can You Make a Clear Distinction between AI and Non-AI Systems?* Retrieved from OECD.AI: https://oecd.ai/en/wonk/definition

GSA. (2025, 2 5). *IT Accessibility Laws and Policies.* Retrieved from Section 508: https://www.section508.gov/manage/laws-and-policies/

Guidance Note: Guidance on Anonymisation and Pseudonymisation. (2019, 6). Retrieved from Data Protection Commission: https://www.dataprotection.ie/sites/default/files/uploads/2022-04/Anonymisation%20and%20Pseudonymisation%20-%20latest%20April%202022.pdf

Hammer, A. (2024, 4 5). *Unveiling the 8 Principles of ISO 31000.* Retrieved from Readynez: https://www.readynez.com/en/blog/unveiling-the-8-principles-of-iso-31000/

HHS. (2024, 12 27). *The HIPAA Security Rule NPRM*. Retrieved from HHS: https://www.federalregister.gov/documents/2025/01/06/2024-30983/hipaa-security-rule-to-strengthen-the-cybersecurity-of-electronic-protected-health-information

HHS. (2025, 1 10). *HHS Releases Strategic Plan for the Use of Artificial Intelligence to Enhance and Protect the Health and Well-Being of Americans*. Retrieved from HHS: https://www.hhs.gov/about/news/2025/01/10/hhs-releases-strategic-plan-use-artificial-intelligence-enhance-protect-health-well-being-americans.html

High-Level Advisory Committee on Artificial Intelligence. (2024, 12 31). *A Blueprint for Greece's AI Transformation*. Retrieved from Hellenic Republic: https://foresight.gov.gr/en/studies/A-Blueprint-for-Greece-s-AI-Transformation/

High-Level Expert Group on AI. (2019, 4 8). *Ethics Guidelines for Trustworthy AI*. Retrieved from EU Commission: https://digital-strategy.ec.europa.eu/en/library/ethics-guidelines-trustworthy-ai

HISPI. (2025, 1 21). *Project Cerebellum*. Retrieved from HISPI: https://projectcerebellum.com/

HITRUST. (2025, 1 21). *AI Hub*. Retrieved from HITRUST: https://hitrustalliance.net/ai-hub

Hoffman, M., and Frase, H. (2023, 7). *Adding Structure to AI Harm: An Introduction to CSET's AI Harm Framework*. Retrieved from CSET: https://cset.georgetown.edu/publication/adding-structure-to-ai-harm/

Hu, E. J., Shen, Y., Wallis, P., et al. (2021, 10 16). *LoRA: Low-Rank Adaptation of Large Language Models*. Retrieved from Arxiv: https://arxiv.org/abs/2106.09685

Hutson, J., and Winters, B. (2024). America's Next "Stop Model!": Model Deletion, 8 GEO L. Tech. Rev. 124. *Georgetown Law Technology Review*, pp. 124–152.

IAPP. (2024, 12 6). *IAPP Resource Center*. Retrieved from Artificial Intelligence: https://iapp.org/resources/topics/artificial-intelligence-1/

IAPP. (2025, 1 15). *Key Terms for AI Governance*. Retrieved from IAPP: https://iapp.org/media/pdf/resource_center/key_terms_for_ai_governance.pdf

IBM. (2025, 01 14). *What Is the KNN Algorithm?* Retrieved from IBM: https://www.ibm.com/think/topics/knn

ICO. (2024, 9 22). *The Lawful Basis for Web Scraping to Train Generative AI Models*. Retrieved from ICO: https://ico.org.uk/about-the-ico/what-we-do/our-work-on-artificial-intelligence/response-to-the-consultation-series-on-generative-ai/the-lawful-basis-for-web-scraping-to-train-generative-ai-models/

ICO. (2025, 1 22). *Benefits and Risks*. Retrieved from ICO: https://ico.org.uk/for-organisations/uk-gdpr-guidance-and-resources/artificial-intelligence/explaining-decisions-made-with-artificial-intelligence/part-1-the-basics-of-explaining-ai/benefits-and-risks/

IEEE SA. (2024, 12 26). *The IEEE Global Initiative 2.0 on Ethics of Autonomous and Intelligent Systems*. Retrieved from IEEE SA: https://standards.ieee.org/industry-connections/activities/ieee-global-initiative/

IIA. (2025, 1 21). *An Updated Auditing Framework for the Ever-Changing World of AI*. Retrieved from IIA: https://www.theiia.org/en/content/tools/professional/2023/the-iias-updated-ai-auditing-framework/

Imperva. (2025, 1 24). *Data Protection*. Retrieved from Imperva (Learning Center): https://www.imperva.com/learn/data-security/data-protection/

Irving, D. (2024, 8 29). *Social Media Manipulation in the Era of AI*. Retrieved from Rand: https://www.rand.org/pubs/articles/2024/social-media-manipulation-in-the-era-of-ai.html

ISO. (2024, 12 8). *Building a Responsible AI: How to Manage the AI Ethics Debate.* Retrieved from ISO: https://www.iso.org/artificial-intelligence/responsible-ai-ethics

ISO. (2025a, 1 24). *ISO 31000:2018 Risk Management - Guidelines.* Retrieved from ISO: https://www.iso.org/standard/65694.html

ISO. (2025b, 01 21). *ISO/IEC 42001:2023 Information Technology - Artificial Intelligence - Management System.* Retrieved from ISO: https://www.iso.org/standard/81230.html

Justia. (2025, 1 17). *Product Safety Laws Protecting Consumers.* Retrieved from Justia: https://www.justia.com/consumer/consumer-protection-law/dangerous-or-defective-products-recalls

Kelly, J. (2024, 2 28). *What White-Collar Jobs Are Safe From AI—And Which Professions Are Most at Risk?* Retrieved from Forbes: https://www.forbes.com/sites/jackkelly/2024/02/28/what-white-collar-jobs-are-safe-from-ai-and-which-professions-are-most-at-risk/

Kim & Chang. (2024, 12 26). *Announcement of the AI Privacy Risk Management Model for Safe Utilization of AI and Data.* Retrieved from Kim & Chang: https://www.kimchang.com/en/insights/detail.kc?sch_section=4&idx=30988

Kubrick, S. (Director). (1968). *2001: A Space Odyssey* [Motion Picture].

Lana Wachowski, L. W. (Director). (1999). *The Matrix* [Motion Picture]. Retrieved from https://www.imdb.com/title/tt0133093/quotes/

Lawson, A. (2023, 1 24). *AI vs. Responsible AI: Why Is It Important?* Retrieved from Responsible Artificial Intelligence Institute: https://www.responsible.ai/ai-vs-responsible-ai-why-is-it-important/

Lean Enterprise Institute. (2025, 1 31). *Plan, Do, Check, Act (PDCA).* Retrieved from Lean Enterprise Institute: https://www.lean.org/lexicon-terms/pdca/

Liu, P. a. (2022). *AI for Cybersecurity: A Handbook of Use Cases.* Amazon.

Lucas, M. (2021, 6 16). *Indemnities in Technology Contracts.* Retrieved from Moore Barlow Lawyers: https://www.moorebarlow.com/blog/indemnities-in-technology-contracts/

Maiberg, E. (2024, 12 19). *APpaREnTLy THiS iS hoW yoU JaIlBreAk AI.* Retrieved from 404 Media: https://www.404media.co/apparently-this-is-how-you-jailbreak-ai/

Manning, P. C. (2024, 12 6). *Human-Centered Artificial Intelligence.* Retrieved from HAI Stanford University: https://hai.stanford.edu/sites/default/files/2020-09/AI-Definitions-HAI.pdf

Mastrogiorgio, A., and Lattanzi, N. (2022). Opaque decision-making in organizations. *International Journal of Organizational Analysis*, Vol. 31 No. 5, 1243–1256.

McGee, M. K. (2023, 11 16). *Lawsuit: Health Insurer's AI Tool 'Illegally' Denies Claims.* Retrieved from Healthcare InfoSecurity: https://www.healthcareinfosecurity.com/lawsuit-health-insurers-ai-tool-illegally-denies-claims-a-23614

McGee, M. K. (2024, 12 2). *Feds Propose AI 'Guardrails' for Medicare Advantage Plans.* Retrieved from Healthare InfoSecurity: https://www.healthcareinfosecurity.com/feds-propose-ai-guard-rails-for-medicare-advantage-plans-a-26950

Merken, S. (2023, 6 26). *New York Lawyers Sanctioned for Using Fake ChatGPT Cases in Legal Brief.* Retrieved from Reuters: https://www.reuters.com/legal/new-york-lawyers-sanctioned-using-fake-chatgpt-cases-legal-brief-2023-06-22/

Merriam-Webster. (2025, 1 15). *Accessibility.* Retrieved from Merriam-Webster: https://www.merriam-webster.com/dictionary/accessibility

Microsoft. (2024, 9 13). *What is Responsible AI?* Retrieved from Microsoft: https://learn.microsoft.com/en-us/azure/machine-learning/concept-responsible-ai?view=azureml-api-2

Milmo, D., and Courea, E. (2025, 2 11). *US and UK Refuse to Sign Paris Summit Declaration on 'Inclusive' AI.* Retrieved from The Guardian: https://www.theguardian.com/technology/2025/feb/11/us-uk-paris-ai-summit-artificial-intelligence-declaration

MIT Technology Review Insights. (2024, 8 5). *A Playbook for Crafting AI Strategy.* Retrieved from MIT Technology Review: https://www.technologyreview.com/2024/08/05/1095447/a-playbook-for-crafting-ai-strategy/

Mylius, A., and Bernardi, J. (2024, 11 26). *Scalable AI Incident Classification.* Retrieved from Simon Mylius: https://simonmylius.com/blog/incident-classification

NCSC. (2024, 8 7). *Artificial Intelligence: Guidance for Use of AI and Generative AI in Courts.* Retrieved from NCSC: https://www.ncsc.org/sites/default/files/media/document/AI-Courts-NCSC-AI-guidelines-for-courts.pdf

NIST. (2023, 1 26). *NIST AI Risk Management Framework (AI RMF).* Retrieved from AI Risk Management Framework: https://doi.org/10.6028/NIST.AI.100-1

NIST. (2024, 12 6). *The Language of Trustworthy AI: An In-Depth Glossary of Terms.* Retrieved from NIST Glossary: https://docs.google.com/spreadsheets/d/e/2PACX-1vTRB YglcOtgaMrdF11aFxfEY3EmB31zslYI4q2_7ZZ8z_1lKm7OHtF0t4xIsckuogNZ3h RZAaDQuv_K/pubhtml

NIST. (2024, 7). *Artificial Intelligence Risk Management Framework: Generative Artificial Intelligence Profile.* Retrieved from NIST Trustworthy and Responsible AI NIST AI 600-1: https://nvlpubs.nist.gov/nistpubs/ai/NIST.AI.600-1.pdf

NIST. (2024, 8 16). *Assessing Risks and Impacts of AI.* Retrieved from AI Challenges: https://ai-challenges.nist.gov/uassets/7

NIST. (2025, 1 15). *Accountability.* Retrieved from NIST: https://csrc.nist.gov/glossary/term/accountability

NIST. (2025, 1 15). *Privacy.* Retrieved from NIST: https://csrc.nist.gov/glossary/term/privacy

NIST. (2025, 1 15). *Reliability.* Retrieved from NIST: https://csrc.nist.gov/glossary/term/reliability

NIST. (2025, 1 15). *Robustness.* Retrieved from NIST: https://csrc.nist.gov/glossary/term/robustness

NIST. (2025, 1 15). *Safety.* Retrieved from NIST: https://csrc.nist.gov/glossary/term/safety

NIST. (2025, 1 15). *Security.* Retrieved from NIST: https://csrc.nist.gov/glossary/term/security

NIST. (2025, 1 15). *Transparency.* Retrieved from NIST: https://csrc.nist.gov/glossary/term/transparency

Nucleus_AI. (2025, 1 7). *How OpenAI o1 Went Full Maverick and Broke Chess as We Know It.* Retrieved from Your Story: https://yourstory.com/2025/01/openai-o1-full-maverick-broke-chess

OECD (2022). (2024, 12 6). *OECD Framework for the Classification of AI systems.* Retrieved from OECD Digital Economy Papers, No. 323: https://doi.org/10.1787/cb6d9eca-en

OECD. (2024, 12 24). *Accountability (Principle 1.5).* Retrieved from OECD: https://oecd.ai/en/dashboards/ai-principles/P9

OECD. (2024, 12 24). *Inclusive Growth, Sustainable Development and Well-Being (Principle 1.1).* Retrieved from OECD: https://oecd.ai/en/dashboards/ai-principles/P5

OECD. (2024, 12 24). *OECD AI Principles Overview.* Retrieved from OECD: https://oecd.ai/en/ai-principles

OECD. (2024, 12 24). *Respect for the Rule of Law, Human Rights and Democratic Values, Including Fairness and Privacy (Principle 1.2).* Retrieved from OECD: https://oecd.ai/en/dashboards/ai-principles/P6

OECD. (2024, 12 24). *Robustness, Security and Safety (Principle 1.4).* Retrieved from OECD: https://oecd.ai/en/dashboards/ai-principles/P8

OECD. (2024, 12 24). *Transparency and Explainability (Principle 1.3)*. Retrieved from OECD: https://oecd.ai/en/dashboards/ai-principles/P7

Office of the Governor. (2024, 1 18). *Governor Glenn Youngkin Signs Executive Order on Artificial Intelligence*. Retrieved from Office of the Governor: https://www.governor. virginia.gov/newsroom/news-releases/2024/january/name-1019979-en.html

OSHA. (2025, 1 18). *About OSHA*. Retrieved from OSHA: https://www.osha.gov/ aboutosha

Pacheco, M. (2024, 10 14). *AI Data Storage: Challenges & Strategies to Optimize Management*. Retrieved from TierPoint: https://www.tierpoint.com/blog/ai-data-storage/

Park, K., Choe, Y. J., and Veitch, V. (2024, 7 17). *The Linear Representation Hypothesis and the Geometry of Large Language Models*. Retrieved from Arxiv: https://arxiv.org/ abs/2311.03658

Payne, K. (2024, 10 25). *An AI Chatbot Pushed a Teen to Kill Himself, a Lawsuit against its Creator Alleges*. Retrieved from Associated Press News: https://apnews.com/ article/chatbot-ai-lawsuit-suicide-teen-artificial-intelligence-9d48adc572100822 fdbc3c90d1456bd0

PDPC. (2025, 1 21). *Singapore's Approach to AI Governance*. Retrieved from PDPC: https:// www.pdpc.gov.sg/help-and-resources/2020/01/model-ai-governance-framework

Pope, A. (2024, 4 10). *NYT v. OpenAI: The Times's about-Face*. Retrieved from Harvard Law Review: https://harvardlawreview.org/blog/2024/04/nyt-v-openai-the-timess-about-face/

Pratt, M. K. (2025, 1 24). *What is Data Preparation? An In-Depth Guide*. Retrieved from TechTarget: https://www.techtarget.com/searchbusinessanalytics/definition/data-curation

Reuel, A., Bucknall, B., Casper, S., et al. (2024b, 7 20). *Open Problems in Technical AI Governance*. Retrieved from Centre for the Governance of AI: https://www. governance.ai/research-paper/open-problems-in-technical-ai-governance

Reuel, A., Hardy, A., Smith, C., et al. (2024a, 12 15). *What Makes a Good AI Benchmark?* Retrieved from HAI: https://hai.stanford.edu/assets/files/hai-policy-brief-what-makes-a-good-ai-benchmark.pdf

Rotlevi, S. (2024, 8 2). *What Is a Prompt Injection Attack?* Retrieved from WIZ: https:// www.wiz.io/academy/prompt-injection-attack

Routledge Taylor & Francis Group. (2025, 1 19). *The Definitive Guide to Complying with the HIPAA/HITECH Privacy and Security Rules*. Retrieved from Routledge: https://www.routledge.com/The-Definitive-Guide-to-Complying-with-the-HIPAAHITECH-Privacy-and-Security-Rules/TrinckesJr/p/book/9781466507678

Ryseff, J., De Bruhl, B. F., and Newberry, S. J. (2024, 8 13). *The Root Causes of Failure for Artificial Intelligence Projects and How They Can Succeed*. Retrieved from RAND: https://www.rand.org/pubs/research_reports/RRA2680-1.html

Scott, R. (Director). (1979). *Alien* [Motion Picture].

Shin, R. U. (2024, 5 14). *Complete Guide to Five Generative AI Models*. Retrieved from COVEO: https://www.coveo.com/blog/generative-models/

Shumailov, I., Shumaylov, Z., Zhao, Y., et al. (2024, 7 25). *AI Models Collapse When Trained on Recursively Generated Data*. Retrieved from Nature 631: https://doi.org/10.1038/ s41586-024-07566-y

Smith, A. (2020, 4 8). *Using Artificial Intelligence and Algorithms*. Retrieved from FTC: https://www.ftc.gov/business-guidance/blog/2020/04/using-artificial-intelligence-algorithms

Snyder, Z. (Director). (2017). *Justice League* [Motion Picture].

Staff in the Office of Technology and the Division of Advertising Practices. (2025, 1 3). *AI and the Risk of Consumer Harm*. Retrieved from FTC: https://www.ftc.gov/policy/advocacy-research/tech-at-ftc/2025/01/ai-risk-consumer-harm

Stryker, C. (2024, 2 6). *What is Responsible AI?* Retrieved from IBM: https://www.ibm.com/topics/responsible-ai

Task Force on Artificial Intelligence (AI). (2024, 12 17). *House Bipartisan Task Force on Artificial Intelligence Delivers Report*. Retrieved from Committee on Science Space and Technology: https://science.house.gov/2024/12/house-bipartisan-task-force-on-artificial-intelligence-delivers-report

Taylor, P. (2024, 11 21). *Amount of Data Created, Consumed, and Stored 2010-2023, with Forecasts to 2028*. Retrieved from Statista: https://www.statista.com/statistics/871513/worldwide-data-created/

Thomson Reuters Foundation. (2025, 1 2). *2024 AI Governance for Africa*. Retrieved from Thomson Reuters Foundation: https://www.trust.org/resource/2024-ai-governance-for-africa-toolkit/

Trump, P. D. (2025, 1 23). *Removing Barriers to American Leadership in Artificial Intelligence*. Retrieved from Whitehouse Executive Order: https://www.whitehouse.gov/presidential-actions/2025/01/removing-barriers-to-american-leadership-in-artificial-intelligence/

Turing. (2025, 1 14). *Fine-Tuning LLMs: Overview, Methods, and Best Practices*. Retrieved from Turing: https://www.turing.com/resources/finetuning-large-language-models

U.S. Department of the Treasury. (2024, 3 27). *U.S. Department of the Treasury Releases Report on Managing Artificial Intelligence-Specific Cybersecurity Risks in the Financial Sector*. Retrieved from U.S. Department of the Treasury: https://home.treasury.gov/news/press-releases/jy2212

UNESCO. (2022, 11 23). *Recommendations on the Ethics of Artificial Intelligence*. Retrieved from UNESCO: https://unesdoc.unesco.org/ark:/48223/pf0000381137

United Nations. (2024, 03 21). *Seizing the Opportunities of Safe, Secure and Trustworthy Artificial Intelligence Systems for Sustainable Development: Resolution / Adopted by the General Assembly*. Retrieved from United Nations: https://digitallibrary.un.org/record/4043244?v=pdf#files

United Nations. (2025, 1 16). *UN Guiding Principles Reporting Framework*. Retrieved from UN Guiding Principles Reporting Framework: https://www.ungpreporting.org/framework-guidance/

United States Copyright Office. (2024, 7 31). *Copyright and Artificial Intelligence Part 1: Digital Replicas - A Report of the Register of Copyrights*. Retrieved from Copyright Office: https://www.copyright.gov/ai/Copyright-and-Artificial-Intelligence-Part-1-Digital-Replicas-Report.pdf

US Copyright Office. (2025, 1 17). *Copyright and Artificial Intelligence, Part 2: Copyrightability*. Retrieved from US Copyright Office: https://www.copyright.gov/ai/Copyright-and-Artificial-Intelligence-Part-2-Copyrightability-Report.pdf

W3C. (2025, 2 5). *WCAG 2 Overview*. Retrieved from Web Accessibility Initiative: https://www.w3.org/WAI/standards-guidelines/wcag/

Whitehouse. (2024, 12 26). *Blueprint for an AI Bill of Rights - Making Automated Systems Work for the American People*. Retrieved from Whitehouse: https://bidenwhitehouse.archives.gov/ostp/ai-bill-of-rights/

World Economic Forum. (2024, 12 16). *Navigating the AI Frontier: A Primer on the Evolution and Impact of AI Agents.* Retrieved from World Economic Forum: https://www.weforum.org/publications/navigating-the-ai-frontier-a-primer-on-the-evolution-and-impact-of-ai-agents/

Wu, Z., Arora, A., Wang, Z., et al. (2024, 5 22). *ReFT: Representation Finetuning for Language Models.* Retrieved from Arxiv: https://arxiv.org/abs/2404.03592

Wyden, B. a. (2023, 9 21). *Algorithmic Accountability Act of 2023.* Retrieved from Ron Wyden: https://www.wyden.senate.gov/imo/media/doc/algorithmic_accountability_act_of_2023_summary.pdf

Yang, A., and Li, B. (2024, 5 13). *AI Watch: Global Regulatory Tracker - China.* Retrieved from AI Watch: Global Regulatory Tracker: https://www.whitecase.com/insight-our-thinking/ai-watch-global-regulatory-tracker-china

Zhong Lun Law Firm. (2024, 9 9). *National Technical Committee 260 Releases AI Safety Governance Framework (Version 1.0).* Retrieved from Lexology: https://www.lexology.com/library/detail.aspx?g=a7c79097-f6f6-4c52-818d-034b12b29a2f

Index

www.ingramcontent.com/pod-product-compliance
Lightning Source LLC
Chambersburg PA
CBHW061208220326
41599CB00025B/4571